W9-CNW-985

The Feud of Language

The Feud of Language

A History of Structuralist Thought

English Version by
Linda Jordan and Thomas G. Pavel

Thomas G. Pavel

Basil Blackwell

First published in French as *Le Mirage linguistique*, Editions de Minuit
Translated with the support of the French Ministry of Culture
First published in this translation 1989

Basil Blackwell Ltd
108 Cowley Road, Oxford, OX4 1JF, UX

Basil Blackwell Inc.
3 Cambridge Center
Cambridge, MA 02142, USA

British Library Cataloguing in Publication Data

A CIP catalogue record for this book is available from the British Library.

Library of Congress Cataloging in Publication Data
Pavel, Thomas G., 1941-
[Mirage linguistique. English]
The feud of language: a history of structuralist thought / Thomas Pavel.
p. cm.
Translation of: Le Mirage linguistique.
Bibliography: p.
Includes index.
ISBN 0-631-16874-5
1. Structural linguistics – France. I. Title.
P146.P3513 1989 89-32241
410'.944 – dc20 CIP

Designed by Chase Production Services, Chipping Norton
Typeset in 10 on 11.25 pt Garamond by Setrite, Hong Kong
Printed in Great Britain by The Camelot Press, Southampton

Contents

Preface vii

1 The Order of Language 1

2 Technology and Regression 18

3 The Transcendental Ties of Linguistics 38

4 Games of Dispersion and the Correspondence Fallacy 74

5 On Conventionalism in Poetics 96

6 On Discretionary Intellectual Behaviour 125

Post–Scriptum: The Heidegger Affair 146

Notes 157

References 165

Index 174

Preface

This book examines French structuralism and poststructuralism from the point of view of their own claims to originality; that is, from the point of view of *language*. In France in the 1960s, linguistics, in particular structural linguistics, brought the promise of a true scientific conversion for the humanities. When this project miscarried, linguistics provided the critics of the scientific approach with the conceptual weapons of their discontent. Cultural, epistemological and metaphysical debates were all expressed in a vocabulary bristling with linguistic jargon.

But the linguistics of French structuralism and poststructuralism was a mirage. Those who used its notions understood neither the technical aspects of linguistics nor the theoretical stakes involved. They mistook the results of a specialized science for a collection of speculative generalities. They believed that breathtaking metaphysical pronouncements could be inferred from simple-minded descriptive statements. They thought that notions elaborated under the influence of behaviourism and logical positivism could be turned against these trends. The story of these misreadings is highly revealing. It proves that the philosophical contribution of structuralism and poststructuralism is flawed in its core: the selection of language as the main concern of human sciences and philosophy. It entails that, to the extent that structuralism and poststructuralism misunderstood the way in which language operates, both their spectacular critique of human intentionality and their resulting hostility to contemporary cultural and political institutions rest on shaky ground. Finally, it demonstrates the need for responsible co-operation between the human sciences and philosophy.

The first chapter surveys some of the French intellectual debates of the 1980s, debates that signal a gradual movement away from poststructuralist thought. Chapters 2, 3 and 4 provide close analyses of texts by Claude Levi-Strauss, Jacques Derrida and Michel Foucault, discussing their intellectual contexts and the twentieth-century linguistic trends that most influenced them. A detailed critique of structuralist poetics in chapter 5 prepares the way for the final socio-cultural explanation of the rise and success of structuralism and poststructuralism. A post-scriptum analysing the stormy controversy over Heidegger in Paris in 1987–8 reinforces my initial claim that a new cultural equilibrium has been reached in France.

I wish to express my gratitude to the Social Sciences and Humanities Research Council of Canada for several research grants, and to Michael Cowan, Dean of Humanities, University of California at Santa Cruz, for research support and flexible teaching schedules.

Many colleagues and friends have provided stimulating and helpful advice. I feel particularly indebted to Viviane Alleton, Marc Angenot, Claude Bremond, Menahem Brinker, Jacques Bouveresse, Dorrit Cohn, Vincent Descombes, Roger-Pol Droit, Gérard Genette, Wlad Godzich, Yves Hersant, Benjamin Hrushovsky, Georges Leroux, Virgil Nemoianu, Michel Pierssens, Gerald Prince, David Schneider, Mihai and Mariana Sora, Douglas C. Walker and Lindsay Waters.

Special thanks are due to Jean Piel, the director of the *Critique* series at Editions de Minuit, who made possible the publication of the French edition of this book. Jacques Poulain graciously organized a symposium on my book at the Collège International de Philosophie, Paris, in June 1988.

Ann Hawthorne's revision of the manuscript was immensely helpful, as was the careful reading by J. E. Hardy. Stephan Chambers has been a most supportive and generous book-editor.

Last but not least, I want to express my affectionate gratitude to Linda Jordan, who has been a marvellous partner in a difficult project.

1 The Order of Language

My generation witnessed the rise and, one might safely add, the *fall* of one of the most influential yet perplexing intellectual trends in this century – French structuralism and poststructuralism. We saw how, in France during the 1960s, the concepts of structural linguistics were transformed into a lasting set of metaphysical notions, which, in turn, played a crucial role in one of this century's most spectacular attempts to achieve intellectual modernization.

As early as the 1960s, many linguists and anthropologists noticed that the linguistic notions used by the various trends in French structuralism had little to do with the discipline patiently developed, from 1929 on, in Prague and Copenhagen, and at Yale and MIT. A major feature of intellectual modernity, it is sometimes assumed, lies in philosophy's influence over the development of the sciences. The structuralists, however, proposed to achieve modernization in the reverse manner, by subjecting speculative philosophy to the influence of one particular science, linguistics. In the following chapters, I shall argue that this singular strategy was an error and that the intellectual stimulation the structuralists sought in linguistics was beyond the means of that modest discipline. The linguistic project, so vigorously promoted by the human sciences in the 1960s and 1970s, had no genuine impact on the results of these sciences. Moreover, a convincing demonstration of the misuse of linguistic concepts would prove that the modernization undertaken in the name of language and semiology was illusory.

Some may doubt the need for belabouring the difficulties and errors of a trend the intellectual legitimacy of which has, in the past decade, been increasingly called into question. In 1980, in the first issue of the bi-monthly *Le Débat*, Pierre Nora's 'Que peuvent les intellectuels?' ('What Can Intellectuals Do?'), attacked poststructuralism and made a resounding appeal to reason, clarity and intellectual responsibility. At the same time, a group of philosophers and literary critics, many of them associated with the monthly *Critique*, began to question the structuralist and poststructuralist paradigm in the name of rationalism. In

1983, Vincent Descombes's *Objects of All Sorts: A Philosophical Grammar* used the tools of philosophical logic to scrutinize semiology. In the same year, *La Troisième République des lettres* (*The Third Republic of Letters*) by Antoine Compagnon detailed the links between the rise of French literary history at the beginning of the century and the Dreyfus affair. Compagnon's analysis suggested, intentionally or not, that structuralism had a similar relationship with the events of May 1968; it also reminded that a triumph of dogmatism usually triggers a countermovement. In 1984, in *La Philosophie chez les autophages* (*Philosophy in the Land of the Self-Eaters*) and *Rationalité et cynisme* (*Rationality and Cynicism*), Jacques Bouveresse denounced the nihilistic turn of poststructuralist thought. In *Literature and Its Theorists*, Tzvetan Todorov criticized ahistorical formalism and negative hermeneutics in literary criticism. The exchange between Marc Fumaroli and Gérard Genette in *Le Débat*, March 1984, delineated the alternatives available in literary theory. Fumaroli, supporting the logical flexibility of the humanities, defended epistemological monism and a defence of the scientific project in the humanities. Fumaroli's recommendation of a return to literary history appeared as the natural counterpart to Genette's plea for poetics and literary theory. In 1985, *La Pensée 68* (*The Thought of 68*) by Luc Ferry and Alain Renaut sharply attacked Lacan, Derrida and Foucault, treating them as mere instances of an ideal type: anti-humanism. In 1986, François Roustang denounced the cult of Lacan in *Lacan, de l'équivoque à l'impasse* (*Lacan: From Equivocation to Impasse*). At about the same time, the polemic between J.-F. Lyotard and Jürgen Habermas on the notion of postmodernism signalled an interest in new forms of rationality, and, *a fortiori*, a dismissal of the structuralist paradigm. Still more recently, in 1987, a debate on the legitimacy of cultural judgements has questioned the cultural relativism or the 1960s, and revived the interest in ethics and theory of value. Finally, the representatives of a new generation of political philosophers, Marcel Gauchet, Jean-Pierre Dupuy, Luc Ferry, Pierre Manent, Bernard Manin, Philippe Raynault, Alain Renaut and Pierre Rosanvallon, among others, have contributed to a renewed sense of moral and political responsibility.

All these developments suggest a gradual movement away from the structuralist and poststructuralist debates. They imply that the study of language has ceased to provide the key to philosophy and to the humanities. And while what has been called 'the linguistic turn' has undoubtedly been one of this century's major intellectual events, the time has come to reflect upon the intellectual tasks of the future. True, each time a new generation finds the concerns of its predecessors irrelevant, it is tempted to turn its back on the old topics of dispute and attend calmly to its own affairs. But simply to dismiss the debates of the recent past would be to sidestep an important and urgent task. Knowledge, in order to prosper, needs well-kept and up-to-date records. And although structuralism and poststructuralism may no longer be at the centre of current intellectual interest in France, surely it is too early to dismiss them altogether, given their persisting influence in England and the United States. Whether one supports or decries structuralist and post-structuralist thought, it is necessary to evaluate the successes and the errors of the waning paradigm. And, as a prerequisite, define it.

THE STRUCTURALIST PARADIGM

From 1945 to 1960, French intellectual life was dominated by a powerful trend which could be called *synchretic humanism* and which generously accommodated Marxism and phenomenology, morality and dialectics, history and modernity. While Sartre's *Critique of Dialectical Reason* is probably the best-known product of this trend, most political and cultural debates during those years (the Atlantic alliance, Indochina, the European Defence Community, Algeria, existentialism, the rise of postwar Marxism, etc.) were shaped by the growth of synchretic humanism. Among its primary tenets was a strong confidence in revolutionary social progress, to be achieved by human agents freed from the alienating chains of mercantile society and imbued with a sense of moral responsibility and political commitment. But synchretic humanism never imposed its authority without meeting some resistance. The articles and books by Lévi-Strauss, Barthes and Foucault, some of them published as early as the 1950s, immediately triggered a strong response. Sartre and Lévi-Strauss decorously debated in the pages of *Les Temps modernes* the respective merits of humanism and structuralism. For a while humanism appeared to have won, and before 1960 it was difficult to predict whether and how it would ever be rendered obsolete.

But disaffection for humanist rhetoric gradually did develop. From 1955 to 1960, the idea of a modernizing discourse inspired by linguistics steadily gained prestige. Under the name of *structuralism*, the new discourse influenced the human sciences, particularly those which were then called 'the sciences of the sign': anthropology, poetics, psychoanalysis and philosophy. In 1968, the term *structuralism* figured in the title of an introductory book, *Qu'est-ce que le structuralisme?* (*What is Structuralism?*) which explained the principles of the trend. Yet after having been for a while closely united around the linguistics of Ferdinand de Saussure, the structuralist disciplines, namely the anthropology of Lévi-Strauss, narrative poetics and the theories of Lacan, Foucault and Derrida, began to differentiate themselves from one another at the end of the 1960s. Soon after substantially contributing to the invention of literary semiology and narrative grammars, Barthes concluded that these disciplines were too subservient to the scientific, hence reductive, practices of linguistics. At the same time, Lacan, Foucault and Derrida, all previously considered as exponents of structuralism, began to criticize it strongly. Replaced in the early 1970s by an approach that focused on notions such as 'desire' and 'power' (Nora and Gauchet, 'Mots-moments' ('Terms-moments') in *Le Débat*, 50, 1988), linguistics has nevertheless passed on a common legacy to the former structuralists. Derrida and Barthes, like the other French poststructuralists, and later like their Anglo-American disciples, continued to organize their thoughts around the theoretical metaphors originating in structural linguistics. For a long time after 1972, signs, texts, discourse, discursive formations, signifiers, signifieds, differences and traces could be found everywhere. The one notion that continued to pervade all aspects of this large family of doctrines was that of language.

But this family was far from homogeneous. There were three major varieties of structuralism. *Moderate structuralism* included those rationalist theorists who were attracted to the results of recent linguistics, but refrained from borrowing its concepts and methods *stricto sensu*. In stylistics and poetics, moderate structuralism was dominant throughout the 1960s and 1970s, defining itself against philology and history on the one hand and the impressionism of literary criticism on the other. This branch of structuralism shared many of the concerns of morphology of culture, German stylistics, Russian and Czech formalist criticism and American New Criticism. Taxonomic attempts to systematize the theory of genre, such as Todorov's *Introduction to Fantastic Literature*, Jean Rousset's and Paul Zumthor's sophisticated literary analyses, J. P. Richard's phenomenological thematics and the poetics and narratology of Claude Bremond, Genette and Todorov are examples of moderate structuralism. These writers were only moderately interested in the methodological problems raised by structural linguistics; in addition to linguistic notions, they made use of various other conceptual tools, such as traditional grammar, the theory of action or, simply, intuition.

Scientistic structuralism borrowed more vigorously from linguistics. This trend was the main representative of the structuralist orthodoxy in France in the 1960s, claiming that linguistics was the most advanced among the social or human sciences. Its most typical thinkers were Lévi-Strauss, Barthes (during the 1960s) and A. J. Greimas. Since they and their disciples strongly believed that the linguistics of Saussure, Hjelmslev and Jakobson offered the most advanced methodology conceivable in the human sciences, they spent a considerable amount of energy developing various applications of linguistics in anthropology, semiology and formal narratology, each deciding in his own way to compensate for the inadequacies of the model through *ad hoc* means without ever questioning its fundamental validity.

Speculative structuralism, uniting the philosophical and ideological branches of the movement, flourished at the end of the 1960s and attracted both intense admiration and violent criticism. From Louis Althusser's efforts to transfer the scientistic message of structuralism to

Marxism, to the stands of *Tel quel* and *Change*, *theory* (used without a complement) became a source of radical political ideologies. At about the same time, less directly related to politics, yet equally remote from empirical concerns, great speculative systems proclaimed the end not only of Western metaphysics but of humanity itself as an object of knowledge. Most of the texts of the founding fathers of speculative structuralism (Foucault, Derrida, and, since the beginning of the 1970s, Barthes) were bursting with an elegant despair. To this branch belonged the school of existential psychoanalysis founded and subsequently abolished by Jacques Lacan.

These three categories are necessarily idealized, and the work of the most important authors, Lévi-Strauss, Lacan, Barthes, Foucault and Derrida cannot be flatly reduced to them: each followed his own winding path. Lévi-Strauss's research does far more than momentarily apply linguistic models. Having in the early 1960s abandoned Marxist concerns in favour of structuralism, Barthes later dramatically converted from scientism to anti-scientism. Foucault, who always rejected the label 'structuralist', changed his theoretical stands more than once during his long and baffling career. Although it is useless to predict the future development of Derrida's thought, it seems clear that from *Speech and Phenomena* to *Glas*, his ideas underwent a dramatic change. These authors not only called into question their own past convictions, they also often criticized each other, either explicitly (as Derrida did with Lévi-Strauss and Foucault), or implicitly (as Foucault frequently did with other structuralist and poststructuralist thinkers).

All these branches of structuralism had several features in common. All used *linguistic concepts*. Though developed by moderate structuralists mostly as heuristic devices, they played a major role in the modernization project of the scientistic group. The speculative thinkers used these concepts to articulate their epistemological misgivings more clearly. The scientific determinism of the early structuralists gradually gave way to scepticism, and linguistic algebra became the model of a new transcendence.

Another striking feature, bitterly resented by the adversaries of structuralism, was the *critique of humanism*. It can be found in Lévi-Strauss's vast research programme, in Foucault's *The Order of Things* (1966), in Derrida's call for the replacement of humanism, as well as in the writings of the Marxist group at the prestigious Ecole Normale Supérieure. Some analysts take this to be the most important feature of French poststructuralism.

Equally striking and equally omnipresent, was the *critique of subjectivity and truth*. Indeed, Lévi-Strauss defined his conception of myths as Kantianism devoid of a transcendental subject. Barthes asserted that the death of the author is the only provider of meaning. Both Foucault and Derrida, so seldom in agreement, believed that the notion of subject should be dispensed with. Truth was discarded by Barthes as a useless prejudice, denounced by Derrida as a logocentric illusion, destroyed in Foucault's theories by the impact of changing epistemes. Only Althusser still believed in it; and, paradoxically, his notion of truth took such rudimentary and dogmatic forms that rather than supporting truth, it undermined it. Notice that the critique of humanism, subjectivity and truth is by no means restricted to French structuralists and poststructuralists. It characterizes all philosophical trends which, after recognizing that subjectivity cannot serve as a foundation for knowledge, looked for new solutions in the realm of language.

Moreover, structuralist philosophers questioned philosophical language to an unprecedented degree. The targets of philosophical meditation changed. Instead of addressing questions of nature, knowledge, or freedom, philosophical discourse withdrew into itself and carefully problematized its own impossibility: self-consuming philosophy, as Bouveresse (1984a) calls it. Indeed, although speculative structuralists declared war on what they decided to call metaphysics, they never attempted to define an alternative conceptual space in which new referents could be constructed and new strategies of understanding could be tested. Deconstruction (Derrida's notion), archaeology (in Foucault's early work) and Althusser's structuralist rewriting of *Capital*, all manifest *the replacement of metaphysics by metacriticism*. The repetition of the prefix *meta* emphasizes that these philosophers perpetuated a speculative pattern of thought even as they explicitly condemned it.

Speculative structuralists, perhaps embarrassed by the conjectural nature of their approach, tried to reconcile themselves with the empirical sciences. Unlike the German philosophers at the end of the eighteenth and the beginning of the nineteenth centuries, the French philosophers of the 1960s avoided, or at least purported to avoid, being absorbed in the examination of subjective consciousness. Instead, they turned to disciplines more closely related to the outside world: hence Derrida's close reading of Rousseau; Lévi-Strauss's theorizing on the origin of language and writing; Foucault's research on the history of medicine, political economy, biology and linguistics; and Althusser's acrobatics through the cogs and wheels of *Capital*. However, their attitude towards empirical work is fundamentally ambiguous. In *Of Grammatology* (1967), Derrida appears to speak both as a linguist and as a theoretician of anthropology. Some of his long commentaries on passages by Saussure and Hjelmslev (ibid., pp. 27–73) would not be out of place in a treatise on general linguistics; several of his remarks on the relationship between writing and violence (ibid., pp. 101–40) seem to be aimed at anthropologists, be they theoreticians or experienced field researchers. But suddenly, as the argumentation seems finally to have taken root in the empirical realm, the discourse flies off without warning into the heavens of transcendental speculation. A lucid analysis of Lévi-Strauss's anthropological biases during his visit to the Nambikwara (ibid., pp. 173–200) abruptly leads to the establishment of one of those ironical and evanescent concepts with which Derrida wants to replace the hard concepts of classical philosophy. In this case, the concept is *the lure*:

To recognize writing in speech, that is to say difference and the absence of speech, is to begin to think the lure. There is no ethics without the presence of *the other* but also, and consequently, without absence, dissimulation, detour, difference, writing. The arche-writing is the origin of mortality as of immorality. (ibid., pp. 139–40)

In just one paragraph, the reader is projected a thousand metaphysical miles from the Nambikwara and their writing anxieties as described by Lévi-Strauss. Noting that Saussure expresses a certain distrust of the written forms of language – a distrust in fact shared by all nineteenth-century comparative philologists, who wanted to avoid the prejudicial confusion between written forms and pronounciation – Derrida develops, without any transition, a theory of how linguistics *expelled* writing, as it were:

Saussure here points at the inversion of the natural relationship between speech and writing. This is not a simple analogy: writing, the letter, the sensible inscription, has always been considered by Western tradition as the body and matter external to the spirit, to breath, to speech and to the Logos. (ibid., pp. 34–5)

A few lines later he points an accusatory finger at the great sacred images of metaphysical thought: 'And the problem of soul and body is no doubt derived from the problem of writing from which it seems – conversely – to borrow its metaphors' (ibid., p. 35). The linguist, seized with admiration, is thus reminded how irremediably provincial is his discipline. At the same time, the critical reference to the true specialists of language is calculated to dazzle philosophers and persuade them that the body/soul distinction derives from the existence of writing.

Similarly, in *The Order of Things*, Foucault oscillates between superficial research into the history of science and glamorous philosophical generalizations. The text is thus made invulnerable, since to the sceptical historian one can answer that, after all, isolated facts count less than the theoretical gains in this kind of project (one of the book's main theses is that in science facts count for little); while to the unconvinced epistemologist, one can modestly argue that the book is just a contribution to the history of science. True, such *empirico-transcendental sidestepping* (to designate this last feature of structuralist thought using an adjective created by Foucault himself) is commonplace in the history of philosophy: it is easily found (proceeding in reverse chronological order) in Friedrich Engels' *Anti-Dühring*, in Hegel's philosophy of nature, and in the physics of the late scholastics and neo-Platonists; consequently, its use by a metaphysician of language or by a philosopher of knowledge, though disconcerting, is by no means exceptional. Yet one cannot help feeling disturbed by the resilience of the old sophisms, ready to spring to life again at any moment, and in places where one would least expect them.

The last two features, namely the transformation of metaphysics into metacriticism and the empirico-transcendental sidestepping, are more stylistic than substantive. By style, I mean the style of thought and not the numerous discursive procedures and special rhetorical effects which, carefully cultivated, gave speculative structuralism its particular physiognomy. In the midst of a relatively civilized and peaceful period, a group of distinguished representatives of the liberal universities spontaneously adopted an apocalyptic idiom, quite similar to that of Puritan preachers and revolutionary tyrants. They talked less of knowledge than of salvation, relied less on logical arguments than impassioned pleas, were interested less in results than revelations. To a certain extent, Tocqueville predicted this development when he wrote that in the twentieth century the style of literary production will often be 'fantastic, incorrect, overburdened and loose, almost always vehement and bold' (1840, p. 62).

Others have criticized the style of poststructuralist authors in more detail. Few, however, have noticed the *narrative technique* embedded in their writings. Jean-François Lyotard is probably correct when he claims that the great Promethean metastories of the nineteenth century have by now lost most of their appeal. But we have not yet attained a perfect indifference to narratives. Lashed to the mast of postindustrial society, we still let ourselves be charmed by the legend of the 1960s and their intellectual heroes. Whether this new myth will supplant the lost stories of Progress and Revolution or whether it will turn out to be only a passing fad is difficult to foresee. In any case, the heroic point of view in the history of science has been around for a long time – and refuted for almost as long. Narrative is, however, inescapable, and I will later use a narrative device myself: the notion of modernization. Before this, it is useful to examine briefly a narrative pattern that is common in structuralist and poststructuralist writings: the rhetoric of the end.

THE RHETORIC OF THE END

The recent challenge to the structuralist paradigm has been accompanied by a reappraisal of many topics that were marginalized during the 1960s. Accordingly, the critics of structuralism and poststructuralism speak of the *return* of the subject, of the referent, of history. Yet the metaphor of the *return* in recent anti-deconstructionist writings is just a belated answer to the concept of the *end*, which was in great favour in the 1960s and 1970s and, more generally, in all anarchist and millenarian approaches, which love to stress how inevitable their arrival is and how fortunate the world is to have them as a last resort after all other intellectual choices have been exhausted. If Foucault is ultimately right in insisting that all discourse involves power, the metaphor of the end (notably the end of all rival concepts and groups) that has recently been so much used and abused implies that the speaker is in a position – or at least a posture – of power. If, forgetting historical fact for a moment, we examine the narrative effect of the notion of end, it becomes apparent that he who announces the end of an era, the end of the onto-theology or of logocentrism, for instance, presents us with a *finished story*, thus implying that the debate is concluded and the file has been closed. The debate over, the speaker plays the role of narrator, hence of judge, thus assuming the right to pronounce verdicts. To conceptualize the end – be it the end of a historical period or a way of thought, not to mention the end of History itself or the entire metaphysical tradition – amounts to inflicting an ontological degradation on the sequence supposedly ended, relegating it, through rhetorical artifice, to the level of passive narrative material lacking the right and the ability to react.

In an insightful analysis of historical discourse, Arthur Danto (1985) noted that any presentation of the past remains essentially incomplete. A historian who, in 1825, narrated a series of past events, say those of the 1789 French Revolution, could hardly claim to have exhausted its meaning, since at any subsequent time, in 1830 or 1848 for instance, new events could retroactively change the perception of the first revolution. But if this is true of all propositions about events, it is equally true of higher-order assertions that add a caesura indicating the end of a sequence of narrative sentences. As Danto put it, 'a complete story of the past presupposes a complete story of the future' (ibid., pp. 17). During the 1950s, social scientists predicted the end of ideologies. Ten years later, their revival took everyone by surprise. In North America today, whether we like it or not, ideologies are as lively as ever. Similarly, are we indeed experiencing, as Derrida claimed, the end of onto-theology? If onto-theology happens to make a comeback in a few years, its so-called end will prove to have been an illusion. Used from within history and about history, the notion of end points less to a *fact* than to a *desire*; far from achieving a real closure, it instead opens a polemic. If, in addition, using the weapons of philosophy, the announcement of the 'end' fails to provide any empirical proof, the period being proclaimed as closed will be as impossible to defend as those political figures in totalitarian systems who are retroactively erased from all records. History's distinctive feature is co-ordination, Jacob Burkhardt said; that of philosophy, subordination. Presumably this is why in philosophy, behind the concept of the end, lurks a project of violence.

The philosophical ambitions of a theory often become evident through the rhetoric of the end, even though the discipline in which this theory takes shape belongs to the empirical sciences. In 1954, when Lévi-Strauss argued in favour of the structural revolution in anthropology, he reasoned in the following manner: by attributing a stable meaning to myths, theoreticians (such as C. G. Jung, with his archetypes) committed an error comparable to that of Socrates in *Cratylus*. During his conversation with Hermogenes, Socrates attributes an affinity with definite meaning to each sound, *r* to express movement, *l* for elision, *o* for roundness. After Saussure elaborated the principle of the arbitrariness of the linguistic sign, however, linguistics achieved the stature of a real science. The arbitrariness of the linguistic sign emphasized the absence of justified links between sounds and meanings and contributed to the successes of structural phonology proving that the sounds of a language, though devoid of all meaning, nevertheless form a system. *As a result*, Lévi-Strauss continued, since the anthropology of myths must also transform itself into a science, it has no other choice than to adopt the principle of arbitrariness and follow phonology's example. Just as the sounds brought together in a word have no meaning on their own, since *t* followed by *r* and *i* signifies 'tree' only by pure convention, so the elements which make up a myth emerge in the same arbitrary fashion and without any direct relationship to the myth's overall meaning. Like phonemes, which, beyond spoken sequences, organize themselves into harmonious abstract systems, the simple narration of myths does not exhaust their meaning, because narration rests on an algebraic foundation that the anthropologist deduces by using conceptual tools borrowed from linguistics. Those who had proposed other methods before this discovery, as well as those who were not converted as soon as it came to light, found themselves relegated to pre-scientific limbo.

Lévi-Strauss's argument divides the history of linguistics into a 'before' and an 'after' separated by the revelation of the principle of conversion (the arbitrariness of the sign) attributed to Saussure. Let us call this narrative model 'the scientific salvation'. It proves so effective that it sweeps away the pre-Saussurian history of linguistics and, at a stroke, assures the converted access to a privileged epistemological domain, that of structural linguistics. In the same way, with anthropology allegedly being in a state of crisis, the principle of conversion already tested elsewhere will bring about the much-needed progress. Setting aside for a moment this highly unlikely account of the development of linguistics, let us examine briefly the fallacy in Lévi-Strauss's reasoning. Linguistics and anthropology have always enjoyed a 'good neighbour' relationship and the free exchange of methodologies and results between the two disciplines has proved profitable from as far back as the missions and grammars of the Jesuits. The methodological borrowings were for a long time limited to the less problematic aspects of research, notably to field techniques. When Edward Sapir and then Benjamin Lee Whorf, updated Humboldt's well-known theses on the mutual dependence between language and worldview within each culture, they reformulated them as substantial hypotheses and not as methodological improvements.

Consequently, Whorf's reflections on the Hopi, far from taking the interdependence between language and worldview for granted, strove instead to establish its existence. Yet when Lévi-Strauss suggested converting the methodologies of the anthropology of myths, the validity of the models adopted was never subject to doubt or to systematic research. Working in this way saves several steps: not only did Lévi-Strauss avoid considering other recent trends in linguistics and phonology, as though the linguistic community had, by 1954, unanimously accepted the results of the Prague school formulated in Roman Jakobson's writings as the best solution for phonology; he also avoided examining how appropriate those models that had supposedly succeeded in structural phonology were to the analysis of myths.

Given these conditions and the lack of any debate, for Lévi-Strauss to label his adversaries 'pre-scientific' was tantamount to pronouncing a symbolic death sentence, to marking out their narrative end, an end which had to bear witness to the inevitable advent of a new regime in anthropology. Such is the force of excommunicative utterances. To proclaim the end of other groups and systems exorcizes the fear of having to confront them. It pours the contingency of new projects into the concrete of necessity and conceals their precarious nature, thus eliminating all the features that would make such projects risky and, perhaps, seductive.

Elsewhere the end appears as *division*. In *The Order of Things*, Foucault avoids the model of scientific salvation, which, as we saw, divides the universe of discourse into a before and an after separated by the advent of a scientific saviour who brings about a revelation. The rudimentary character of such a model, however satisfactory it may be for the anthropologist searching for certainty, would hardly have escaped the historian of sciences who, because of his training, is familiar with the evanescent promises of scientific salvation. Since the history of every discipline is but a series of theoretical upheavals, it is tempting to enhance the notion of epistemological end by attributing to it the virtues of periodicity. Somewhat similar to Cuvier's conception of the successive creation of animal kingdoms, which successfully emphasized but avoided explaining the morphological discontinuities of fossils, the Western world, according to Foucault, experienced a series of epistemological mutations, the reasons for which remain shrouded in obscurity. For example, at the end of the eighteenth century

> European culture is inventing for itself a depth in which what matters is no longer identities, distinctive characters, permanent tables with all their possible paths and routes, but great hidden forces developed on the basis of their primitive and inaccessible nucleus, origin, causality and history ... What changed at the turn of the century, and underwent an irremediable modification, was knowledge itself as an anterior and indivisible mode of being

between the knowing subject and the object. (ibid., pp. 251–2)

These famous lines fail to explain the nature of the epistemological change, even though everything that follows ensues from it. Perched atop giant unstable tectonic plates, we wait for the next movement as unpredictable as the preceding ones. Yet again, before our very eyes, the shift within epistemology drastically alters the horizon:

the entire modern *episteme* ... was bound up with the disappearance of Discourse and its featureless reign, with the shift of language towards objectivity, and with its reappearance in multiple form. If this same language is now emerging with greater and greater insistence in a unity that we ought to think but cannot as yet do so, is this not the sign that the whole of this configuration is now about to topple, and that man is in the process of perishing as the being of language continues to shine ever brighter upon our horizon? (ibid., pp. 385–6)

This beautiful and often-quoted sentence illustrates not only the post-structuralist themes, from anti-humanism ('man is in the process of perishing') to the linguistic turn ('the shift of language towards objectivity and ... reappearance in multiple form'), acknowledging on the way the end of philosophy ('the disappearance of Discourse') and the dissolution of the truth ('as the being of language continues to shine ever brighter'). It also resonates with those specifically Foucauldian motifs of the *Götterdämmerung* ('the whole of this configuration is now about to topple') and of the giant thinker, Zarathustra, with a smile on his face, throwing out his challenge into the cataclysm: 'a unity that we ought to think but cannot as yet do so'.

Beneath its pure literary beauty, beneath its explicative complacence – because it avoids the thorny problem of the *cause* of the change – the vision of history as an eternal return of flames and twilights commends itself by the convenient justification provided for at the end of the present era. The single narrative thread peculiar to models of salvation dissipates here into a multiplicity of ends of projects, the futile ambition of each being revealed by the speaker with Argus-like eyes. Whereas Lévi-Strauss naively explains the end of pre-scientific anthropologies by their refusal to accept grace and conversion, Foucault uses a periodical twilight which inevitably descends, on average, once every two hundred years: with the exception of the sage who describes the process, the epistemological holocaust annihilates all servants of knowledge, without distinction.

The position of the sage, who is contemplating this destruction from his plateau top, is no less precarious as a result of this wholesale slaughter. He no longer deludes himself about the irreversible contingency of systems of knowledge or sustains activist illusions or hopes in method. The Foucault of the 1960s did not aim at the conversion of sinners, but dispassionately speculated upon their fall together with that of the righteous. His universe, therefore, does not include norms exterior to the transient epistemes; nor, beyond periodic revolutions, does it provide a cognitive space safe from tremors. Bound to configurations which topple or rise up, knowledge, 'an anterior and indivisible mode of being between the knowing subject and the object' (ibid., p. 252), can no longer separate subject and object. Yet if no one can detach himself from these shifting landscapes, who will have the power to describe them? And from which focal point? Radical relativism, because of the very thesis it defends, excludes the cognitive locus from which it is spoken. The giddy interplay of the epistemes hides the inconceivable place of the sage who claims to control them. When the rhetoricians of scientific salvation announce the end of the infidels, they disguise the desire to annihilate the adversary and ensure complete mastery of a field circumscribed by knowledge, a field, after all, well defined by the history of the discipline in question but simply poorly cultivated in the hands of those whose influence has to be eliminated. In Foucault's model of periodic twilight, the stakes are much higher: this model does not involve a succession of hegemonies within such and such constituted discipline, but, rather, beyond disciplinary boundaries, it claims the utopian right to recount the end of all other discourses. Like the tyrants of Elias Canetti, who measure their own immortality by the number of subjects they unceasingly put to death, radical epistemology feeds on the decay of every discipline and on the collapse of every configuration. Hearing such voices, we would be wise to remember how groundless, fragile and overrated their pretensions are.

The most subtle rhetoric of the end, as practised by Derrida, at least freely acknowledges its weaknesses and the precariousness of its condition. Yet Derrida's critics cannot accuse him of setting forth an excessive project, since he turns the *exorbitant* into the main feature of his work, thereby cutting the ground from under their feet. 'I wished', he writes in *Of Grammatology*, 'to reach the point of a certain exteriority in relation to the totality of the age of logocentrism' (ibid., p. 161). The *age* of logocentrism, a temporal notion, coincides, we are told, with the development of Western rationality, to which Derrida attributes unparalleled coherence, since it includes at one and the same time Greek metaphysics, Christian theology and modern science. Does temporality here imply completion, genuine end, the destruction of ideas and methods, as in the model of recurrent twilight? Nothing could be less certain, since Derrida avoids prophesying catastrophes, and his work aims less at the total denunciation of a model of knowledge than at the examination of a few sutures which reveal the heterogeneity of the surfaces they are holding together. 'Starting from this point of exteriority', he continues, 'a certain deconstruction of that totality which is also a traced path, of that orb (*orbis*) which is also orbitary (*orbita*), might be broached'. The final effort consists therefore in deferring the invisible yet ineluctable authority of logocentrism so that the mind can invent new courses. Departing from the traced path, venturing into the unknown and the unheard-of, these urges to explore the out-of-the-ordinary are certainly not accompanied by new certainties or new rules: 'The first gesture of this departure and this deconstruction, although subject to a certain historical necessity, cannot be given methodological or logical intra-orbitary assurances'. This approach attempts to go beyond classical conceptual oppositions 'particularly the one within which the value of empiricism is held: the opposition of philosophy and non-philosophy, another name for empiricism' (ibid., p. 162). The end of philosophy, therefore, is revealed not as a state already attained which merely requires recording, nor as an irreversible progression that 'we glimpse only as a thin line of light low on the horizon' (Foucault, 1966, p. 384) but, more problematically, as a project of demolition.

According to Derrida, a metaphysics of the presence-to-oneself, a will-to-signify sustained by the speaking breath, underlies the history of Western thought; the intention of deconstruction is to leave this history without wanting to and without being able to wish for its death. In the sinuous analyses of *Speech and Phenomena*, as we shall see later, Derrida stresses that transparence, meaning and the phreatic rhythm of the pneuma are aligned with presence and the metaphysics of the spoken word, and that, inversely, the thought process of writing is partly linked with the ideality of undefined repetition, with the absence of the 'I', with death and with silence. Thus we read the humble wish of philosophy's maverick:

The opening of the question, the departure from the closure of a self-evidence, the putting into doubt of a system of oppositions, all these movements necessarily have the form of empiricism and of errancy. At any rate, they cannot be described, *as to past norms*, except in this form. (*Of Grammatology*, p. 162)

And although he dissociates himself from these norms with a weary gesture, the metaphysical adventurer does not even lay claim to initiating the process:

No other trace is available, and as these errant questions are not absolute beginnings in every way, they allow themselves to be effectively reached, on one entire surface, by this description which is also a criticism. We must begin *wherever we are* and the thought of the trace, which cannot not take the scent into account, has already taught us that it was impossible to justify a point a departure absolutely. (ibid.)

Derrida had already presented these themes in 1963:

> Our discourse irreducibly belongs to the system of metaphysical oppositions. The break with this structure of belonging can be announced only through a *certain* organization, a certain *strategic* arrangement which, within the field of metaphysical opposition, uses the strengths of the field to turn its own stratagems against it, producing a force of dislocation that spreads itself throughout the entire system, fissuring it in every direction and thoroughly *de-limiting* it. (*On Writing and Difference*, p. 20)

In the *Tel quel* milieu of 1968, this project (rightly or wrongly, it is difficult to decide) was deemed to be 'subversive'. Some reservations about the political connotations of such subversion are justified; the purely philosophical connotations perhaps suggest nothing more than attention to the seismic echoes, to the faint tremors which secretly run through the great conceptual mechanisms surrounding us. The end, according to Derrida, is the term for separation and conversion; the philosopher who has had the vanity of the logos revealed to him will not rest until he has made the empty labyrinths echo his discovery.

RADICAL QUESTIONS AND THE QUESTION OF LANGUAGE

Although the notion of appearance does not play an important role in Derrida's writings, his critique of logocentrism invests it with those traits traditionally assigned to phenomenal illusion: its superficial gleam, its perfect closure, its urgent yet impossible replacement. The kinship between logocentrism and illusion is stressed in numerous passages where the deconstructor openly acknowledges the anti-natural, even anti-logical, character of his methodology. But nature and logic are the cornerstones of the building which he endeavours to destroy. Neo-Platonism likewise rejected the world of the senses, and Kant deployed the stealthy movement of reflection in the small rift between conscience and the empirical world. But even though the *whole* of the given – or, as here, of logocentric thought – falls suspect, we still can *point* to it. Indeed, every expressed thought requires, as a starting point, a pre-logical grasp of the universe as a totality, a simple act of showing, an act which, before the crystallization of meaning and objectivity, separates Being from the gaze to which it is presenting itself. Just as, in the infinite reflexiveness of the subject, idealist systems draw on the reserves of energy they need to overcome the gravity of phenomena, Derrida calls this act 'the supplement': 'the indefinite process of supplementarity has always already *infiltrated* presence, always already inscribed there the space of repetition and the splitting of the self' (*Of Grammatology*, p. 163).

Beyond the novelty of Derrida's formulation, we recognize a question which has been around since the beginning of philosophy. Conquered only with difficulty by the work of reflection, confronted with what Derrida calls *presence*, the splitting of the self appears as inscribed in the world of presence merely because of the strategic – and therefore contingent – choice of terrain on which Derrida conducts his arguments.

This terrain belongs to language and, more precisely, to language in its specifically grammatical formality. But other options could have been selected. Derrida's justification, at the beginning of *Of Grammatology*, is one of the rare occasions when a poststructuralist thinker clearly reasons about the *choice* of language. He sounds quite hesitant, as if he wants to win the reader's complicity with an allusion to immediate actuality:

However the topic is considered, the *problem of language* has never been simply one problem among others. But never as much as at present has it invaded, *as such*, the world horizon of the most diverse researches and the most heterogenous discourses, diverse and heterogenous in their intention, method and ideology. (ibid., p. 6)

These memorable sentences, by taking philosophy's contemporary interest in the analysis of language and the linguistic hegemony in the human sciences *for granted*, gives these trends the stature of a 'world' phenomenon. World is related to worldly, therefore to fashions, and fashions are quickly rejected:

The devaluation of the word 'language' itself, and how, in the very hold it has upon us, it betrays a loose vocabulary, the temptation of a cheap seduction, the passive yielding to fashion, the consciousness of the avant-garde, in other words – ignorance – are evidences of this effect. (ibid.)

World is, therefore, perhaps used in an ironical sense to emphasize the grotesque character of the universal passion for what Derrida calls the problem of language: with too much in circulation, coinage loses its value. He adds, however, that the global triumph of such inflation is a sign of impending crisis: 'It indicates, as in spite of itself, that a historico-metaphysical epoch *must* finally determine as language the totality of its problematic horizon' (ibid.).

Must? Is this a must of necessity or a must of normative obligation? or, perhaps, a must of intention or a must of probability? In other words, is the conversion to language inevitably inscribed (as Derrida would say) in the evolution of metaphysics, or does it perhaps represent just one of many ends which would be of some particular advantage to metaphysics to select and head towards? Was the French linguistic turn the inevitable destiny of metaphysics, or was it more a contingency of the intellectual climate in France some twenty years ago? The inventory of possible connotations of the word *must* indicates how problematic the relationship between the history of philosophy and the French linguistic turn is, and also how riddled with contingency is the attempt to impress necessity upon it. Why would *we* see in 'the problem of language' the same amorphous and irresistible wave that Derrida witnessed in 1967? If, at that moment in history, the linguistic turn benefited at all from the confused prestige and the urgency of fashion, then, by examining its history, we would perhaps learn more about the strategic position of philosophy in France in the 1960s – and of the philosophy of language in particular – than about the timeless destiny of metaphysics. Looked at from the particular and contingent point of view of Derrida in 1967, the interest shown in language in this century could then be experienced as the crest of a relentless universal wave. It is nevertheless true that the selection of another horizon could lead to a different perception of the linguistic turn and help explain the anxiety it caused in French philosophical circles. Since, however, Derrida and his generation inherited the concern for language from earlier structuralists, we shall next examine Lévi-Strauss's formulation of the linguistic problem.

2 Technology and Regression

Structuralism's complexity became apparent as early as the 1950s. In his articles published between 1945 and 1956, Lévi-Strauss blended the traditional tone of academic discourse with the bold postwar drive to intellectual modernization. His treatment of the legitimate precursors was, therefore, harsh. They were replaced by past masters from neighbouring disciplines: Saussure, Marx and Freud. These came to play an essential role in the reform of the humanist disciplines in France. But the modernizing drive inevitably created tensions in the disciplines that it invested.

MODERNIZATION AND DISCIPLINARY TRADITIONS

Not unlike commercial and industrial modernization, the intellectual modernization of the human sciences in the past two centuries aimed at creating a system that would allow for rapid change and the easy circulation of information and ideas. To achieve this goal, the reformers encouraged the fermentation of new ideas through the creation of new disciplines, as well as the reformation of the traditional, established ones. They also vigorously encouraged the diffusion of the most advanced scientific methodologies. Whereas the creation of new *disciplines* in the social sciences and the humanities rarely met with opposition, the diffusion of new *methodologies* periodically aroused anxiety, because it challenged the internal balance of the existing disciplines affected. But methodological unity was an important objective of the intellectual modernizers, who intended to remove the barriers between disciplines.

The reformers' sustained effort to weaken disciplinary traditions had little to do with the 'epistemological breaks' or 'scientific revolutions' so often invoked by historians of science influenced by Foucault or Thomas Kuhn. Take the example of linguistics. As Foucault himself shows in *The Order of Things*, the assumptions of philology at the beginning of the nineteenth century were strikingly different from those of the general grammars of the previous two centuries. The opening up of the field, chiefly exemplified by the discovery of Sanskrit, had made possible the solution of an old puzzle: the kinship among Greek, Latin and the Germanic languages. As a consequence, comparison between related languages became a priority, leading to the creation of a new methodology. The transformation, however, was by no means revolutionary: philologists often used known techniques and data to achieve methodological innovation. Comparative grammar of Greek and Latin had long been the object of detailed description, and, although the discovery of Sanskrit made the relationship between the two classical languages fully comprehensible, the comparative method had been in use long before William Jones, Rasmus Rask and the Grimm Brothers transformed it into a precise instrument of historical reconstruction.

The theoreticians of the new philology, notably Friedrich Schlegel, justified comparatism by reference to natural history; but their purpose was not so much to borrow new techniques from biology, as to confer a new legitimacy on well-tested philological methods. The biological method which, according to some historians of linguistics (including Foucault), played a crucial role in the development of nineteenth-century comparative philology was in fact only one of several models that influenced linguistics. It was also the weakest model, occasioning the least reputable linguistic speculations. From Schlegel to Schleicher, the influence of the natural history enhanced the belief in the evolutionary progress of languages. In the middle of the nineteenth century, Schleicher distinguished among crystalline forms (isolating languages, such as Chinese), vegetal forms (agglutinating languages, such as Turkish), and animal forms (inflecting languages belonging to the Indo-European family). The last group was deemed superior.

As Hans Aarsleff (1982) has shown, during the second half of the nineteenth century Michel Bréal in France, J. N. Madvig in Denmark, and W. D. Whitney in America forcefully rejected these speculations. But natural history was not the only model available to nineteenth-century linguistics: physics also exercised a strong influence on linguistics: the New Grammarians modelled the phonetic laws, supposed to act blindly and without exception, in line with Lavoisier's deterministic universe. History also exercised increasing influence on linguistics, especially after the rejection of pseudo-biological theories. At the end of the century, Hermann Paul in Germany and Bréal in France firmly placed linguistics among the historical sciences.

Seen from the late 1980s' point of view, after the rise of structuralism, the late nineteenth-century methodology of the New Grammarians may appear as a victory of positivism over earlier speculative thought. In fact, during the entire nineteenth century, from the pioneering work of Rask, Bopp and Grimm to the later findings of Venner, Paul and Brugmann, philology was based on empirical research. It developed its methodology solely through a series of *ad hoc* solutions, most often improvised in order to answer pressing descriptive needs. The organic metaphors of Schleicher had virtually no impact on the enormous mass of descriptive work in Indo-European and other languages. The theoretical theses of the New Grammarians (the law-abiding character of phonetic change and the principle of morphological analogy), modest and innocuous though they appear today, aroused considerable hostility among anti-speculative philologists, such as Curtius. Clearly, a purely atheoretical science is an impossibility. Yet there must be degrees of theoretical abstractness, and comparative grammar is on the lower end of the ladder.

In our century, the reform of methodology became an urgent goal of epistemological modernization. Rather than following the nineteenth-century habit of creating new methods when new disciplines needed them, the humanities and social sciences created new tasks and new disciplines for methodological reasons. The project of unity of science, behaviourism in psychology, and structuralism in linguistics all reflected fascination with the precise methodology of the pure sciences. At the turn of the century, Rickert and Dilthey had warned human scientists against such a fascination. They attacked historical positivism and mechanist doctrines in psychology and aesthetics, attempting to separate the natural sciences from the moral sciences (or sciences of the spirit) in the name of divergent methodologies. Yet, despite its considerable influence on aesthetics and art history, their epistemological dualism soon encountered hostility on two fronts: on one, Husserl's monism claimed to lay the foundations of all knowledge, including mathematics and science, on the experience of the knowing subject; on the other, the scientific philosophy of Ernst Mach and the Vienna school proposed the total exclusion of subjectivity and introspection from science and advised the social sciences, notably psychology, to adopt the methods of experimental physics.

The success of monism weakened the boundaries between disciplines in a way which would have been difficult to imagine a century before. In contrast, the emphasis on the historical dimension at the beginning of the nineteenth century reinforced those borders. A hierarchy of disciplines was then established: history was accepted as occupying a higher place than linguistics, and paleography as being less important than either. The hierarchy was little resented as long as increasing specialization reinforced both the autonomy and the prosperity of each discipline. At the end of the nineteenth century, thanks in large measure to the efforts of Bréal, Whitney and Saussure, linguistics had become quite different from comparative philology and had evolved into a vast federation of disciplinary fields covering all languages of the world and all domains of language, from phonetics to stylistics. Any significant innovation was unreservedly accepted into the discipline. For instance, although over the long term they contributed to the erosion of comparatist practices, the experimental phonetics of Abbé Rousselot and Jules Gilliéron's linguistic geography easily won recognition in an environment which encouraged exhaustive description and was less keen on methodological convergence. Thus, when Saussure, in his *Course in General Linguistics*, advocated that linguistics be freed from the tutelage of other disciplines (history, anthropology, and psychology) in order to achieve its own autonomy, he was not defining a utopian situation to be reached through revolution but rather describing a prevailing state of affairs in an era when the organic interdependance between the humanities, as recommended by Humboldt, had long ago given way to specialization.

Saussure was a moderate. In a period of disciplinary proliferation, his thought, shaped by the New Grammarians' views on comparative philology but equally influenced by the functionalism of Claude Bernard and the new Swiss and French sociology (Durkheim, Walras and Pareto), realized that the autonomy of linguistics was inevitable. Like a medium-sized nation which resigns itself to becoming a republic after vainly offering its throne to members of several European royal families, nineteenth-century linguistics had unsuccessfully turned to biological, physical and historical models, only to discover each time its own irreducible originality. Schleicher's adversaries had demonstrated that the analogy of language with living beings and their evolution was not supported by the available evidence on linguistic evolution; linguistic geography had shown how uncertain was the effect of phonetic laws and how unwarranted were the analogies between linguistics and physics; finally, the links between the history and the science of language were rendered problematic by the absence of any clear interdependence between linguistic change and historical events. In relation to history, moreover, linguistics found itself dangerously relegated to an auxiliary role. The autonomy advocated, or rather, recognized, by Saussure could succeed only if all branches of linguistics were given a respectable place. The rejection of external models made an inventory of internal resources necessary: hence the recognition granted to traditions other than comparative philology. Hence, too, Saussure's remarkable timidity about his own theories: his role of a benevolent peacemaker precluded the expression of clear-cut theoretical positions that might have jeopardized the much desired harmony within linguistics.

Today, the admirers of the *Course in General Linguistics*, content to repeat over and over again the same few quotations on signs, values and syntagmatic and paradigmatic relations, neglect the integrative aspect of Saussure's teachings, and focus instead on its 'revolutionary' aspects. They forget that the book, published by Saussure's students, devotes as much attention to synchronic linguistics as to historical grammar, linguistic geography and experimental phonetics.

Lévi-Strauss's references to Saussure are no exception. Saussure is mentioned in *Structural Anthropology* only in connection with the arbitrariness of the sign (vol. 1, pp. 88, 91, 209) or, in an even vaguer manner, as the founder of structural linguistics (vol. 1, pp. 20, 52, where Saussure shares the honour with Antoine Meillet). In all five cases there is noticeable on the one hand a lack of interest in the detail of Saussure's doctrines and, on the other, a firm conviction of how important these doctrines are for the healthy development of a rejuvenated anthropology.

Rejuvenated, that is, in the sense of being ready to desert the descriptive–interpretative disciplines for the camp of the methodologically based sciences. Unlike linguistics and experimental psychology, which reached methodological modernization as early as the 1920s, anthropology continued through the first half of the century to subordinate methodological concerns to pursue descriptive goals. Thus, research by the American school of anthropology led by Franz Boas was, in large part, oriented towards descriptive tasks, with a minimum of general theory and little methodological discussion. When, after the First World War, the followers of Boas resolutely ranged themselves on the side of cultural determinism against the partisans of biological determinism, the new theoretical priorities did not lead to greater methodological awareness. In fact the opposite happened. By endeavouring to prove that the biological behaviour of humans depends on social conventions, they showed themselves ready to compromise on method in order to arrive at the desired results more quickly. Margaret Mead's research on Samoa is an excellent example of methodological negligence. British functionalists were practising a more rigorously empirical methodology, but they did not really concern themselves with its theoretical implications.

Whereas Lévi-Strauss did not specifically comment on the inadequacies of these approaches, he declared himself more generally in favour of methodological modernization, not unlike those American anthropologists (W. Goodenough, K. L. Pike and F. Loundsbury) who were also impressed by the recent results in linguistics. On the one hand, he stressed that the situation had become so irremediable within the discipline that only potent solutions borrowed from elsewhere could change it; on the other hand, to evade the burden of tradition, he resorted to exotic models heralded as a new foundation:

> Linguistics occupies a special place among the social sciences, to whose ranks it unquestionably belongs. It is not merely a social science like the others, but, rather, the one in which by far the greatest progress has been made. It is probably the only one which can truly claim to be a science and which has achieved both the formulation of an empirical method and an understanding of the nature of the data submitted to its analysis. (1958, p. 31)

He also claimed that 'the Saussurean principle of the *arbitrary character of linguistic signs* was a prerequisite for the accession of linguistics to the scientific level' (ibid., p. 209). Juxtaposed, these two fragments reveal a strategy: post-Saussurian linguistics is singled out among the human sciences to receive the enviable status of science because it allegedly understands both the nature of its object and the methodological exigency imposed by it. But since anthropology and, more particularly, the analysis of myths have not reached this exalted state and are continuing to lose ground, the reformer assumes exceptional powers.

Lévi-Strauss's confidence in Saussurian linguistics betrays a good many illusions. Aspiring to the second stage of intellectual modernization, that of methodological unification, he subscribes to the idea that true science is formal and deterministic. Otherwise, why couldn't the functionalist anthropology of a Radcliffe-Brown or a Malinowski, perfectly empirical and completely lucid in its treatment of fact, qualify as real science? Because, answers Lévi-Strauss, these scholars did not succeed in discovering *necessary* relationships as structural linguistics had done (ibid., p. 33). In contrast, thanks to the application of Saussurian principles, the phonology of Troubetzkoy and Jakobson would have accomplished precisely this feat! Saussure's canonization as the unwitting pioneer of scientific modernity is thus based upon the belief that his linguistics, like all true sciences, formulates necessary laws.

Yet, the traditional strength of human sciences comes from practices of description and understanding. Sometimes cumulative, sometimes subject to the leaps and bounds of the dialectic, these practices guarantee the object of study its empirical stability and afford each successive generation of scholars a sense of common purpose. Beyond differences of opinion, beyond polemics and schools of thought, each human science defines its horizon, which embraces research but does not compel it to stay within its flexible boundaries. A feeling of belonging develops, and tacit rules and customs emerge. Every discipline develops its own culture, but the human sciences, not having been governed by harsh or explicit rules like medieval theology or modern science, are fashioned more intimately by the acceptance of informal agreements, *savoir-vivre* and intellectual tact.

A discipline's relevance clearly depends on the intellectual practices which crystallized during its development. This in no way implies the dissolution of rigour and even less an apology for relativism, since the differentiation of these practices leads to well-defined intellectual controls. If intellectual integrity, for example, is judged according to different precepts in literary criticism, linguistics and mathematics, it is because in each field the accepted values, just like the principles which confer legitimacy on the results, depend on local traditions and the material being studied. As grammarian or as historian of the language, the linguist is concerned with the formal patterns of language and not with its experiential context. Under these conditions, the arbitrariness of the sign, far from being the founding discovery of modern linguistics, in fact represents the very condition of possibility of historical grammar, dialectology and lexicography. In so far as there are no motivated links between sound and concept, historical phonetics can have an objective: to follow modifications in sound independently of semantic variations; in so far as sense cannot be deduced from the phonetic form of a word, the lexicographer can record myriads of accepted uses under the same keyword. Read from the point of view of their first audience rather than in retrospect after three-quarters of a century of synchronic linguistics, Saussure's passages on the arbitrariness of the sign appear as *an attempt to generalize a truth which had already been tried and tested in historical grammar onto descriptive grammar*. Saussure (1916) writes, referring to his considerations on language change:

> Above we had to accept the theoretical possibility of [linguistic] change: further reflection suggests that the arbitrary nature of the sign is really what protects language from any attempt to modify it. (ibid., p. 73)

In anthropology and myth analysis, however, the disciplinary tradition rests on the examination of meaningful objects in close relation with their social and cultural context. The study of archaic institutions and the so-called primitive mentality has, from the descriptions of the missionaries on, always involved accounting for the *networks of motivation* which relate certain forms of social organization to their tacit functions, to the representations they legitimate, and to the self-consciousness of social groups. Such networks of motivation were essential for all anthropologists independently of their specific methods and objectives. In the same vein, the interpretation of myths and religious beliefs always attempted to decipher the links between these and the moral and social experience embodied by myths and religion, whether they express their content transparently, or use symbolism to convey a message inaccessible to the believer. The myth of Demeter speaks of death and mystical rebirth to the scholar of hermeneutics, of the unfolding of agrarian rites to the historian of religion: yet in both cases interpretation gives access to and motivates the text.

In anthropology, meaning cannot be reduced to the order of signs. Whereas no linguist has ever tried to find anything but contingent relations between the sound /tri:/ and the concept 'tree', the anthropologist inquires about the nature, not the existence, of motivated links between cultural products and their meaning. Clearly, the anthropologist's biases regarding the nature of social phenomena may influence his interpretation of the facts, if not their very selection: it was not by chance that functionalist anthropology avoided studying ritual or that C. G. Jung's analyses quietly passed over the American Indian tradition of myths. Wishing to conceal this bias, the structuralist programme defended the theoretical neutrality of its analyses. Structuralism thus claimed to surpass its predecessors in objectivity and in precision in the same way that classical mechanics had made Aristotle's physics obsolete in the seventeenth century. Sharing the formalist ideology of methodological diffusion with modern science – although we will shortly see how vague its applications remain – structural anthropology defied any attempt to explain social phenomena causally or functionally. It attempted only to describe dependencies and relationships. In the final analysis, structuralist speculations on social or human nature identified it with its ability to generate these relationships, just as Descartes and Newton defined nature according to number and not according to quiddity.

Modernization somehow feels duty-bound to separate its targets from natural frameworks of explanation. The dismissal of essences in post-Galilean science differs little from the modernization's loosening of the old ties between the individual and the cosmos. In the first case, mathematical formalism usurps the place of Being; in the latter, Being is gradually converted into Use. Through one further operation, the useful separates from the rational norms that constitute it: the useful becomes the arbitrary. In the human sciences, the search for necessary relations puts too much pressure on a domain ill-prepared to undergo the process. To postulate, as Lévi-Strauss does, that the relation between the visible form of a social structure or a myth and its hidden content is arbitrary, gives unwarranted priority to randomness. Far from being a faithful application of Saussurian principles to anthropology – for, as we have just seen, the arbitrariness of the linguistic sign is a prerequisite of *any* theoretical statement on language – Lévi-Strauss's professed admiration for Saussure stems rather from the fact that, in the linguistic practice made explicit by Saussure, the anthropologist finds a model of modernization which, despite its dangerous implications for anthropology, can be promoted in the name of solidarity between the social sciences. Hence Lévi-Strauss's insistence on the primacy of linguistics among the human sciences: his aim is to pre-empt any questions about the new methodology and about the epistemological consequences of transferring the principle of arbitrariness to anthropology. Hence also his need to present the 'discovery' of the arbitrariness of the linguistic sign as a recent breakthrough marking the end of a long dark age in linguistics: this manoeuvre aims at convincing anthropologists that the principle of arbitrariness is a legitimate instrument of modernization. In fact, the transfer of the arbitrariness principle to anthropology represented the transformation of a *traditional* linguistic notion into a weapon against current mythological analysis.

But once the arbitrariness of the sign was used as a lever to separate anthropological facts from any network of motivation, a radically new formality had to be imposed on these facts. With this end in view, Lévi-Strauss relied on the phonological models of structural linguistics, the only models which, in his view, could prove the existence of 'necessary relationships' in the natural languages. In fact, the New Grammarians thought they had already found necessary relationships postulating that phonetic laws act as blindly as the laws of nature. In 1878, Saussure's *Mémoire sur le système primitif des voyelles indo-européennes* developed the idea of a phonic system. The phonologists of the Prague school developed this longtime concern of historical grammar into what remained one of the best developed structural disciplines until the late 1930s. Moreover, by the mid-1940s a flexible and sophisticated structural morphology had come into being and in 1946 the first attempts in formal syntax were published: Zellig Harris's 'From Morpheme to Utterance' and Bernard Bloch's important article on Japanese syntax. Linguistics shifted the emphasis of research on 'necessary relationships' from phonetics to syntax. This remarkable transition culminated in 1955 in Noam Chomsky's thesis *The Logical Structure of Linguistic Theory*. Lévi-Strauss's analysis of the Oedipus myth, which drew on phonological principles and applied them to a cultural object, was published in the same year.

THE PHONOLOGY OF MEANING

According to Lévi-Strauss's reading of the Oedipus myth, just as the linguistic sign is composed of two sides (sound and concept) joined by arbitrary bonds, each myth contains an apparent story and a hidden structure. The relationships between the two levels are arbitrary, and any interpretation of a myth which uses only its apparent story is by definition mistaken. To discover the hidden structure one must employ phonological techniques, since it is phonology which best reduces spoken sounds to simple underlying systems.

Reading a myth, Lévi-Strauss tell us, is a misleading operation, as if one was looking at an orchestral score not as the simultaneous organization of a set of instruments but as a continuous single line, beginning, say, with the whole flute score, followed by the entire oboe part, then by the clarinet part, and so forth. Read as such, the score obviously does not make musical sense. The musician who receives a copy of a Haydn symphony mistakenly arranged 'in succession' must, in order to understand it, copy the scores for each instrument one under the other in accordance with the laws of harmony, orchestration, counterpoint, and so on. Likewise, Lévi-Strauss continues, the anthropologist examining a myth the narrative thread of which is but a disorderly mixture of disparate elements must separate the mythical story into discontinuous elements and then redistribute them into a coherent structure in accordance with the laws of myth organization. In these theoretical metaphors, we recognize the arbitrariness of the linguistic sign, the non-coincidence between signifier and signified, and the phonological operation through which, by dividing the sound continuum, the phonologist finds the inventory of phonemes which he then organizes into a phonological system.

In the Oedipus myth, the system takes the following form (notice that the arrangement vaguely resembles an orchestral score):

Cadmos seeks his sister Europa, ravished by Zeus			
		Cadmos kills the dragon	
	The Spartoi kill one another		
			Labdacos (Laios' father) = *lame* (?)
	Oedipus kills his father, Laios		Laios (Oedipus' father) = *left-sided* (?)
		Oedipus kills the Sphinx	
			Oedipus = *swollen-foot* (?)
Oedipus marries his mother, Jocasta			
	Eteocles kills his brother, Polynices		
Antigone buries her brother, Polynices, despite prohibition			

One unravels the myth by reading the rows from left to right and from top to bottom; one makes the myth comprehensible by considering the columns as units and reading them one after another from left to right. Thus, the telling of the myth involves going from one event to the next: first, Cadmos seeks his sister, Europa, ravished by Zeus; then the Spartoi kill one another; then Cadmos kills the dragon; and so on. Since the order of the elements in this arrangement follows the story chronologically, Lévi-Strauss calls it diachronic. Conversely, synchrony consists in the comparison of the four columns, which leads to an understanding of the myth as a system. The analysis produces a definition of the four columns as, respectively, the overrating of blood relations (manifested by Cadmos' love for his sister, Oedipus' incest and Antigone's devotion to her brother's memory); the underrating of blood relations (the Spartoi mutual murder, Oedipus' killing of his father, Eteocles' slaying of his brother, Polynices); the slaying of monsters (the dragon, the Sphinx); and, finally, the difficulties in walking straight and standing upright suggested by the meaning of Labdacos' and Oedipus' names. Comparing the first two columns, Lévi-Strauss notices that they seem to weigh the overrating against the underrating of blood relations; while the two last columns respectively deny and assert the links between humans and the earth. The unexpected interpretation of the third and fourth columns rests on the observation that the slain monsters belong to the category of chthonian creatures, while the faltering gaits implied by the various proper names can be attributed to the insufficient autonomy of man with respect to his mother, Earth.

Thus, in Lévi-Strauss's reading, the Oedipus myth relates ideas about blood relations to ideas about the autochthonous origin of man. Though invisible during the normal reading of the myth, these ideas form a proportional relation of sorts: 'the overrating of blood relations is to the underrating of blood relations as the attempt to escape autochthony is to the impossibility to succeed in it' (Lévi-Strauss, 1963, p. 216). The proportional or analogic correspondence between these ideas, each accompanied by its negation, testifies to the intellectual tension felt by the culture in which the myth was created when the culture was confronted by apparently insoluble problems: 'The myth has to do with the inability, for a culture which holds the belief that mankind is autochthonous . . . to find a satisfactory transition between this theory and the knowledge that human beings are actually born from the union of man and woman' (ibid., p. 216).

The theory which underlies this analysis rests on several assumptions about the relations between myth and language, assumptions that could be formulated as follows:

1 The meaning of myth does not reside in its 'diachronic' unfolding but is present only in the myth's totality; its components do not possess meaning

in or by themselves.
2 Myth is a linguistic phenomenon enjoying specific properties.
3 These properties are certainly more complex than those of other linguistic phenomena.

While there is nothing wrong with assumptions (2) and (3), which simply indicate the methodological decision to import linguistic models, assumption (1) asserts something about the nature of myth and consequently has empirical content. But, whereas propositions possessing empirical content need to be supported with empirical proof, (1) here represents the starting point of the entire approach; it is asserted dogmatically as if it were a matter of common knowledge. In fact, Lévi-Strauss's claim that the elements of myths do not possess an autonomous meaning appears as a consequence of the introduction of linguistic, more specifically phonological, models into mythology. Absence of autonomous meaning is, indeed, a characteristic of isolated phonemes; yet, as many critics of Lévi-Strauss have remarked, the meaning of linguistic utterances does not come from an agglomeration of phonemes. The arbitrariness of linguistic signs and the systematic character of phonology notwithstanding, the meaning of linguistic utterances still derives from the meaning of their components, the words. This property, which has been called the componential character of natural semantics, is evident at any level of language: complex words, phrases, sentences, etc. The question, therefore, is why, once language has been selected as the regulatory model of anthropology, the methodological decision was taken to apply phonological notions to myth analysis without either exploring alternative linguistic models which may have proven more adequate, or producing independent evidence showing the meaninglessness of the isolated elements of myths.

Put more generally, the problem raised by Lévi-Strauss's analysis is how to justify theoretical borrowings from one discipline to another. When discipline D wishes to borrow the methods and categories of another discipline, D', what principles regulate the relation between the elements of D and the elements of D'? When anthropology uses a linguistic model, how are linguistic notions to be paired with their anthropological counterparts? To take only one mythological concept, that of mythological pattern (understood as a sequence of mythological elements which occurs with a certain constancy in different myths belonging to various cultures) and to use it in conjunction with a simplified linguistic set of notions, we have to decide whether (and why) the mythological pattern is to be paired with the phoneme and not with the morpheme, the word (as Paul Ricoeur suggested long ago), the morpheme sequence (complex word or word group), or the sentence. The decision is crucial: if mythological patterns are treated as phonemes, they will be meaningless and play a major role in constituting and distinguishing higher level units which, in turn, will have to resemble the morphological level of natural languages. If mythological patterns are similar to morphemes, they will possess meaning, be irreducible to smaller meaningful units, and contribute to the global meaning of the next level. If we want these patterns to be broken down into independent meaningful units (for example, if we want to decompose the archetype of the guilty king into the elements 'king' and 'guilty'), we might prefer the mythological pattern to correspond to complex words. Finally, it might be fruitful to assimilate them with sentences, especially when they contain actions and not just characters or situations. Clearly, of these choices, the least illuminating for the anthropologist is the treatment of myths as phonological structures. Suppose none the less that, despite these considerations, we still want to select the phonological method. In that case, we must ensure that the use made of phonology in myth analysis does not contradict linguistic practice, or, if it does, that the differences are clearly explained in terms of the properties of the new field of application.

The primary purpose of structural phonology was to discover the system of invariants underlying all phonetic utterances of a given natural language. Accordingly, once the invariant elements were discovered, the phonological analysis of a language had to be able to assign a phonological representation to each phonetic sequence in that language. If, for instance, the invariant elements are phonemes, the phonologist should have no difficulty in transcribing any utterance in terms of phonemes; if the invariants chosen are distinctive features, phonological representation would translate phonetic sequences into sequences of distinctive features. The phonology of each language, the structural linguists thought, could be described in various equivalent ways; nevertheless, the phonologist was not free to act as he pleased. The phonological description of a given language, that is, the representation of phonetic sequences in terms of phonological units was subjected to a set of theoretical constraints destined to prevent the phonologist from freely manipulating the data. In 1964, Chomsky (who entertained his own, very different ideas on phonology) formulated classical phonology in terms of five conditions:

1 phonetic specifiability
2 invariance
3 linearity
4 biuniqueness
5 local determinacy

The phonetic specifiability condition required that phonological theory incorporate a general phonetic theory consisting of a universal phonetic alphabet and a set of general laws concerning phonetic combinations and contrasts. In other words, the phonologist did not carry out his analyses without having his feet on firm phonetic ground.

The linearity condition meant that once the list of phonemes corresponding to the sounds was established, the phonemic representation of any sequence of sounds had to be such that if the phoneme A preceded phoneme B in the phonological representation, then in the phonetic sequence the realization of A had to precede the realization of B. The purpose of this requirement was to limit the possible arbitrariness of the analyses by imposing a strict parallel order between the phonetic transcription and its phonological representation. For example, if a phonological analysis of English assigns the sounds [kh], [aê] and [th], respectively to the phonemes /k/, /ae/ and /t/, then the phonetic string which manifests the phonological representation /kaet/ 'cat' must be [khaêth], with the sounds arranged in this particular order and not, say, [khthaê]. This requirement seems so obvious that one is almost astonished to see it formulated with such care; yet we shall soon see that Lévi-Strauss's mythological analysis failed to take it into account.

In its strongest form, the invariance condition prevented a single sound from serving as the realization of two different phonemes. If, for instance, in certain circumstances the sound [d] was assumed to represent phoneme /d/, it could not represent the phoneme /t/ in another context. When expressed in this manner, the invariance constraint made it difficult to describe the phenomena of neutralization. Consequently, some linguists adopted a weaker form of the requirement without modifying its aim which was, once again, to minimize the arbitrariness of the analysis and to secure a strong link between the theoretical constructs (the phonological representations) and their empirical base (the sequence of sounds).

This link was further strengthened by the biuniqueness condition, which required the phonological representation and the phonetic transcription of a given segment to be unequivocally deducible from one another. For technical reasons, linguists also adopted a related condition, often called the condition of local determinacy, which asked that the information used in deducing a phonological representation from a phonetic one be limited to phonetic facts and, conversely, all information used in building a phonetic representation from phonological data be of a phonological nature. This rule aimed at excluding potential vicious circles from phonology by not presupposing as known what was going to be discovered. The general purpose of these restrictions is thus apparent: they strove to guarantee the phonological description with a high degree of precision, to minimize the role of random decisions, to attach abstract representations firmly to empirical content, and to endow phonology with a procedure for evaluating research results.

Now let us see how these conditions are reflected in Lévi-Strauss's adaptation of phonology to the study of myth. The phonetic specifiability condition required the phonologist to master detailed knowledge of the raw material of the phonological system, namely, to have a phonetic theory. This theory was assumed to be largely independent of the phonological theory, although in the later stages of research the two had to be related. Linguists labelled the considerations of linguistic substance *etic* statements (from the ending of the word *phonetics*), opposing them to *emic* or formal statements (from *phonemics*) which describe the abstract form of language. In the analysis of myths a roughly similar condition of etic specifiability would require that the researcher first prepare a universal theory of mythological raw material which would render the pre-systematic description of myths possible. But what could be considered as the raw matter of myths; the narrated events? – in which case the etic side of mythology would coincide with narratology; the mythological archetypes? – which would give Jung's analyses a privileged place; the motifs described by folklorists following the ideas of Aarne and Thompson? The question never even arises. In Lévi-Strauss's work, the etic level did not qualify as an independent domain of the theory in relation to which the emic level could be discovered or at least defined.

The linearity condition compelled theoretical representations to follow the raw material closely with regard to the order of elements. A major difficulty in evaluating the application of this condition in Lévi-Strauss's structural anthropology is the absence, noted above, of an explicit etic level. It is possible, however, to determine how such a level, if it existed, would relate to the emic level in Lévi-Strauss's analyses.

Let us assume that the etic level is composed of the events of a myth. This assumption does not deviate too much from Lévi-Strauss's practice, at least regarding the Oedipus myth. Indeed, the proposed reading to the myth proceeds as if Lévi-Strauss has constructed his four-column model, which can be thought of as the emic level, from a selective list of events. The emic unit 'underrating of blood relations' for instance, includes the etic units 'the Spartoi kill one another', 'Oedipus kills his father', 'Eteocles kills his brother Polynices', etc. As long as we limit our survey to the first three columns, the linearity is preserved. Indeed, as clumsy as such an analysis would be, there is nothing wrong with matching an etic sequence such as:

'Oedipus kills his father', then 'Oedipus kills the Sphinx', then 'Oedipus marries his mother'

with an emic representation such as:

'Underrating of blood relations', then 'denial of the autochtonous origin of man', then 'overrating of blood relations'

But as soon as we try to account for the fourth column the linearity condition is violated, because the units of the fourth column are situated outside the narrative flow of the myth. In the myth's sequence of events, we cannot find anything like:

'Oedipus kills the Sphinx', then 'Oedipus' name means "swollen-foot"'

since, except for the cases where names are conferred to recall memorable exploits, the names of heroes do not constitute events and, consequently, have no particular narrative importance in the myth. True, phonology has developed the conceptual apparatus needed to deal with cases of etic properties which cannot be localized at a specific moment in the spoken chain. Intonational contours resemble proper names since, just as intonation covers the entire phonetic segment, a proper name accompanies a character throughout a story. But in order to account for this kind of phonetic phenomena, phonologists have carefully distinguished between a segmental level, which includes phonemes that can be identified at a specific location in the spoken chain, and a supra-segmental level, comprising phonemes 'added' to the segment: intonation, stress, pitch and length. Each level respects its own linearity.

Lévi-Strauss's analysis incautiously mixes events and proper names for the very reason that the study of myth has little to do with phonology. Accordingly, some constraints, such as linearity, which make sense for phonological representation, are too restrictive for meaningful phenomena. It is quite likely that at least some semantic properties of texts are not ordered linearly; French semioticians would later call such phenomena the 'isotopies' of a text. But if this is indeed the case, how can we still claim that phonological models are adequate of the needs of myth analysis? And if, for some reason, the linearity condition must be suspended, shouldn't the conditions under which the transition from linearity to nonlinearity is allowed be explicitly stated?

As for the invariance condition, the lack of etic specifiability in Lévi-Strauss's analyses almost makes its discussion superfluous. The violation of linearity does not make the task easier. Let us assume, however, that only local violations of linearity occur and that there are some unspecified ways of relating theoretical units to the etic level. The invariance condition ensures that the assignment of etic entities to emic ones is performed uniformly: once a given etic unit has been associated with an emic one, it cannot be linked to another emic unit except in specific, strictly defined circumstances. In the analysis of the Oedipus myth, for example, the action of killing a close relative is assigned to the theoretical unit 'underrating of blood relations'. According to the strongest form of the invariance condition, every time the analyst claims that the myth contains the emic unit 'underrating of blood-relations', the text of the myth should contain the slaying of a close relative. In Lévi-Strauss's scheme this is indeed the case. Quite correctly, the murder of a close relative is never associated with another abstract emic unit. Nevertheless, strict application of the invariance condition can take place only if the theoretical units are themselves narrowly defined. The first column shows that such is not the case: to include under the same theoretical item ('overrating of blood relations'), elements as different as the burial of a brother and marriage to a woman who happens to be the bridegroom's own mother treats identity and difference in an unconstrained and haphazard manner. The capricious matching of etic to emic elements gradually becomes more visible in Lévi-Strauss's later work. In the analysis of Oedipus, in which invariance is still respected, this apparent regularity is obtained only because of the great freedom allowed in assigning etic elements to their abstract theoretical counterparts.

The biuniqueness and the local determinacy conditions further constrain the range of choices available to the analyst. They are particularly difficult to observe, especially when the phonologist is not permitted to make use of non-phonic information: local determinacy, for instance, obliges the linguist to draw up a language's list of phonemes before the division of the spoken chain into words is known. Keeping the levels of analysis separate may make some sense in linguistics, where the hierarchy of domains (phonology, morphology, syntax) has been long given; but it would be useless in anthropology, where so little is known about levels of representation. Since, moreover, local determinacy is not unanimously accepted, even by structural linguists, the two last conditions will be discussed together.

The two conditions essentially require that the rules stating the correspondences between the etic and the emic levels be devised so as to allow each etic description to be matched with one and only one emic representation and, conversely, to associate only one etic description with each emic description. In linguistic practice, however, it has become clear that although the passage from phonological representations to the corresponding phonetic descriptions is entirely specifiable in terms of the rules of phonological correspondence, the reverse does not necessarily hold, that is, the phonetic representations do not necessarily lead to phonological representations in an unambiguous way. There is nothing surprising about this asymmetry. That it is easier to recover an etic representation from an emic one than the reverse agrees with the commonly accepted view concerning the relations between theory and data. A description of the data together with a set of scientific laws is usually compatible with several theoretical explanations. On the other hand, the theoretical representation accompanied by the laws of that domain should yield a unique set of predictions; in the ideal case, the correct ones.

It is less baffling that the analysis of the Oedipus violates the biuniqueness and local determinacy conditions than that this violation comes about in an unusual way. In fact it is easy to establish a set of rules to show how Lévi-Strauss arrived at his scheme. Their form would be somewhat like the following instruction:

Read the text of the myth, and every time you come across the killing of a close relative, mark it with the symbol 'underrating of blood relations'.

For the Oedipus myth we need five such rules: four for the columns and one for the deletion of everything else. Their application combined with an instruction such as:

Place all events marked by the same symbol one under another.

will result in the four columns. But carrying out the reverse operation, that is, moving from the emic to the etic level, is impossible. The events of the myth deleted during the construction of the four columns are too numerous to recover by using only the five rules above. In other words, we cannot reconstitute the myth of Oedipus from the four columns and the rules that led to their establishment. What we are left with is an unintelligible sequence of events and proper names.

Trying to explain why certain events traditionally considered as essential are missing from his theoretical representation, Lévi-Strauss noted that Jocasta's suicide and Oedipus' self-inflicted punishment, which are absent from the oldest versions of the myth, can easily be integrated into the four-column scheme, the former as a slaying of a chthonian being (column three) and the latter as a confirmation of Oedipus' name (column four). But even if we were to agree with this improbable reading of what readers and students of the myth have felt for thousands of years to be a double punishment, a central component of the myth remains unaccounted for: the interrelated movement of guilt and knowledge. Even the most archaic variants emphasize that since Oedipus did not know who he was when killing his father and marrying his mother, both were crimes of ignorance. It is also common to most variants that Oedipus' offences attract the wrath of the gods, who, after a period of silence, answer the insistent inquiries of the unhappy king and inform him of his identity and crimes. The absence of this essential part of the myth, namely, the relation between guilt and knowledge, is the most serious violation of the biuniqueness/local determinacy condition. What else can we conclude but that, from both the theoretical and methodological point of view, Lévi-Strauss's analysis of the Oedipus myth has little to do with classical phonology's regard to empirical justification of its descriptions, or with its constant preoccupation with the principles of scientific inquiry and intersubjective verification? After all, Lévi-Strauss's lack of genuine interest in the rigorous methods of structural linguistics demonstrate that his disciplinary instincts were correct. Practice made phonology and linguistics dispensable: beyond them, in Lévi-Strauss's analysis of the Oedipus myth, we recognize the perennial concern of mythologists for the meaning of sacred stories.

THE RETURN TO GNOSIS

Lévi-Strauss's concern, however, differed in certain respects. Structural linguistics, Lévi-Strauss claimed, reveals the unconscious character of language operations. The fact that a phonological system does not really have to take the mind of its speakers into account is what perhaps attracted him most, since he wanted not so much to submit to new constraints as to escape hermeneutic controls. Yet the urge to reform took place, out of necessity, within the long-established parameters of the discipline. The past was more than ever present; despite the impetus of modernization, old habits furtively re-emerged, legitimated by the new ideology. Divergences between textual evidence and the distortions of interpretation were already common in medieval Jewish and Christian exegesis of holy texts. The theoreticians of the four meanings of Scripture aimed at giving textual legitimacy to the dogmatic interpretations least constrained by the letter of the Bible. Going even further, the cabalists utilized a principle of spontaneous permutation of the phonological and lexical units: since, in their view, the text of the Torah contained all possible meanings, every possible combination of letters was entitled to meaning despite violations of linearity. Born of divine understanding, the Torah goes far beyond what mortals believe they are reading; discovery of its message consequently comes through the radical decomposition of its apparent cohesiveness. As with Lévi-Strauss, the perceptible text becomes frozen in a mysterious jumble of currents of meaning legitimated at a completely different level. The principles of humanist philology transformed biblical criticism in the seventeenth century. In *Tractatus theologico-politicus*, Spinoza established a clear distinction between mystical reading and historical exegesis. One consequence of this sharp distinction was the creation of nineteenth-century linguistics and its structuralist offspring. Another branch of this tradition links biblical criticism with work on the history of religions in the eighteenth and nineteenth centuries. Frazer, Cornford, Jung, Malinowski, Eliade, Jaspers and Bultmann, all belong in different ways to the movement which, as far back as Bayle and Spinoza, examined the Holy Book and, consequently, myths in general in accordance with the principles of philological rationality – with the emphasis either on historical criticism or on the interpretation of the message.

The anthropology of myths derives from the same project. Methodology did not give rise to any problems from Spinoza to Saussure, even to Troubetzkoy. Yet, between Troubetzkoy and Lévi-Strauss, or even between Frazer and Lévi-Strauss, despite the persistence of the same concerns, methodological techniques underwent a dramatic change. The use of medieval exegetical methods, now radicalized, became possible once more. Since Spinoza, the ethos of biblical philology and the disciplines of man have been defined in exact opposition with the medieval use: it follows that Lévi-Strauss's practice reverted to archaic practices, but without going as far as openly assuming regression.

Lévi-Strauss's later stances confirm this epistemological confusion. Comparing mythology to music, the 'Finale' to *The Naked Man* (1981) asserts the emptiness of a theoretical approach that hesitates to dissolve into its object:

> The myths are only translatable into each other in the same way as a melody is only translatable into another which retains a relationship of homology with . . . But while one can always . . . translate one melody into another . . . as in the case of mythology, one cannot translate music into anything other than itself without falling into the would-be hermeneutic verbiage characteristic of old-fashioned mythography and of too much musical criticism. This is to say that an unlimited freedom of translation into the dialects of an original language forming a closed system is bound up with the radical impossibility of any transposition into an extrinsic language. (ibid., p. 646)

It remains to be established whether such a 'radical impossibility' really comes from the nature of the object studied or instead from an unforeseen return to techniques of pre-critical exegesis.

3 The Transcendental Ties of Linguistics

During the 1950s and 1960s, methodological modernization based on structural linguistics moved into disciplines that were seeking rigour and formalism, namely, psychoanalysis and literary criticism. However, it gradually became apparent that linguistic methodology would soon no longer suffice as a model of rigour. Both Lévi-Strauss in anthropology and Jacques Lacan in psychoanalysis had often warned against slavish imitation of linguistic models. Other sources of intellectual modernization were needed. Thanks to Roman Jakobson, Paul Garvin and Tzvetan Todorov, innovators in literary studies discovered the works of Vladimir Propp, the Russian formalists and the aestheticians of the Prague school. These works, though independent from linguistics, shared its concern for formal rigour. Furthermore, during the same period linguistics itself was undergoing a crisis which would completely detach it from the structuralist doctrines and methods. For these reasons it seemed necessary, at the end of the 1960s, to consolidate the different attempts at renewing the human sciences into a single movement, if not even into a single discipline, one that would be better prepared to meet the theoretical needs of various human sciences in search of a formal base. In fact, the discipline already had two names: Saussure had spoken of a *general semiology* of which linguistics would be only one branch; the term *semiotics* had been used for some time in the United States. Despite their differences, both Roland Barthes in *Elements of Semiology* and Umberto Eco in *A Theory of Semiotics* agreed that a programme was needed to bring together the human sciences under a single methodology.

STRUCTURALISM AND HERMENEUTICS

A great many different semiologies and semiotics were proposed during this period, all of which aimed of excluding reference to reality and concentrated on the purely instrumental categories of language. Similarly to the linguistic approach, semiology disregards the links to empirical reality and the notional wealth of human sciences. Lévi-Strauss's treatment of the Oedipus myth is a striking example. In a semiological system, language schemata are supposed to provide human sciences with the type of foundation that mathematics has given to physics and astronomy: concepts are reduced to linguistic formality. In Saussure's linguistics, this operation begun with the reduction of *meaning* to the *sign*. Semiology, according to its creators, would eliminate from contemporary thinking everything that went beyond pure articulation, beyond the emptiness of the new formality.

In 1963, structuralism possessed only the groping methodology of Lévi-Strauss. Yet others were beginning to see it as a legitimate auxiliary of hermeneutics. Structuralist explanations, Ricoeur noted in 1963: '(1) relate to an unconscious system which (2) is made up of differences and oppositions [of meaningful distinctions] (3) independently of the observer' (P. 621). In contrast, hermeneutic interpretations 'consist in (1) the conscious examination (2) of an overdetermined symbolic background (3) by an interpreter who situates himself in the same semantic field as the object of his understanding and thus enters into the hermeneutic circle' (ibid.). Nevertheless, Ricoeur believed that the two activities could be linked together.

Similarly, in 1966, Gérard Genette predicted linkages between structuralism and hermeneutics 'not of mechanical separation and of exclusion, but of complementarity: with regard to a single work, hermeneutic criticism would speak the language of the recreation of meaning and interiority and structural criticism that of the distant speech and intelligible reconstruction' (1966, p. 61).

Not everyone welcomed the expansion of structuralism. In 1965 the literary historian Raymond Picard attacked the structuralist method in its most vulnerable spot: its claim to be scientific. In an analysis of Barthes's (1963) essay on Racine, Picard denounced the pseudo-scientific vocabulary, the lack of patience with the text – philology's cardinal virtue – and the absence of the regulatory notion of truth. Barthes's response (1965) minimized the importance of truth, intimating that the advanced wing of structuralism, far from peacefully adding a surplus of technical knowledge to the foundations of the philologico-hermeneutic edifice, openly set about its demolition. Reference and meaning were not left aside for a short while for the sake of better studying the articulation of signs. Structuralism worked relentlessly towards the *replacement* of reference and meaning by signs.

In 1967, following Chomsky's long and devastating criticism of linguistic structuralism, Ricoeur advocated establishing a complete science of language that could perhaps accommodate linguistics and could take into account the dynamism of discourse as well as its speaker, meaning and reference:

it is not enough to juxtapose a vague phenomenology of the act of speaking to a rigorous linguistics of the language system. Language and speech must be bound together in the work of discourse. (1967, p. 810)

A fine plan, perhaps too fine. In the past twenty years linguistics has, contrary to Ricoeur's hopes, become even more rigorous and more firmly grounded on a mathematical base than the old structuralism. On the rare occasions when linguists analyse discourse, they use purely formal relations. Each science treats its objects in accordance to its own methods. It is therefore as futile to suggest that linguistics should open itself to the wealth of meaning by studying discourse, as to expect anatomy to become religious through the study of the heart or the brain. If Ricoeur failed to differentiate linguistics from phenomenology and hermeneutics, it is perhaps because for some time French philosophers neglected to examine the tensions between the thinking subject and his language.

FROM CONSCIENCE TO LANGUAGE WITHOUT PHENOMENOLOGY

The philosopher Brice Parain had subtly described these tensions as early as 1947. Focusing on the disturbing property of every language never to be at rest, Parain noted that 'philosophy is today still in the same state as physics . . . before Einstein's intervention. It continues to reason as if the observer, here the individual conscience, were immobile' (1947, p. 78). This specious immobility according to Parain was a vestige of classical metaphysics, which rests on the concept of an eternal, unchangeable God. It affected even Hegel's philosophy, since the dialectical movement of the conscience, self-induced, too closely resembles the notion of *causa sui*. The self-generating dialectical movement cannot account for events which interrupt our thinking: births, deaths, crises, wars and revolutions (ibid. p. 79). Though producing a movement as perfectly regular as a chiming clock, the Hegelian dialectic succeeds no better than metaphysics in explaining the ruptures – which come from elsewhere – or the beginning – which is not imaginable within a philosophy of the conscience. Since it is impossible to conceive an irregular movement without a force moving it and stopping it, philosophy, in neglecting to study this force, obliges conscience – today we would say the subject – to play a role that it has not learned: that of God.

Because the drama featuring conscience has more than one character, a model involving two distinct forces was necessary. Long before the advent of structuralism, Parain introduced the supporting player: language. With the entrance of language, conscience can no longer be thought of as autonomous and self-generating. This model presents a limited conscience folded back on itself that language opens up to the idea of universality. The upheaval caused by language's intervention will go on indefinitely, like the ripples on a pond hit by a stone. These inevitable oscillations, which have initiated drama, also make up its plot; from now on the two characters will be unable either to live without each other, or to resolve the tensions between them, to the point that nothing will seem more threatening for conscience than the possibility of a rupture with language:

> We know that we cannot stop breathing without our bodies ceasing to exist ... But we know that we may or may not say what we first feel like saying, without its immediately having fatal consequences. There is therefore the possibility of at least a momentary rupture between breathing and speaking. (ibid., p. 82)

The dependence of the subject *vis-à-vis* language is real, yet uncertain. Purely automatic linguistic behaviour is impossible: meaning cannot be reduced to context, be it intra- or extra-linguistic context. The pressure of the linguistic context, which is a product of the force of language can never totally suppress the presence of a subject providing meaning and imperfectly bound to language. The extra-linguistic context is just as powerless, because even if the rupture between language and existence is always possible, it is never total. The freedom to remain silent does not eliminate the need to speak, and in order to explain an utterance one cannot just describe the surrounding situation: speech is not simply a mirror in which the external stimulus is reflected as reaction, it is rather 'the means to bring into being what does not yet exist' (ibid., p. 83). Although humans often dream of a pre-linguistic state, of being 'creature[s] among the creatures', such a state can never be captured outside language. Language binds existence to history, and transforms necessity to the possible.

This linkage between conscience and language is not necessarily identical with *freedom*. For Parain, and later for Barthes, language is above all a master, and its presence the sign of our servitude. According to Parain,

> individual conscience exists in an imaginary moment of time only to vanish just as quickly in the name it assumes, similar to imaginary numbers in algebra, which no longer figure in the final formula once their role has been accomplished. (ibid., p. 86)

Even corrected by such assertions as 'Conscience is, this is indisputable', this perpetual obliteration of individual conscience foreshadows the dogmas of structuralist. For, objects Parain, if conscience created language, who would guarantee its semantic stability? And how can we regain intersubjectivity from transcendental idealism? More simply, how is it that our neighbours can understand what we are saying, unless a common intellect, now called language, historically precedes our birth and governs our words? This is not to say that conscience is paralysed and entirely consumed by language. Quite the contrary: whereas the subject passes language from one state to the next, conscience, in giving life to language, also changes it:

At every moment, every conscience is destroying a little of the vocabulary that it has received and against which it cannot not revolt because it is not its own; immediately, however, it recreates another into which it disappears again. (ibid., p. 87)

This formulation is technically unsatisfying because it is concerned only with vocabulary. Nevertheless, beyond the clumsy identification of language with nomenclature, the formula makes it clear that language is subjected to the action of the mobile conscience down to its lowest levels – and not only in its vocabulary. This mobility, Parain observes, is not synonymous with autonomy: 'individual conscience is mobile because it belongs to a mobile whole that it helps move along, but whose movement is different from its own' (p. 90). Conscience feels at one and the same time its own mobility and that of the whole; perhaps it sometimes perceives a dissonance between the two movements and wants to re-establish agreement. It can do so only by *speaking*, by taking risks, which are considerable, since 'all my being refracts the world to which it belongs all the time, according to its index which is unlike any other', (Parain 1942, p. 61). Nothing is worse, therefore, than to despair of language, to try to abandon it, to become a *misologist*. We must accept the stakes and try to reduce the distance between ourselves and our language as much as possible, knowing that we are subjected to perpetual mobility and inevitable refraction.

The obstacles become evident with the mind's first operation: the act of naming, which makes us feel the separating power of language: 'the object detaches itself from me as soon as I name it' (ibid., p. 21). True, in saying the word *road* we are sure to utter 'the road itself made from stone and sand'. Yet do our words ever bring before us the thing itself? Do utterances have any power over reality?

At this point, Parain, as the structuralists and their critics did later, could have defined the linguistic sign as the absence of the object signified. Instead, he heads off in the opposite direction towards a resolutely anti-semiotic doctrine. The word 'is not identical with the thing because it never represents either an object or a person in its individuality' (ibid., p. 30). Words invoke the *possible*: they are 'orders and promises at the same time, not natural signs that would communicate the knowledge of things directly to us, nor conventional signs on which a perhaps out-of-date logical thought would act, but the seeds of being' (ibid., p. 55).

The problem is thus less one of differentiating meanings than of accomplishing what is signified in an action whose norm is language. The possible, which is another name for language, most certainly amounts to more than the possibility of the logical emptiness which astounded Aristotle in the arguments of the sophists. It heralds a task to perform:

To become real, it [language] will use poets and inventors, but it will have to find an entity, a time and a place to establish itself. The bird-man of mythology is now the pilot whom we hear fly overhead every day. The goat-deer has perhaps already appeared in some circus. Truth, justice, immortality are as much goals towards which we unceasingly strive whether we meet with failure or success ... Instead of looking at the word *goat-deer* as a monster so that other words seem real in comparison, it is from its point of view that all words must be considered. (ibid., p. 54)

Being thus subjected to the transcendence of language, we see language as the only promise of certainty. But, by submitting to this promise, we cannot avoid the delay which separates us from its fulfilment.

Conscience and language, despite being irreversibly intertwined, are always separated by a tissue of differential signs – the language of linguistics and semiology – about which Parain, like all other philosophers before 1960, worried little. When Saussurian notions were put back into circulation, the stakes of the argument changed dramatically. The generation of the 1960s aimed less at reconciling language's semiotic immobility to the incessant movement of the conscience than at choosing between these alternatives. When, at the end of the 1960s, Derrida attempted a synthesis between the phenomenology of language and Saussurian semiology, he was not so much offering semiology a supplement of meaning as imposing the reign of the sign.

THE SIGN AND THE FREEZING OF THE SUBJECT

As soon as language is no longer considered as an instrument of thought, obeying the authority of conscience, two topics emerge: the mobility of conscience and the delay as its relationship to language. For Parain, pure self-sufficient conscience was a myth, since it had already met the transcendent force of language with which it must come to terms. The outcome of this compromise is the delay. Parain did not use this term, yet, given our inability to prove the truth of our words immediately, by what name can we call the obligatory recourse to time? Our words are not like those of the pharaoh who possessed the divine ability of realizing them instantaneously. We can only promise; therefore, our relation with our utterances must take the form of postponement, of a reprieve. Both of these topics are found in Derrida's writings of the 1960s, as if mobility and postponement were so clearly inscribed in the relationship of conscience to language that two readings done from two different points of view could not help but decipher it.

In *Speech and Phenomena*, Derrida starts by showing that Husserl's distinction between the *indicative* and the *expressive* sign had always dominated philosophy of language. The indicative sign (e.g., red spots on one's face indicating measles) is one that has no intended meaning, or, in Husserl's German, *Bedeutung*. Since Derrida hesitates to identify *Bedeutung* with meaning, he translates the German word by *vouloir-dire*, 'will-to-signify'. An expressive sign (e.g., someone's uttering the word 'hello!') is a sign which possesses intended meaning or *vouloir-dire*; it is a sign endowed with a 'will-to-signify'. What arouses Derrida's interest is not as much the actual content of the distinction as its *radical* character. Why should Husserl make such a clearcut distinction, especially since the expressive signs are never seen or heard without being covered by an indicative layer? For, when uttering 'hello', the speaker indeed indicates (but does not express) the existence of thoughts and a desire to communicate. Given the constant intertwining of expressions and indications, can they be considered as radically different?

What then is a sign in general, Derrida asks. Can the unity of the sign beyond the heterogeneity of the indication and the expression be imagined or at least assumed? And, at the same time, can we try to *define* the sign? Classical philosophy had no difficulty in providing such a definition and subjecting (imprudently in Derrida's opinion) the 'sign to truth, language to being, speech to thought and writing to speech' (1967a, p. 24). But if the sign, instead of simply signifying the truth, 'in some way preceded what we call truth or essence' (ibid., p. 24), would we still have the right to 'speak about the truth or essence of the sign'? Should we not content ourselves with describing the possibility of its emergence, which '*produces* truth or ideality rather than ... records it' (ibid., p. 25)?

In order to arrive at this possibility, Derrida carefully examines Husserl's discourse. He first directs his suspicions towards the short passage where Husserl eliminates indicative signs from logic: 'indicative signification in language will cover everything that falls subject to the "reductions": factuality, worldly existence, essential nonnecessity, non-evidence, etc.' (ibid., p. 30). By supposing that phenomenological reduction was ushered in 'in the form of a relation between two modes of signification', that is, between indication and expression, Derrida then shows how Husserl also reduces expression to arrive at a pre-expressive, pre-linguistic layer of meaning. For Husserl, expression is the exteriorization of the *content* of thoughts: it 'comes to reflect, "to mirror" ... every other intentionality ... There is no expression without the intention of a subject animating the sign, giving it a *Geistigkeit* [a spiritual character]' (ibid., p. 33).

Derrida's irritation is similar to Parain's: the conscience that masters and supervises its language is only another form of the immobile conscience that Parain had denounced in 1947. In opposition to the will-to-signify, the indicative signs will be the locus of *the involuntary*. Gestures, physiognomy, everything which is corporeal and worldly will form part of the indicative crust, which instantly envelops expression as soon as it appears, like the whiteness which covers a photographic film incautiously exposed to light. If 'the essence of language is in its telos; and its telos is voluntary consciousness as meaning [comme vouloir-dire]' (ibid. p. 36) expression to be successful, must overcome the obstacle of indication.

For Derrida, however, expression ends in failure: 'The indicative sphere which remains outside expression so defined circumscribes the failure of this telos' (ibid.). Derrida makes his statements from a phenomenological point of view. As understood by Saussure's linguistics and semiology, however, natural language *is indication to its very core*. The sound–meaning combination which 'produces a form, not a substance' along the 'borderland' where they meet (Saussure, 1916, p. 113) is not in fact an expressive semantic structure combined with an indicative phonic structure. The phenomenological opposition between expression and indication does not correspond to the semiological opposition between sound and meaning, if only because the semiological meaning is different from the phenomenological meaning. The first is the product of an empirical, concrete system which is not *the* language but *a* language, a systematic organization linking meanings to sounds in a stable synchronic structure. According to Saussure:

Language can also be compared with a sheet of paper: thought is the front and the sound the back; one cannot cut the front without cutting the back at the same time; likewise in language, one can neither divide sound from thought nor thought from sound . . .' (ibid., p. 113)

He adds, as if to remove any shadow of a doubt:

the idea of value, as defined, shows that to consider a term as simply the union of a certain sound with a certain concept is grossly misleading. To define it in this way would isolate the term from its system; it would mean assuming that one can start from the terms and construct the system by adding them together when, on the contrary, it is from the interdependent whole that one must start and through analysis obtain its elements. (ibid., p. 113)

Each language is, therefore, nothing but a well-ordered system of indications; at this level it is impossible to speak of spiritual meaning animating a body: semiological meaning is melded to sound in an indicative unit. (Need one add that analysing the phonological level into distinctive traits and content into semantic traits does not really change the situation? According to Saussure's semiology, these analyses presuppose the interdependence between the two sides of the linguistic sign. To carry the analysis through, one systematically suspends the *semiosis* uniting the signified and the signifier; but this liaison, which, according to the Saussurians, remains the most important phenomenon of language, is continually assumed by the analysis.)

Language is an indicative structure with two inseparable levels: an external phonetic one and an internal semantic one. Since, according to Saussure, the linguistic sign is based on the solidarity between sound and meaning, the semantic level cleaves to exteriority: therefore, the linguistic meaning is the last imaginable limit of interiority which already no longer belongs to interiority. It is through language that indication penetrates still more deeply into the domain that Husserl reserved for expressivity. Far from being the medium of expressivity, speech is already indicative in so far as it belongs to a natural language.

Derrida, like Saussurian semiologists, is uneasy with the distinction between indication and expression. For the semiologists, however, speech and orality represents only one – albeit the best-known – part of language. For his part, Derrida doubts the presumed difference in nature between outwardly directed speech and the audible interior monologue in the solitary life of the soul, without needing to resort to a theory of the imagination. ('In the interior monologue, a word is thus only represented. It can occur in the imagination' (1967a, p. 43). To show that expression does not coincide with the function of linguistic manifestation, Husserl touched upon the problem of natural language:

So far we have considered expressions as used in communication, which last depends essentially on the fact that they operate indicatively. But expressions also play a great part in uncommunicated, interior mental life. This change in function plainly has nothing to do with whatever makes an expression an expression. Expressions continue to have meanings as they had before, and the same meanings as in dialogue. *A word only ceases to be a word when our interest stops at its sensory contour, when it becomes a mere sound-pattern.* But when we live in the understanding of a word, it expresses something and the same thing, whether we address it to anyone or not. (Husserl, 1913, pp. 278–9; emphasis added)

The italicized sentence has a very precise meaning from the point of view of Saussurian semiology: in considering the word a mere sound-pattern, one suspends the semiotic function, that is, the link between the signified and signifier. In Hjemslev, this suspension coincides with the very beginning of linguistic analysis. It is to this analysis that Saussure refers when he maintains that by separating sound from thought we would obtain an abstraction which 'would be either pure psychology or pure phonology' (Saussure, 1916, p. 113). But we may wonder whether, when writing the sentence quoted above, Husserl had the suspension of the semiotic function in mind. Since Aristotle the philosophy of language has considered the spoken word as the sign of the pre-phonetic thought. It was Saussure's innovation to shift the boundaries of the linguistic sign to include the signified as well, and to distinguish between the linguistic sign, including meaning, and the 'confused mass' that surrounds natural language, that is, thought and reality. Husserl who worked at the heart of what Saussure called the 'confused mass' and who, at the same time, was unaware of the boundaries of the *linguistic* sign, had neither the interest nor the means to think of the suspension of the semiotic function. For him, the solidarity between signified and signifier, in the Saussurian sense, was quite simply still not existing. Doubtless, he considered the phonic level as dispensable, meaning being sufficient for the constitution of a *phenomenological* word.

The last attribute is essential, since it reveals an ambiguity which may well upset Husserl's methodology, as well as Derrida's – although the latter advances in the same direction as the semiologists. Since the linguistic sign is an interdependence of a spoken form (the signifier) and a semantic form (the signified), the suppression of the spoken form, were such a suppression possible, would also entail the disappearance of the sign, possibly a more radical disappearance than that provoked by the suspension of meaning. But to do away with the sound is not to abolish the signifier; this cannot be absent or the linguistic sign would disappear.

Even when discourse withdraws into the solitary life of the soul, the Saussurians would say that it continues to speak a language and therefore is still governed by the interdependence of signified and signifier. The mode of existence (or persistence) of the silent signifier – representation, imagination – remains a secondary question at least for the semiologist. What is certain, and here we come back to the objections that Derrida brings against Husserlian analysis, is that the indication persists in interior monologue even after reduction of the communicative manifestation: *orality* (if by orality we metaphorically understand the presence of the linguistic sign) *is not reducible within a natural language*. If one tries to reduce it, one has to renounce that particular natural language.

It may seem strange that neither Husserl nor Derrida (who knew Saussure when he wrote *Speech and Phenomena*) ever considered the possibility of this renunciation, even though it is still not a renunciation of language in general but simply a setback in relation to the particular semiological system used. This negligence in the succession of reductions is easily pinpointed. When Husserl speaks of 'what an expression expresses', by differentiating expression and meaning, he also carefully separates expressed objectivity and meaning.

Each expression not merely says something, but says it *of* something: it not only has a meaning, but refers to certain *objects* ... The necessity of distinguishing between meaning (content) and object becomes clear when a comparison of examples shows us that several expressions may have the same meaning but different objects, and again that they may have different meanings but the same object. (Husserl, 1913, p. 287)

Before studying these possible divergences, Husserl quickly brushes aside a clearly secondary consideration devoid of interest:

There is of course also the possibility of their differing in both respects and agreeing in both. The last occurs in the cases of synonymous expressions, e.g., the corresponding expressions in different languages which mean and name the same thing ('London', 'Londres'; 'zwei', 'deux', 'duo'; etc.). (ibid.)

The examples chosen are characteristic: to be able to claim that words or expressions which correspond in different natural languages are *perfect synonyms*, Husserl must limit himself to marginal examples, proper names or cardinal numbers, that is, pre-eminently univocal expressions. What would he do if he had to deal with less synonymous expressions? To find them, we need not resort to the example of the names of colours in various languages, dear to semiologists; we have an example at hand concerning the difference between the French word *signification* and the German *Bedeutung*, a difference which led Derrida to translate the latter as *vouloir-dire* or to use the German word frequently in the French text. What happens when Derrida writes a sentence such as: 'The ideality of *Bedeutung* here has by virtue of its structure the value of a testament' (1967a, p. 96). Isn't the use of the German word the result of a *failed reduction of the natural language?* Isn't resorting to a foreign word the sign of an attempt to go outside the system of a given language? Even if we consider the use of French as belonging to an empirical and therefore contingent level, what is no longer empirical is the systematic unity of this language, the property which Hjelmslev and the semiologists considered as linguistically fundamental, and the reason why a language remains identical to itself in all its diverse uses. From this point of view, as far as the semiologists are concerned, every language is closed. A message which, while using a certain language – in Derrida's case, French – even once uses a foreign word (*Bedeutung*) reveals a sense of dissatisfaction with the system of the given language, the presence of some inadequacy, of a distance between the speaker and the system he employs.

I deliberately use the expression 'the speaker'. I could also expand it to 'the speaker who searches for words'. For what are the choices of the person speaking and searching for words if, after having unsuccessfully scoured the entire surface of the semiological system, he realizes that the word he is seeking is, strictly speaking, not to be found, and that perhaps the very arrangement of the system is preventing the word from appearing, that is, is preventing his vague sense of frustration from being satisfied? The speaker thus finds himself faced with three possibilities: (1) He can use a word that he feels is partially inadequate but that has the advantage of existing in the system used. As often happens in such cases, a slight shift occurs in the word's usage and the word's relationship with other lexical items in the language undergoes a modification. Or (2) he can use a foreign word, as Derrida does in the example quoted, which implies a withdrawal from the natural language in question. This withdrawal attests the inadequacy of natural languages – and thus puts in peril the doctrine of expressibility, which would have any natural language adequately expressing any idea. In fact the choice of the foreign word clearly indicates that behind each natural language there is still something irreducible to it. This something is nevertheless elusive, since the person speaking draws back only to make immediate use of the system of differences and resonances of another natural language. Or, of course, (3) the speaker can keep quiet.

Silence, the insertion of a foreign word, and the change in semantic weight are therefore closely related phenomena; having their starting point in the linguistic system, they extend towards a region which is no longer controlled by the semiological system, but which is no longer identical with the silence of the 'state of creature' about which Brice Parain was speaking either. The momentary silence of alternative (3) is only the feeling of a given language's inadequacy with respect to something which, by nature, should be linguistically expressible, as proved by the possibility of the alternative (2), that is, the insertion of the foreign word. We already see that this evasion – silence or momentarily resorting to the resources of another language – signals the irreducibility of language (*langage*) in general to natural language (*langue*),* if not the irreducibility of meaning to sign.

Derrida refrains from tackling the details of linguistics, and his philosophical generalizations on structuralist doctrines begin only when he expresses doubts concerning the reality of the pre-expressive silence. The pre- is perhaps too clear-cut: perhaps this silence too is not *pre*-expressive but, as we have just seen, more *intra-indicative*, since like semantic change and recourse to other languages it signals a level different from natural languages, a level that Saussure designated as language in general. It is undoubtedly difficult to seize this silence called language (*langage*) before its translation into the internal or external discourse

* The English 'language' translates both the French *langue*, a natural language or tongue such as German or French, and *langage*, which refers to language in general. Where the English *language* could lead to confusion, the original French has been inserted to make the distinction clear.

that takes place in a given natural language (*langue*); but can it not be seen when we speak, in those brief momentary lapses of silences, the slip-ups, the hesitating between two languages?

Yet the sign does regain its integrity. According to Derrida, if Husserl first separates indication from expression, then expression from the pre-expressive layer, it is because for him conscience is nothing more than a pure presence-to-itself of a voice that understands itself and says what it wants to say. Analysis of the inward conscience of time leads Derrida to uncover a continuous delay – a *deferral** – within the presence-to-itself, which is nothing more than the work of temporality. The *now* is perpetually postponed; the delay precedes and generates it. In a bold stroke, by bringing together the delaying impulse of the conscience and the substituting nature of signs, Derrida manages to see the possibility of the latter in the former: the sign would be inscribed in the delaying impulse, in the *deferral*. The concept of *deferral* contains both the mobility of the conscience and at the same time its relationship to language as delay. According to Derrida, the self-assurance of phenomenology, worked on by the *deferral*, which erodes all attempts at fully assured discourse, collapses, because, like classical metaphysics, phenomenology too blindly believed in the link between language and truth:

> the genuine and true meaning is the will to say the truth ... *In truth*, the telos which announces the fulfilment, promised for 'later', has already and beforehand opened up sense as a relation with the object. This is what is meant by the concept of *normality* each time it occurs in Husserl's description. (1967a, p. 98)

This normality is made questionable by the incessant movement of the *deferral*. It is easy to understand why the irretrievable non-presence-to-itself is the phenomenological condition of the instability of discourse, as this instability is, perhaps, the origin of the noncoincidence between language in general (the intra-indicative silence) and natural languages.

Deferral, however, entails neither the disappearance of intentionality (the death of the subject, in Derrida's terms) nor its replacement with the notion of transcendental writing. For the mobility of discourse cannot be entirely explained by the work of the *deferral*. The distant swell of *deferral* is only the phenomenological background of the *voice's hesitation* betraying language's inadequacy. One cannot operate back and forth between language (*langage*) and tongue (*langue*) relying solely on the behind-the-scenes work of the *deferral*. It is especially impossible

* *Deferral* translates Derrida's neologism *différance* which comprises the two meanings of the French verb *différer*: one indicates 'difference' or 'differentiation', the second denotes the notion of delay, postponement, or deferral, thus bringing into play the idea of temporality.

to give up the notions of intention and intuition, even if it means reformulating them in an idiom less strongly influenced by classical metaphysics. For what would happen if the discourse on meaning gave up using these notions? The last chapter of *Speech and Phenomena* offers an eloquent example:

we might be tempted to maintain not only that meaning does not imply the intuition of the object but ... essentially excludes it. What is structurally original about meaning would be the *Gegenstandslosigkeit*, the absence of any object given to intuition ... This is to say that the language that speaks in the presence of its object effaces its own originality or lets it melt away; the structure peculiar to language alone, which allows it to function entirely *by itself* when its intention is cut off from intuition, here dissolves. (ibid., p. 92)

The essence of discourse being, ideally, its comprehension by anyone, at any spatial or temporal distance.

my nonintuition, my *hic et nunc* absence are expressed by that very thing that I say, by *that* which I say and *because* I say it ... The absence of intuition – and therefore of the subject of the intuition – is not only *tolerated* by speech; it is *required* by the general structure of signification, when considered *in itself*. (ibid., p. 93)

Faced with the infinite variation of possible combinations between intention and intuition, and the infinitesimal degrees for fulfilling intention by intuition, and their more or less exact reciprocal adjustment, we sense in Derrida's attitude the same exasperation which earlier brought Leonard Bloomfield, the founder of American linguistic structuralism, to exclude meaning from linguistic study, or impelled Hjelmslev to banish these agonizing questions into the substance of content, and even further, into the elusive 'matter' of language. Curiously, just as in Bloomfield and Hjelmslev the revolt against mentalism led to extreme mechanism, the dogmatism of assured discourse which Derrida denounces in Husserl's writings reappears in Derrida's own approach. Once Husserl's 'normality' has been turned upside down, Derrida's analysis brings no more freedom. We very quickly realize that as a result of this upheaval a new normality, perhaps more threatening than the old one, is preparing to take over. After denying 'an initial limitation of sense to knowledge, of logos to objectivity, of language to reason' (ibid., p. 99), after perceiving the slight faltering of the *deferral* in the apparently assured voice (the phenomenological voice), Derrida does not let this hesitation develop. On the contrary, he stops it in the name of *writing*, 'the common name for signs which function despite the total absence of the subject because of (beyond) his death'. Writing, according to Derrida, is 'involved in the very act of signification in general and, in particular, in what is called "living" speech' (ibid., p. 93). Involved? The notion of writing soon attains a much more important place.

The pretext for setting up the new normality is provided by the analysis of one of the most debated passages of *Logical Investigations*, a passage that causes Husserl inextricable difficulties because of the absence of distinction between linguistic meaning and phenomenological reference. The passage in question deals with the analysis of the meaning of the pronoun *I*. 'The expressions which name the momentary content of intimation belong to a wider class of expressions whose meaning varies from case to case', writes Husserl, adding:

> This happens, however, in so peculiar a manner, that one hesitates to speak of 'equivocation' in this case. The same words 'I wish you luck' which express my wish, can serve countless other persons to express wishes having 'the same' content. Not only do the wishes themselves differ from case to case, but the meanings of the wish-utterances do so too. (Husserl, 1913, pp. 314–15)

Here Husserl attributes a variation in meaning to a change which takes place, as is always the case for indexical, or deictic expressions (personal pronouns, demonstratives, adverbs like *here, now*) on the referential level. The linguistic signification of the wish remains constant whoever utters it, and the referential variation and, consequently, the phenomenological meaning only develop around this linguistic constancy. But Husserl considers that there exist *essentially occasional* expressions: 'Only by looking to the actual circumstances of utterance can one definite meaning out of all this mutually connected class be constitued for the hearer' (ibid., p. 315). On the linguistic level, exactly the opposite happens. 'The word *I* names a different person from case to case, and does so by way of an ever altering meaning'. How can this be proved? The constant meaning of *I* should be 'whatever speaker is designating himself', but the substitution of these words in a sentence which contains *I* produces strange effects: instead of *I am pleased*, we have *whatever speaker is now designating himself is pleased* (ibid.).

Derrida reacts violently to this clumsy treatment of indexical expressions and justifiably observes: 'Just as I have no need to perceive in order to understand a statement of perception, I have no need of intuition of the object *I* to understand the word *I*' (1967a, p. 107). That goes without saying. It should be added that Husserl's proposed substitution is vitiated from the start: before attempting the substitution, he should have realized that the sequence 'whatever speaker who is now designating himself is pleased' is not a *paraphrase*, but an *explanation* of the meaning of the word *I*. As a consequence, the pronoun *I* in the proposition *I am pleased* cannot be replaced with its *explanation*. The failure of the substitution merely emphasizes that the actual signification of the indicative term *I* cannot be paraphrased by an explicative statement. 'Whatever speaker who is now designating himself is pleased' does not repeat the *I* at its own level (as 'biped without feathers' repeats *man*), but explains it at another linguistic level, thereby naively neutralizing the special effect that the *I* represents in speaking. Structuralist linguists have cautiously undertaken effective substitutions in situations of this type, establishing classes of equivalence based not on *identity of meaning* but on *acceptability in a certain context*. Meaning cannot be grasped with the help of these classes; rather, meaning is 'frozen' as it appears in speech. The *I* is therefore understood as a deictic element of language, having a function in the language and relating in its own way to other elements in that language. Once again, therefore, it is the absence of a linguistic level that hampers Husserl's analysis. Or else, at the logical level, the signification of *I* can be captured by distinguishing between expressions which refer to classes of objects, actions, qualities and so on, and indexical expressions whose reference cannot be established outside the spoken context. But, again, the proposed substitution by Husserl does not capture the meaning of the sentence containing the *I*.

For Derrida, however, the word *I* is neither a purely logical instrument nor a deictic possibility offered by language which, when spoken, indirectly refers to the act of utterance itself:

there is no need to intuit the object *I* in order to understand the word *I*. The possibility of this nonintuition constitutes the *Bedeutung* as such, the *normal Bedeutung* as such ... The anonymity of the written *I*, the impropriety of the *I am writing*, is ... the 'normal situation'. (1967a, pp. 96–7)

And more strongly still:

the signifying function of the *I* does not depend on the life of the speaking subject. Whether or not perception accompanies the statement about perception, whether or not life as self-presence accompanies the uttering of the *I*, is quite indifferent with regard to the functioning of meaning. My death is structurally necessary to the pronouncing of the *I*. (ibid., p. 96)

Noting the glissando in the passage (to begin with, the word *I* does not depend on the life of the subject; later, the relationship between the life and the utterance of *I* is perfectly indifferent, but, in the end, death is structurally necessary for the *I* to be spoken), we can assert that this situation is, ultimately, *possible*. But why invest it with all the prestige and all the force of normality? How does the violence of this new normality differ from that other normality denounced elsewhere by Derrida? To renounce the hard-won flexibility of language, to forsake the hesitation of the finally audible voice in order to impose the new law of writing – is this not, using Derrida's own apt expression, 'to freeze light at its source'?

GLOSSEMATICS AND TRANSCENDENTAL WRITING

The new normality is therefore established on a misunderstanding about the nature of linguistic systems (*langues*) in its relations with the most general notion of language (*langage*). The absence of a true linguistic level in Husserl, an absence which persists in *Speech and Phenomena* despite Derrida's allusions to Saussurian doctrines, suggests that nothing in phenomenological thinking opens the path to a reading of the *General Course in Linguistics*. Phenomenology naturally diverts thought to the generality of language and the sign, whereas the concern of the linguist is to define the property of the linguistic sign and the formal specificity of natural languages. This is why a science unique to language embracing linguistics, logic, phenomenology and poetics could not fail to resemble the medieval bestiaries and lapidaries which described their objects from all possible points of view. Since the modern – scientific and hermeneutic – disciplines do not derive their specificity solely from their object but in equal measure from the point of view and formality that they adopt with regard to it, can we, once the discussion leaves the phenomenological realm and begins to drift towards linguistics, treat Saussurian notions of sign and difference as if they had been established inside philosophy?

This bias is accentuated in *Of Grammatology*. The terms in which Derrida refers to linguistics are symptomatic: 'The science of linguistics', he says, giving the word *science* its Hegelian meaning as was the practice in the 1960s, 'determines language – its field of objectivity – in the last instance and in the irreducible simplicity of its essence, as the unity of the *phoné*, the *glossa* and the *logos*' (1967b, p. 29), that is, sound, language and words. But does linguistics in fact aim at determining its field of objectivity 'in the irreducible simplicity of its essence'? And does it really take language as object to begin with? Wasn't the science (in the non-Hegelian sense of the word) called linguistics constituted outside – if not in opposition to – philosophical thinking on language as a discursive faculty? Among the creators of comparative philology, as in Saussure, we find the concern for delimiting an empirical object different from the faculty which it serves; they study natural language (*langue*), even languages (*langues*), but not language (*langage*). As for the irreducible simplicity of essence, linguistics, as any science, seeks it through the unity of its method and not, as Husserlian phenomenology does, through the contemplation of the object offered to the conscience. The linguistic method originates *in separating* sound from meaning; for Saussure, the solidarity of fact – and not the unity of principle – between sound and meaning is less an essential determination of language (*langage*) than a property of natural languages (*langues*). The Saussurian principle of the arbitrariness of the sign, read from a linguistic rather than a phenomenological point of view, has nothing more to say.

The narrowly linguistic point of view matters little, however, in *Of Grammatology*, as Derrida himself stresses in later commenting upon Hjelmslev's *Prolegomena to a Theory of Language*. This revealing passage merits closer consideration. Speaking about arche-writing, the transcendental back-drop of linguistic systems, Derrida is of the opinion that Hjelmslev would have undoubtedly contested its necessity, seeing in it 'one of those appeals to experience which a theory should dispense with' (ibid., p. 60). Going on to say that the type of experience from which Hjelmslevian theory aims at breaking away corresponds to 'factual or regional experience (historical, psychological, physiological, sociological, etc.), giving rise to a science that is itself regional and, as such, rigorously outside linguistics', Derrida asserts that arche-writing does not fall under the influence of these restrictions, since 'the parenthesizing of regions of experience or of the totality of natural experience must discover a field of transcendental experience' (ibid., pp. 60–1). This field of transcendental experience appears when the linguist, after having found the language system by eliminating non-linguistic data from the field in which he is interested, asks 'the question of the transcendental origin of the system itself ... and, correlatively, of the ... system which studies it: here ... glossematics' (ibid., p. 61). Hjelmslev's linguistics thus finds itself setting phenemological tasks for which it may not be ready; yet the slightest hesitation in carrying them out would lead, Derrida warns us, to the scientistic objectivism 'often noticeable in the work of the Copenhagen School' (ibid.). In the passage, the frequent use of the word *transcendental* causes Derrida some remorse. He immediately explains his approach and reminds us of his anti-idealist doubts to exonerate himself: 'It is to escape falling back into this naive objectivism that I refer here to a transcendentality that I elsewhere put into question' (ibid.).

His attempt to associate a field of transcendental experience with Hjelmslev's glossematics says more about Derrida's own theoretical aims than those of glossematics. The latter starts out from different premises. The bibliography and the table of contents for the *Prolegomena to a Theory of Language* (1943; Eng. trans. 1961) clearly show that Hjelmslev's project represents the meeting point of structural linguistics and logical empiricism. Hjelmslev cited Saussure, Leonard Bloomfield, Joseph Vachek, Rudolf Carnap, Otto Neurath, Alfred Tarski, Georg von Wright, Eino Kaila and Jørgen Jørgensen: three linguists, the last of whom belongs to the Prague school; two influential members of the Vienna school; a Polish logician associated with the work of the Vienna school; and three eminent representatives of logical empiricism in Finland and Denmark. At the end of the introduction to the *Prolegomena*, Hjelmslev, usually so sparing of notes and references, expresses his indebtedness to Jørgensen, author of a treatise on formal logic (1931), member of the editorial board of the *Einheitswissenschaft* series, headed by Neurath between 1934 and 1938, and tireless promoter of logico-positivism in Denmark. There is only one reference to phenomenalism (1961, p. 123) in the sense attributed to it by the neopositivists:

> To what extent it is possible to consider ultimately all entities in any semiotic whatsoever, in its content and expression, as physical or reducible to the physical is a purely epistemological question of physicalism *contra* phenomenalism. This question has been the object of a debate on which we shall not here take a position and on which the theory of the linguistic schema need not take a stand. (ibid., pp. 123–4)

A note to this passage mentions Bloomfield, Neurath and Alf Ross, a Scandinavian philosopher of ethics and law. The debate which Hjelmslev mentions is the positivist controversy about the nature of atomic facts, the elemental particles which make up our world. Defined by Carnap in 1928, in the empirical tradition of Ernest Mach, as phenomenal data, minimal units will be devised by Neurath and by Carnap too at the beginning of the 1930s as physical states of affairs.

These references went unnoticed by French philosophers of the 1960s. But the outline and direction of Hjelmslev's work alone should have enlightened his readers. What Derrida calls scientistic objectivism is not simply a danger threatening the outcome of a project essentially oriented elsewhere; it is the main thrust of the glossematic approach. Throughout the *Prolegomena*, the scientistic theme determines the main choices and gives form to the main connecting ideas. It is true that experimental science is rejected, as evidenced, for example, in the severe rebuttal of Daniel Jones, who wanted to base phonology on phonetic observation (Hjelmslev, 1961, pp. 62–4). This was to be expected. The old positivism had been discredited for a long time in the philosophical circles Hjelmslev was close to. From 1920 on, a new scientism, infinitely better equipped than the old one and no longer focused on experimental objectivity but on theoretical rigour, quickly spread in Central Europe, the English-speaking countries and Scandinavia. Hjelmslev's attempt to transfer new epistemological norms onto linguistics must be judged in the light of work by Carnap, Neurath and their Finnish and Danish colleagues. Looked at from this perspective, the dominant themes of the *Prolegomena* do not as much emphasize loyalty to Saussurianism as try to make the science of natural languages logical. Responding to the recent progress made in symbolic logic and in the theory of science, this effort readily welcomed certain Saussurian notions, but only when it seemed that they could serve the new theoretical orientation.

Yet Derrida's analysis of the *Prolegomena* is not the result of sheer misunderstanding either. Hjelmslev's alliance of Saussurianism and logical empiricism and his transition from epistemological considerations to linguistic practice are not accomplished smoothly. Hjelmslev's hesitations are especially apparent in the initial legitimation of the methodology; later when he establishes his two competing formalities, that of the object and that of the theory; and, finally, in his outline of linguistic functions.

In the first few chapters, the *Prolegomena* resolutely sides with logico-positivism: the science of language will have to break first with naive empiricism, which is not interested in language but in its *disiecta membra* (ibid., p. 5); it will then build a formal theory of the specific structure of language. The object of this theory will be the 'constancy that makes a language a language, whatever language it may be, and that makes a particular language identical with itself in all its various manifestations' (ibid., p. 8). Though there is nothing that directly contradicts phenomenology in such a formulation, what follows removes any shadow of a doubt: in accordance with logical positivism, Hjelmslev adds that any process is subtended by a system and requires the linguistic description to be free and contradiction, exhaustive and simple. Whereas such principles would be the fruit of patient observation in phenomenology, here, in accordance with Carnap, the methodology moves from the formal theory established outside experience to confrontation with the facts. Hjelmslev calls the principle of description 'empirical' (ibid., p. 11) obviously referring to logical empiricism, and his hesitations regarding the aptness of the term reflect the debates which took place in logico-positivist circles after 1935 concerning the relationships between scientific hypotheses and observed evidence. In accordance with these debates and with the principle of empiricism as defined by Carnap (1936), Hjelmslev designates as 'empiricist' the rule requiring linguistic descriptions to be free of contradiction, exhaustive and simple. He calls the linguistic theory both 'arbitrary' and 'appropriate', since on the one hand it constitutes a purely deductive system 'in the sense that it may be used alone to compute the possibilities that follow from its premisses', and on the other hand 'A theory introduces certain premisses [which] fulfil the conditions for application to certain empirical data' (1961, p. 14). Such duality, formulated so explicitly, clearly demonstrates that Hjelmslev conceived his theory with Carnap's model in mind, as a logical calculus in which only the terminal points will be tested empirically.

Empirical verification, mentioned in passing on page 14 of the *Prolegomena*, is far, however, from occupying an important place in the glossematic project. The absence of any verification procedures or, as they are later called, confirmation procedures, an essential element of the sciences formalized according to the logico-positivist norms, becomes obvious when the *Prolegomena* is compared to the early writings of Noam Chomsky. Having, like Hjelmslev, experienced the influence of logico-positivist epistemology, especially the debates on verification between Carnap and Popper, Chomsky devotes a good part of his *Syntactic Structures* (1957) to the construction of abstract calculi (the finite number of states model, syntagmatic grammars) submitted to the test of linguistic data. This procedure, after having allowed Chomsky to disprove two important structuralist models, gave rise to an astounding number of new linguistic models, each proposed to remedy the inadequacies of its predecessors and then abandoned as soon as phenomena discovered in natural languages disproved the expectations. The success of Chomsky's ideas is certainly related to this dexterity in the construction of formal models which are likewise readily abandoned when a difficulty arises. In contrast, glossematics has had relatively little influence in linguistics, because of the weak links it establishes between the formal calculi and the empirical data.

At the same time, the *Prolegomena* reveals the emergence of a divergent project within scientism. On the one hand, Hjelmslev correctly begins by constructing a science that is specifically linguistic in form, including a deductive calculus and provisions for verification, and takes care not to wander too far into the preserves of logic and epistemology ('No mention has been made here of axioms or postulates. We leave it to epistemology to decide whether the basic premises explicitly introduced by our linguistic theory need any further axiomatic foundation'; ibid., pp. 14–15). But further into the *Prolegomena*, there is a sort of gradual exhaustion of the specific linguistic theory, which borrows from logic the technique of constructing models that it should then apply to empirical material. Taking care to use only the most general notions – class, hierarchy, analysis, part, chain, paradigm, etc. (ibid., pp. 29ff.) – Hjelmslev seems to lose sight of the possible return to natural languages; instead he aspires to construct a model the generality of which is comparable to that of logic, and thus impervious to empirical refutation.

In defining the different notions of his theory, Hjelmslev constantly emphasizes its formal character in accordance with logico-empirism. But as his work progresses, not only the *theory* is formal, but also its *object* exhibits a formality of its own which seems to compete with that of the deductive calculus. So unusual a case is worthy of attention. When an astronomer calculates the trajectory of a planet, the geometric formality of its course is, in a realist interpretation, a reliable representation of the orbit, or, in an instrumentalist view, it lays down a rule approximating a movement that is not definable in itself. In the same way, the formal model of the structure of natural languages that a generative and transformational grammar puts forward is likely to be understood in a realist manner, as in Chomsky, who identifies it with the biological properties of the human brain, or it may be taken simply, as in Quine, for a useful instrument of knowledge. In none of these cases does the *object* possess a formality of its own, independent of that of the theoretical calculus. It could not be any different, since this new formality would presuppose a new calculus which establishes it and not just the thematic analysis of the intrinsic properties of the object.

In Hjelmslev, in addition to the formal network, each natural language – the object being analysed – possesses, as if through onto-logical endowment, a form unique to it alone. This form is a specific property of the natural language in question, just as some planet shines with reddish brilliance, or as in Latin there are five declensions. The presence of this second form originates, Hjelmslev emphasizes, with the Saussurian doctrine. Cited by Hjelmslev, the *Course in General Linguistics* defines language as:

as a series of contiguous subdivisions marked off on both on the indefinite plane of jumbled ideas ... and the equally vague plane of sounds ... language works out its units while taking shape between two shapeless masses ... *their combination produces a form, not a substance.* (Saussure, 1916, pp. 112–13)

Since language is, of its own virtue and independently of the formal calculus which describes it, a formal network applied to phonic and semantic substances, an irreversible shift takes place in Hjelmslev's argu-ment, from the *formal character of the calculus* to the *formal character of the object*, such that the latter gradually takes on traits of the former. Relationships which at the beginning seemed to have been introduced by the theoretical calculation outside any experience finally find them-selves among the formal properties of language itself. And when Hjelmslev, by taking up a well-known term from the *Course*, assigns the task of constituting 'an immanent algebra of languages' to his theory (Hjelmslev, 1961, p. 80), we cannot easily see whether this algebra belongs to the hypothetico-deductive step of research or whether it is part of the functioning mode of language itself.

Throughout the *Prolegomena*, by virtue of this new formality, language acquires the characteristics of a universal proto-logic. Once language in general is defined as a formal combinatory (ibid., p. 107), the natural languages, 'a special example of this more general object', are no longer considered as the ultimate object of linguistic research. Although, ac-cording to Hjelmslev, the linguist should primarily concentrate on natural languages, leaving the study of other languages to other specialists, notably logicians, it would be a mistake for the linguist to 'study language without the wider horizon that ensures his proper orientation towards these analogous structures'. In other words, natural languages, far from being simply the *target* of a logical description, form *part of the family* of logical structures. In the penultimate section of the *Pro-legomena*, Hjelmslev takes another step forward. Starting from the double distinction expression/content and form/substance, he proposes a general classification of all the possible semiotic configurations, a classification organized around natural languages. In the process, linguistic theory is completely changed into a kind of general epistemology based on semi-ology which, in the final pages of the work, includes the description of the entire universe as just of its meta-semiological subdivisions: the substance of linguistic content (ibid., p. 124).

As formulated in the *Prolegomena* and several of Hjelmslev's articles, notably 'La stratification du langage' (1954), the undertaking, ambiguous as it is, could be carried out in two different directions: on the one hand, if he keeps his composure, the linguist will easily understand what is gratuitous in these semiological speculations based on natural languages, and, without necessarily depriving himself of such speculations, he will accept the dialogue with philosophical logic and epistemology, and be prepared to recognize the primacy of their results. With this option, the linguist's main task will be to invent formal models specific to the natural languages. On the other hand, the theoretician of language may be seduced by Hjelmslev's typological conclusions and, renouncing the logico-epistemological foundation, take 'the immanent algebra of language' as a starting point for a linguistically based universal semiotics.

The temptation to follow this second path is even greater because the first option requires serious effort in refining the formal models that describe natural languages. Even if Hjelmslev's disciple admits that the first task of the linguist consists in adequately describing the immanent algebra of natural language, the system of notions proposed by Hjelmslev is not sufficient to accomplish this task. Like most structural linguistics, Hjelmslev's description of this algebra isolates a list of invariant elements obtained through commutation (1943, p. 73) and formulates three types of relationships that these elements foster among themselves: determination, interdependence and constellation or autonomy (ibid., pp. 35–6). Determination joins together two elements of which only one is necessary (for example, the relationship between a vowel and a consonant in a syllable, in which only the vowel is required); interdependence links two units which are always mutually dependent, like tone and syllable in tonal languages; constellation indicates the reciprocal independence of the elements – accent and vowel length, for example, in contemporary French. It is easy to see that determination corresponds in set theory to inclusion, interdependence to the identity between sets and constellation to the negation of the two other possibilities. But these relationships between sets are so elementary that by themselves they cannot in any way exhaust the immanent algebra of language. The representation of the formal properties of the syntax of natural languages, to take a familiar example, needs a considerably more complex mathematical set-up, one that is separated from elementary set theory by a number of intermediary steps. To define a formal language, for example, a notion which in its turn represents only the starting point of the formal syntax of natural languages, one needs notions like the Cartesian product between sets; relation, function and operation as subsets of the Cartesian product; the operation of concatenation leading to the definition of formal chains of which the formal languages make up one variety. The theory of recursive functions, on the other hand, leads to the definition of axiomatic systems, of which formal grammars form a subset.

These tools were not available when Hjelmslev's linguistics came into being, since the work of S. Kleene and E. Post on recursive functions appeared in the mid-1930s and mid-1940s. The rudimentary character of the formal glossematic mechanism dissuaded linguists from a project which promised a complete algebra of language only to offer an elementary set-theory. Given the dearth of formalisms to which he had access, it is understandable why Hjelmslev, after having set out his programme at the beginning of the *Prolegomena* within the limits of logico-empiricist norms, turned towards semiological speculations. Read from a non-technical point of view, these speculations could easily be separated from the scientistic programme, and, because of their audaciousness, would appeal to the imagination of a philosopher nurtured on phenomenology.

Derrida's *Speech and Phenomena* and *On Grammatology*, which started as a critique of Husserl, acquired their own special features from the addition of various Nietzschean themes filtered through Heidegger's philosophy (the radical criticism of metaphysics, the problem of origins and absolute foundation, truth as revelation and occultation and the ontological difference between Being and existing), and incorporated a *sui generis* interpretation of Saussure's and Hjelmslev's semiology. This interpretation played a crucial role in the strategic system worked out in Derrida's philosophy.

Derrida's strategy consists in setting up an imaginary protagonist against an ideal target and specifying both the rules of the argumentation and the illegal moves. As has always been the case since Kant, the target is pinned to the already mutilated body of classical metaphysics. The rules of the game include the dialectics of revelation and occultation; finally, it is illegal to formulate doubts about the existence of a transcendental domain. Considered from this perspective, the Heideggerian themes are little more than the means – though undoubtedly privileged means – used by Derrida to elaborate his own doctrine. But his doctrine cannot be reduced to any of the elements used for its construction. Its peculiar message, which results from the unexpected angle of attack on metaphysics, is determined by the constraints which, from the outset, limit the choice of solutions, and by the phenomenological interpretation of semiological notions.

The early writings of Derrida, from *Edmund Husserl's 'The Origin of Geometry': An Introduction* (1963) to *Margins of Philosophy* (1972), are a meditation on the nature of ideal objects. The status of mathematical objects, in particular those of geometry, constitutes a troublesome puzzle for the phenomenologist, since phenomenology, which is a technique for examining the contents of pure consciousness, lacks the means to distinguish strong idealizations, such as those characterizing geometrical objects, from more flexible forms of transcendental constitution, such as the opposition between the real and the imaginary. It is quite significant in this respect that Husserl thinks that he can grasp mathematical ideality through *re-enacting* the original moment of invention. But although re-enacting is an important aspect of the actualization of ideal objects, it cannot account for many essential properties of these objects. The difficulty stems from the fact that phenomenological descriptions take as their target structures filled with temporality while, by definition, mathematical ideality escapes temporality. In his article 'The Origin of Geometry' (1936), Husserl attempted to solve this difficulty by taking into account the historical and inter-subjective dimensions of mathematical knowledge. For him, the supra-temporal existence of geometry, which in principle is universally accessible, must be read against a temporal horizon, since geometry must have been born at a particular moment in time from an unknown mind and evolved in relation to the history of those cultural communities that inherited and developed its first achievements. An admirable solution, Derrida says in his *Introduction*, for, by avoiding both conventionalist Platonism and historicist empiricism, this solution gives priority to truly phenomenological questions, that is, it reconciles the universality of geometry with the particularity of time and consciousness and describes the mode of transmission of geometrical truths. Yet, Derrida admits, the solution fails to throw light on the *nature* of mathematical idealities.

In his penetrating remarks on Husserl's text, Derrida emphasizes why the nature of mathematical ideality cannot be grasped by phenomenological analysis: the latter is already informed by – and subordinated to – a set of norms similar to those that govern mathematics. By going back to the Kantian Idea, the authority of which he detects in the constitution of geometric objects as well as in the ideality of phenomenological descriptions, Derrida rightly notices that there is no phenomenology of the Kantian Idea, since the latter

> cannot be given in person, nor determined in an evidence, for it [the Kantian Idea] is only the possibility of evidence and the openness of the '*seeing*' itself; it is only *determinability* as the horizon for every intuition in general. (1963, pp. 138–9)

And, later:

> If there is nothing to say about the Idea *itself*, it is because the Idea is that starting from which something in general can be said. Its own particular presence, then, cannot depend on a phenomenological type of evidence. (ibid., pp. 138–9)

Turned in this direction, the phenomenological gaze does not meet *anything*: 'Thus, for once, nothing appears in a specific evidence. What does appear is only the regulative possibility of appearing' (ibid., p. 139). The certainty of idealization has no corresponding evidence.

Two important consequences follow. First, the search for an ultimate foundation of knowledge in and through the visible activity of the consciousness stumbles against a founding yet elusive norm, which is ideality itself. To examine the living activity of the transcendental subject as it becomes apparent in the effervescence of the present requires neglecting the norm that makes knowledge possible by invisibly governing the subject's activity. This consequence is quite dismaying, since it shows that phenomenology is bound to fail by virtue of having selected the life of the subject as the main target of its attention.

It is possible to avoid this impasse by simply abandoning the phenomenological project and its pernicious ambitions. A whole set of insoluble problems would instantly vanish, notably the search for an absolute foundation of knowledge and, with it, the ruinous obligations phenomenology imposes on the transcendental subject. This would not instantly solve the question of mathematical objects, but at least in order to address it one would not have to find one's way through a phenomenological labyrinth. At the same time, empiricist solutions, including that of Carl Hempel which has many points in common with Husserl's views, Platonic solutions like Karl Popper's, and conventionalist solutions like Wittgenstein's, would no longer be rejected without examination. Also, phenomenologists would not so easily dismiss with contempt the debates led by mathematicians themselves.

The question of *ideality* in general, that is, ideality independently of its regional determinations, would certainly have less chance of ever being raised. Once freed from foundationalism, philosophy would not need to derive the legitimacy of various fields of knowledge from the same unique source. In addition, if the search for a universal foundation were replaced by particular methods for establishing disciplinary validity, the role of the transcendental subject would lose its absolute primacy and could be redefined in a flexible way, in accordance with the more limited needs of non-foundationalist philosophy.

The redefinition of the tasks of the subject would in no way entail its 'death', as proclaimed by 1960s' rhetoric, but rather a smaller place within a new epistemological economy. Liberated from earlier foundationalist requirements, which were impossible to satisfy in any case, the subject would receive the guardianship of a smaller domain better suited to its powers. For instance, nothing would prevent a more modestly conceived subject from overseeing morality and human rights. It is obvious that this option cannot yet be taken for granted, and at the present stage of the debate only moderation would avoid new setbacks for the notion of subject. The prodigious influence exercised by this notion on European thought in the wake of Kant's Romantic legacy explains the exaggerations of the anti-humanist revolt of the 1960s, as well as contemporary attempts to give the subject a new lease on life. But isn't the violence of these reversals a French singularity? Contemporary English, American and Scandinavian philosophy can comfortably manage ethical questions without the Romantic notion of a founding subject, yet is not confined to utilitarian or naturalist solutions. All non-naturalist and anti-utilitarian theories originating from this horizon, in particular John Rawls's philosophy of justice, successfully avoid the problem of the transcendental subject. Even if a reopening of this problem were genuinely necessary in France, should French philosophers grant the former sovereign a role different from the strictly ceremonial function of modern monarchy accompanied, perhaps, by a small number of well-controlled prerogatives? In such situations, excessive nostalgia often endangers the delicate balance between tradition and political realism.

In France today, philosophical liberalism has assumed the task of maintaining this balance. In the early 1960s, when Derrida discovered the impossibility of establishing mathematical ideality, in fact *any* ideality, on the self-examination of the subject present-to-itself, it was clearly inconceivable in France either to discard the phenomenological project or to search for an alternative non-foundationalist perspective. Fidelity has many faces, and it may not be by chance that, in his *Introduction*, Derrida cites the moving passages dedicated to the Earth by Husserl. Well hidden beneath the objectivism of Copernican astronomy, Earth is, for Husserl, the transcendental certainty and foundation of mechanics (Derrida, 1963, pp. 83–5). Likewise, Derrida's fidelity to phenomenology survives the discovery of its vulnerable point. First, if the life of the subject present-to-itself is discovered to be an insufficient foundation for ideality and, second, if the problem of the subject is still haunting philosophy, two options become available for the philosopher who decides to confront the dissociation between ideality and the subject: either to concede the fragility of the subject and, starting from there, build an atheoretical image of truth – Heidegger's path; or to reject the transcendental subject and the correlative idea of well-founded ideality.

But the latter option, which is Derrida's, encounters a considerable problem, since deprived of its conceptual cornerstone – the subject – the phenomenological edifice fractures beyond repair. Hoping for some kind of an epiphany, the phenomenologist patiently dismantles the eroded structures. Paradoxically, with the discovery of each new fissure and widening crevice, a growing faith attaches him to this shaky ground. This agony presides over Derrida's thinking. The deconstruction of the conceptual work achieved by what Derrida quite lightly calls 'Western metaphysics' may represent a transference of guilt: bitterness towards the failing father (Husserl) spreads to the entire ancestral line, starting with Plato, the tribe's patriarch, who must assume the mythical responsibility for this latest failure. The unattainable ideality is pursued and denounced at its ancestral hearth. Finally, the frail subject is broken at the heart of phenomenological territory by the uncontrollable forces of protention and retention whose composition is called deferral. As for describing what could some day replace the condemned edifice, only terms like 'unheard of', 'exorbitant', 'unthought of', 'unimaginable' are used.

Secondly, and as important as the dissociation between subject and ideality, Derrida indicates in the *Introduction* where new sources of ideality should be sought. As we just saw, criticism of Husserl led him to discover that one cannot grasp and master the nature of ideality within the limits of phenomenology; yet this critique lacked the means to conclude that the Kantian Idea is equally vulnerable. Within the phenomenological approach, Derrida proves that the subject present-to-itself, being an idealization, cannot *produce* ideality. But nothing should prevent the subject, distorted as it is by the effects of deferral, from *receiving* ideality from elsewhere. This is precisely Derrida's solution. Yet without explaining why, he decides against giving the subject access to a source of ideality similar to the Kantian Idea. Such a source, though not explicitly ruled out by Derrida's argumentation, would have made intelligible if not the foundations of mathematics and science at least the possibility of their existence. It would also have accounted for the distance between ideal and natural languages and, perhaps, the fragility of the transcendental subject notwithstanding, favoured the establishment of a scale of ideality, ranging from the strongest to the weakest, in relation to the different domains of knowledge.

Instead, Derrida turns to language: 'ideal objectivity not only characterizes geometrical and scientific truths; it is the element of language in general', he comments on Husserl's remark, according to which ideal formations 'must always be capable of being expressible in discourse and translatable . . . from one language into another' (*Introduction*, p. 66). The translation requirement shows that here the notion of language is, just as in the discussion of the first *Logical Investigations*, a general notion whose properties do not depend on the natural languages that manifest it. At a more determinate level, the ideal identity of a word in its various usages is an excellent example of this notion. The ideal character of a word can be dissociated at a truly linguistic level – the level at which the word, say, the German *Löwe*, is empirically attached to a linguistic and historical community – and a second, more abstract level at which it cannot be distinguished from the English word *lion*, since, just like the English word, it refers to the unity of meaning, hence to the object, 'lion'. In language however – and this is the direction that Husserl is already taking – the ideal object separates itself from its exclusive rapport with the individual subject in order to serve an entire community. In going beyond the concrete communal bounds, *writing*, Derrida comments, immobilizes the ideal object in 'the purity of its relation to a universal transcendental subjectivity' (ibid., p. 87). Through writing, communication continues in a virtual mode within a kind of 'autonomous transcendental field from which every present subject can be absent' (ibid., p. 88). This property of writing establishes it as the highest possibility of any constitution of ideal objectivity and as an image of the indestructibility of ideal meaning. The theme runs through Jewish and Christian traditions: writing brings together the transcendental absolute viewed as divinity with the transcendental absolute viewed as intersubjectivity or historical community (ibid., p. 147). The relationship to writing, which is also the relationship with a well-established, even indestructible ideality, at the same time accommodates the reactivation of an original act of foundation, the trace of which writing faithfully preserves, and announces the search for a finality already contained in the original act. The reactualization of the former and the pursuit of the latter imply that 'delay is the destiny of Thought itself as Discourse' (ibid., p. 152). The double reference to the origin and the finality of thought confirms the impossibility of founding knowledge on the living present. The originating Absolute is '*present* only in being *deferred-delayed* [*différant*] without respite' (ibid., p. 153), and only the pure consciousness of Difference's undefined work can give its meaning to transcendence. 'The Difference would be Transcendental', Derrida concludes, 'the pure and indeterminable disquietude of thought striving to "reduce" Difference by going beyond factual infinity toward the infinity of its sense and value, i.e., while maintaining Difference – that disquietude would be transcendental' (ibid.).

The enigmatic transcendental space from which the Kantian Idea had withdrawn will thus be conceded to writing understood as a mixture of deferral and dissonance that gauges the performance of the thinking subject. Consequently, at the junction of the two forces – deferral and disharmony – the temptation will become irresistible to postulate a kind of hyperspace of dissonant subjectivity for whose epiphany no classical philosophy has prepared us, since in the past all philosophies of paradox and disorder preferred to look for them in the subject itself. Only Nietzsche, as some of his fragments suggest, seems to have had a glimpse of a transcendental disorder which he conceptualized (ironically?) as biological energy.

Phenomenology comprises, however, a principle of quietude. Seen only from a phenomenological viewpoint, the combination of writing as the matrix of objectivity with difference-deferral as origin and end of thought opens an unexpected transcendental space. By themselves, they could not create the explosive blend at work in *Of Grammatology*. Heidegger's later work unambiguously testifies that such is the case. Although it is indeed possible to trace Derrida's notion of difference-deferral back to the Heideggerian difference between Being and existing, in Heidegger's writings this concept preserves the peaceful connotations and the piety of Platonism. For the postwar Heidegger, the search for Being involves waiting for its revelation and as such belongs to contemplative life. Wandering along paths that lead nowhere, the thinker, like the poet or the pilgrim, welcomes the revelation of Being disguised as difference. Though rejecting Husserl's variety of foundationalism and thus the entire tradition of intellectualist phenomenology, Heidegger inherits the longing for certitude as well as the calm technique for approaching it. But since the certitude of Being does not give itself up once and for all, since the road which may lead to it never decisively overcomes the difference between Being and existing, the philosopher can only follow the endless twists and turns of ontological difference. He feels attracted towards ontological difference, elicits a question from it which, like an echo, contains its own answer, and finds in it the appeasing source of something that could be called wisdom.

In *Of Grammatology*, however, difference is on the side of distraction, of sound and fury. Between the *Introduction* of 1963 and the books published in 1967, Derrida found that ingredient capable of transforming the transcendental writing/difference mixture into a remarkably powerful explosive: Saussurian linguistics revised and radicalized by Hjelmslev. Thus Derrida's references to linguistics, which, according to some, constitute the innovative nucleus of his thinking and, according to others, are but a minor theme of his philosophy, can be described as a *metaphysical trigger* which activated the conceptual movement of *Of Grammatology*.

Again let us follow Derrida's reasoning: first, he shows that objective knowledge cannot be legitimated by the activity of the knowing subject. Secondly, he attaches the name of *writing* to the transcendental regularities that govern our knowledge. Thirdly, he demonstrates that knowledge is based less on stable certainty than on restless *deferral*. Fourthly, *writing* and *deferral* are identified with *language*. The result is a perceptible shift in the nature of epistemological inquiry. For, if the play of transcendental regularities (writing) and of temporality (deferral) were designated as language, philosophy would be ready to dispense with the notion of the transcendental subject. All thinkers who saw language as the source of objectivity eliminated the individual subject as a provider of meaning. Here, in spite of the melodramatic tone that enhances his discourse, Derrida stays surprisingly close to many analytical philosophers, especially those belonging to the anti-intentionalist trend: Quine, for example.

At the same time, the opposition between the transcendental and the empirical *seems* to disappear, since the subject (which justified it) withdraws from the game. Just like the early analytical philosophers, Derrida loudly expresses the premature satisfaction of having brought metaphysics, even philosophy, to an end through the examination of its language. Therefore, since the demon of metaphysics has been exorcised, philosophy, according to Derrida – and to early analytical philosophers – is left with just two final tasks: to construct a formal theory of language and to expose the emptiness of old speculations. It is clear here how similar Wittgenstein's *Tractatus* is to the project of grammatology; both attempt to build a general science of language/writing as transcendental objectivity. It is also clear how close the denunciation of 'pseudo-philosophical problems' in the writings of the Vienna School is to Derrida's deconstruction of metaphysical concepts.

But a general and formal science of language, whether inspired by logic and mathematics or having the evanescent properties of grammatology, is not at all assured of avoiding the pitfalls of metaphysics. In fact the distinction between the empirical and the transcendental is still present at the very core of linguistic philosophy: since language becomes the general form of the possibility of knowledge, *it inherits all the determinations previously attributed to the transcendental domain.* After a long period of anti-metaphysical puritanism, this fact is now recognized again by post-positivist analytical philosophers and provides renewed interest in metaphysics. The work of Arthur Danto, Daniel Dennett, Jaakko Hintikka, Saul Kripke, Alvin Plantinga and Hilary Putnam, among others, reformulated traditional metaphysical questions in the idiom of analytical philosophy. They were able to do so because for decades innumerable research projects proposed so many models of natural and formal language. By virtue of its strategic positioning in Derrida's system, grammatology is set a task similar to that of logic in Russell's and Wittgenstein's philosophy: it must examine the organization of language as the ultimate source of objectivity. And it is precisely here that both the particularity and the weakness of Derrida's strategy become apparent. For, by choosing Saussurian linguistics, and not formal logic, as the model of ideal objectivity, Derrida postulates a kind of pre-existing harmony between, on the one hand, his own theory of temporality and objectivity (deferral and writing) and, on the other, the immanent, arbitrary algebra which, according to Saussure and his disciple Hjelmslev, governs the form of language.

The two sides of Derrida's system – the phenomenological and the linguistic – are linked at three conceptual locations. First, in order to distinguish writing as the transcendental order of objectivity from empirical writing – our everyday notation systems – Derrida designates the former *arche-writing* and identifies it with the semiological system that Saussure calls *langue*. This, incidentally, does not prevent Derrida from frequently protesting against Saussure's anti-writing prejudice (1967b, pp. 30ff). Commenting on a brief chapter on writing in Saussure's *Course in General Linguistics*, a chapter that differs very little from the standard treatment of the topic in the linguistic handbooks at the turn of the century, Derrida claims to have found the undesirable trace of logocentrism. To grant spoken language priority over writing, to assert that writing represents a merely accidental variety of the spoken word, would betray the linguist's complicity with the subject present-in-itself in the vividness of his own speech. The abstract linguistic system and its objective structure that can be indefinitely repeated are embodied in writing, Derrida argues; therefore, it is the spoken word – that is, the oral manifestation of the language system – which should be called an accidental variety of writing. The polemics is clearly spurious, since the distinction between empirical writing (Saussure's notion) and arche-writing (or transcendental linguistic system) is necessary in Derrida's theory. But then both empirical writing *and* the spoken language are equally dependent on arche-writing (the transcendental language system). And it is difficult to see why empirical writing would manifest the exemplary objectivity of arche-writing better than speech, especially given the circumstance that the systematic character of language, beginning with phonology, has been discovered through the study of speech. In fact, in *Of Grammatology*, by playing down the radical distinction between writing and arche-writing, Derrida attempts to conceal the presence of a resilient distinction between the transcendental and the empirical domain.

After relating *arche-writing* to the *linguistic system*, Derrida links his notion of deferral (*différance*) with the Saussurian *difference*. The operation is quite complex and involves two notions that in French are written differently but pronounced in the same way: *différence* (difference) and *différance* (deferral). Phenomenologically speaking, the starting point is deferral, that is, postponement and temporality, signifying both the temporal activity of the human consciousness advancing through time and the relationship of ideal objects – words, texts, mathematical theorems – to their origin and end. But at the same time, the *différance* refers to difference, that is, to what Heidegger calls the ontological difference between Being and existing beings. The combination of these two ideas leads to the truly Derridian notion of *différance* which supposedly captures the silent movement of ontological difference independently of the Being and existing that – this difference – separates. How can we paraphrase such meanderings in plainer language? By considerably simplifying this conceptual labyrinth, we could say that arche-writing corresponds to the form of objectivity while deferral defines its mode of operation. The linguistic difference – the Saussurian principle – is associated by Derrida with deferral (*différance*) as arche-operation or the transcendental dynamics of objectivity. This dynamics, Derrida claims, works by deploying endless spacings (*espacements*) in the inconceivable silence of the arche-writing. To a phenomenologist, this may appear quite similar to the linguistic algebra Saussure spoke about and to the pure immanent form of languages as conceived by Hjelmslev. But such similarity is an illusion. For Saussure's algebra and Hjelmslev's immanent form are regional notions, not transcendental ones. They attempt to characterize the semiotic arrangement of our everyday instrument for communication rather than the source of objectivity itself. Can the structure of the sign system be extrapolated and attributed to thought itself? Is the realm of meaning reducible to that of signs? Derrida answers in the affirmative, but the reasons he presents prove disappointing. At this point in his argument and in order to consolidate his mastery over the notion of language. Derrida should have attempted to move away from the rarefied air of transcendental considerations and supplement his purely thematic thought with genuine methodology, if such a manoeuvre was compatible with the general orientation of his thought.

This move is certainly attempted several times in the long chapter 'Linguistics and Grammatology' (1967b, pp. 27–73). Yet, for some reason, Derrida always pulls up short. This indecision may be attributed to two complementary failures. On the philosophical side, the Hegelian use of the term *science* – accepted by Derrida – makes the recognition of an autonomous, properly scientific, level of thinking impossible. (I am speaking here of *science* in both the classical *and* the contemporary acceptations of the term, referring to an epistemological activity that pursues its objectives independently of transcendental considerations.) In Derrida's view, contemporary linguistics is *threatened* by the desire to be autonomous, that is, independent of philosophy. For example, after explaining that for Saussure writing does not belong to the internal system of language, Derrida continues in an irate tone:

> External/internal, image/reality, representation/presence, such is the old grid to which is given the task of outlining the domain of a science. And of what science? Of a science that can no longer answer to the classical concept of the *episteme* because the originality of its field – an originality that it inaugurates – is that the opening of the 'image' within it appears as the condition of 'reality'; a relationship that can no longer be thought within the simple difference and the uncompromising exteriority of 'image' and 'reality', of 'outside' and 'inside', of 'appearance' and 'essence', with the entire system of oppositions which necessarily follows from it. (ibid., p. 33)

In simpler words, linguistics initiates (or should initiate) the abolition of classical metaphysics in so far as it takes language as its *object*, language being just the *image* of reality. The reality of linguistics will be the image of reality. The essence of language is appearance: therefore, linguistics performs the neutralization of the opposition between appearance and essence! But such an understanding of linguistics requires it to perform a task for which it is certainly not qualified. Original as its field may be, even if the old metaphysical oppositions indeed appear to play a lesser role within its parameters, linguistics is still fully determined by the classical notion of science, which requires, in addition to purely thematic concepts, a methodology. The smallest conceptual investment is expected to produce empirical dividends through methodology. In other words, there is little difference between a purely thematic science and philosophy. This is why in Derrida's text the two notions are so often used indiscriminately: 'The constitution of a science or a philosophy of writing is a necessary and difficult task' (ibid., p. 162). And this may be why Derrida rejects both science and philosophy in the name of *thought* (*la pensée*), which, he claims, goes beyond the old epistemological distinctions: 'a *thought* of the trace, of difference or of reserve, having arrived at these limits and repeating them ceaselessly, must also point beyond the field of the *episteme*' (ibid., p. 93). He thus solves the tensions between thematics and method, between philosophy and science, by rejecting method and, in the end, by abandoning thematics as well. Thought, as governed by the pure movement of difference, is 'in the play of the system, that very thing which never has weight' (ibid.).

This flight towards indetermination, this appeal to randomness, is not at all moderated or rationalized by the reference to linguistics. True, Derrida thinks that a convergent set of notions can be found in linguistics; for the indeterminate play of transcendental deferral (*différance*) seems to coincide with the random economy of arbitrary signs, each defined only by its oppositions to all other signs. Didn't the most scientific of all approaches lead Hjelmslev to the notion of a linguistic form defined as pure negativity and freed from any substantial determinations? True, these themes can be found both in Saussure's *Course in General Linguistics* and in Hjelmslev's *Prolegomena to a Theory of Language*. Yet these *themes*, at the margins of Saussure's and Hjelmslev's scientific project, signal the end of *methodology*. They do not relate to the circuits that link conceptual work to its empirical consequences, but indicate the limits of the formalism and thus the place where the poverty of methodology forbids anything but speculation. Deriving from a saturated formalism that lacks scientific appeal, this linguistic metaphysics captures the attention of those who work outside linguistics itself. It offers them an enigmatic and, by now, out-of-date image of linguistics, an image that encourages speculations that have little to do with its object. Similarly, in the nineteenth century, Laplace's demon, another myth originating in the saturation of a formalism, haunted physicists much less than it did philosophers. When, later, the development of thermodynamics outmoded determinism, Laplace's demon ceased to inhabit the world of speculative philosophy. And it is noteworthy that, after the rise of generative systems in linguistics, the idea of language as a pure system of differences ceased to be mentioned by linguists. The new themes of reflection that dominate contemporary linguistics involve grammar not system, syntax not signs, creativity not the play of differences. In other words, there is no good reason why the metaphor of the differential system should still fascinate philosophers reflecting on language.

Thirdly, after pairing arche-writing with the linguistic system and deferral with linguistic algebra, Derrida brings together the *trace* and the *linguistic sign*. He takes as a starting point the Heideggerian notion of trace of Being – the phenomenal world endlessly displaying such traces – and adds to it the Saussurian notions of linguistic – and differential – signs. Just like Saussurian signs, traces constitute an open framework in which each position is defined by its non-identity with the surrounding positions. In Derrida's anti-epistemology, this structure of traces is essential and is located in the transcendental space that legitimates (or, rather, delegitimates) knowledge. The endless – random – play of empty traces deprives knowledge of any stable foundation and of any hope for such foundation. But the appeal to linguistics miscarries. The reason why systems of signs adopt such a structure is the economy of means and not transcendental negativity. Linguists found instances of differential networks precisely in those areas where language, having only *limited* means at its disposal, must make the best use of them. In phonology, for instance, where each language has only about thirty sounds – consonants and vowels – from which it must build tens of thousands of words, a quasi-differential structure represents an elegant semiotic solution. In contrast, the attempts to apply the idea of a differential system to semantics have been less persuasive. In grammatical semantics, the examples supporting a purely differential view of meaning are far from compelling. Saussure's argumentation distinguishes between linguistic values and conceptual content. Speaking of grammatical tenses, Saussure remarks that

> Distinctions of time, which are so familiar to us, are unknown in certain languages. Hebrew does not recognize even the fundamental distinctions between past, present and future ... The Slavic languages regularly single out two aspects of the verb: the perfective represents action as a point, complete in its totality; the imperfective represents it as taking place and on the line of time. The categories are difficult for a Frenchman to understand, for they are unknown in French; if they were pre-determined, this would not be true. (1916, pp. 116–17)

And he adds: 'Instead of pre-existing ideas then, we find in all the foregoing examples *values* emanating from the system' (ibid., p. 117). In other words, grammatical categories do not depend on the *same* system of ideas in all languages, but are each time defined as differential structures. But 'differential' here should be taken with a grain of salt, since every grammatical category possesses its own well-determined meaning. The Russian verb, for instance, displays *two* aspects, each with its own *specific* meaning, rather than two values emanating only from the linguistic system. If, on the one hand, just as in phonology, grammatical categories offer patterns of *means of expression* arranged as quasi-differential systems, on the other hand, and in contrast with the domain of sounds, these categories already possess a determined semantic weight the meaning of which will be perceived in all messages that employ them. And yet these categories do not determine the expression of ideas. In the Semitic languages, to stay with Saussure's example, tense is not entirely absent or impossible to express, but is signified through the category of aspect. This is why Arab grammarians of the eight and ninth centuries called the perfective aspect *al-mâdî*, 'the past'. The present is expressed through the imperfective aspect, while the future tense, called *al-mustaqbil*, requires the addition of prepositions to the present or is understood through contextual interpretation. Finally, in vocabulary, aside from a few semantic fields (names of colours and of furniture) which may resemble the systems of grammatical categories, the interplay of values and of differences remains rather occasional. It could not be otherwise for the very reason that whereas the inventory of elements is rather limited in phonological and grammatical systems, vocabulary consists of a much vaster and more flexible set of units. Accordingly, there is no need for an economy of means in vocabulary, since words can be invented or forgotten on a daily basis, homonyms and synonyms cause both shortages and surpluses, and lexical creations and borrowings maintain a constant state of fermentation.

Thus, the linguistic analogies of trace and deferral fail to accomplish the philosophical tasks required of them. Natural language seems to be an instance of general grammatology only to the extent that the philosophical argumentation borrows from linguistics either thematic speculation divorced from formal analysis, or technical details isolated from their context. But the deconstructionist philosopher is little worried whether or not he has found a formalism that genuinely fits his thematics. All he wants is to produce the *illusion* of such a fit. In the economy of his doctrine, objectivity, loosened from its old moorings, acquires a random force that no constraint can stabilize. If the only foundation of meaning resides in the silent tremor of pure deferral, then no conceptual achievement would be able to defend itself and no theory would be allowed to spell out its own legitimacy. Decay will not set in from the pressure of facts nor as a result of the success of rival theories, but through a kind of inner unravelling, a self-effacement, a dissipation of the inheritance. The transcendental deferral abolishes unexpected and real differences, the arche-trace erases the heavy traces that mark the face of the Visible; arche-writing obliterates the rough, salient inscriptions on the tablets of the world.

4 Games of Dispersion and the Correspondence Fallacy

Kepler put forward a provocative argument on the infinity of the world: if the universe actually extended in all directions the heavenly bodies would be distributed uniformly, since there is no reason why one region of a limitless homogeneous space would be treated any differently from another. The Creator, operating on the principle of sufficient reason, would not have been able to choose one particular structure for an infinite universe. The world subjected to our observation exhibits such a structure, however, because geometry brings us to the conclusion that the aspect of the universe, contemplated from one of the fixed stars, differs considerably from the image we get of it from Earth. Therefore, since infinite systems exclude singularities by definition, our universe is not infinite.

The outdated astronomical data on which Kepler based his deduction by no means lessen his theoretical insight. In this argument, the geometric world endowed with a particular structure, which was to become that of universal mechanics, already enters into conflict with the universe in dispersion described later by thermodynamics. A principle of infinite dispersion, the source of homogeneity, contradicts the principle of cohesion based on the indubitable existence of empirical singularities. We know that Kepler had an inkling of the name of this cohesion – gravity – but, despite intriguingly precise descriptions, he abandoned the notion, probably because of the metaphysical connotations that could arise from the idea of some force acting mysteriously from afar.

The question of the universe's finitude or infinitude worried subsequent cosmologists, who continued trying to reconcile the principle of uniformity with visible singularities. Soon they found a way of avoiding contradictions by working with orders of magnitude such that the details of the system were no longer perceptible. But the uniformity obtained through increasing the field of vision to such a degree led to contradictions. Olbers's paradox, formulated at the beginning of the last century, demonstrated that to claim that the universe is uniformly filled with stars – today we would say galaxies – makes it impossible to attribute spatial and temporal homogeneity, known valid physical laws and the absence of great systematic movements to this universe all at the same time. In other words, *all uniformities cannot coexist without contradiction in the same theory*. The notion of a stable universe was the first to be abandoned, after the discovery that galaxies grow farther apart at a rate which increases with the distance travelled. Two divergent hypotheses resulted: either the universe began to expand with the initial explosion of a single atom, or it extends indefinitely into uniform space and time, provided that new galaxies, and therefore new matter, are continually created out of nothingness. The first hypothesis abandons the universe's temporal uniformity since it introduces an absolute beginning, whereas the second waives the general validity of physical laws since, on the cosmic scale, the conservation of matter is inconsistent with the postulate of continual creation.

Kepler's argument retains traces of Aristotelian cosmology's reticence towards actual infinity. The problem lurking here, a problem common to all thinking that seeks to abandon classical metaphysics, is how well the concepts are defined. In Kepler's view, postulating the infinity of the universe involved not so much an intolerable increase in the dimensions of the object of astronomy as an infinite weakening of its particularity. The goal of the scientist, however, is to keep this particularity intact and not to let it vanish; furthermore, by virtue of the principle of sufficient reason, the means to do this must be the most simple and the most elegant available. The uniformity of natural laws is not identical with indetermination. To go from a system of circular rotation with many epicycles to the pure ellipses the planets describe around the sun simplifies the representation of the solar system but also allows the movement to be better understood. As we have known since Nicholas of Cusa, in infinity, all geometric figures coincide and all specificity disappears. The networks of geometry and observation would no longer have any hold on an elusive infinite universe.

Powerful mathematical means have since been brought into play to characterize infinite sets, so that the notion of infinity today is no longer necessarily equivalent to that of indetermination. But the researcher avoids such an equivalence only at the expense of laborious formal research, and in its everyday usage the notion of infinity continues to threaten the degree to which we can define our concepts. One of the consequences of the notional device arche-writing/deferral/arche-trace, which takes the place of transcendental ideality in Derrida's thought, is to let go of indeterminate infinity. Derrida's first texts, we have seen, centre on the endless game of writing, the incessant work of the arche-trace, the unbounded spacing of differences in deferral. It is certainly not an infinity laid out before our eyes, like that of Giordano Bruno or Heinrich Olbers, but of an infinity hidden behind (beyond? within?) the singularities endowed with meaning and in which thought guesses at the negative play of the archies, always already there and always eluding us. The mechanism remains the same, however: a single space, called Western metaphysics, which imperceptibly ends up incorporating any significative operation, defines and closes the philosophical horizon. Presumed to liberate thought from its traditional limitations, the new principle of indetermination does not explain, indeed cannot explain, the sedimentation of the singularity upon which it is casting doubts. Again, Saussure's and Hjelmslev's algebras, however rudimentary they may be, avoid this reproach in so far as linguistics, despite its speculative flights of fancy, remains a science of means and not ends of thought. We need not unduly concern ourselves that the mechanisms of natural languages include a source of indetermination, seeing that the flexibility of language will be constrained in its use. Extended to the operation of thought itself, this flexibility no longer receives singular determinations from elsewhere. In the pure form of these archies, all forms disperse, the already-there dissolves irreversibly into the always-already.

INDETERMINATION AND CORRESPONDENCE

The replacement of concrete determinations by randomness and of form by uniformity, and the fear of singularities haunt all structuralist inspired philosophers, since they cannot help hoping that the real will eventually emerge from the pure work of negativity without any need to explain the principles that constitute it. They disregard the slow growth of the tangible, contingency and haecceity. To take them into account, they seem to say, would be a sign of complicity with what they are aiming not to understand but to eliminate. Those who believed in an infinite universe at the turn of the seventeenth century, including the unfortunate Giordano Bruno, embraced their conviction without solid astronomical arguments and used an undeveloped cosmology in order to hasten the downfall of Aristotelian metaphysics. Their attack proceeded not from cosmological arguments in the modern sense of the term but from a fanciful interpretation of the Copernican system. Hence the reserve of professional astronomers who harboured different concerns with regard to the problem of infinity. In the same vein, the methodological results in the human sciences, especially in the linguistics of the 1930s led to speculations of the 1960s and 1970s. No doubt Lévi-Strauss's borrowings from linguistics reflected his desire to increase the credibility of his cognitive speculations. What is known as the linguistic method did not arouse his interest any more than geometric considerations concerned Bruno. No doubt the attack on the notion of the subject directed Derrida's choice of concepts, at the risk of resorting to logico-positivist conceptual tools in an argumentation that was supposed to demolish logocentrism. But as Kepler's argument emphasizes, it is not enough to resort to a theme because one likes its innovative aspects, or because it can reveal what an existing system of thought explains *poorly*; it is also important to consider what will happen to the phenomena that earlier systems explained *well*.

The matter is not limited to explaining the already-there. Often, thought that comes up against existing dogmas gains momentum through generalizations of unprecedented force. The difficulty raised by Kepler disappeared in the subsequent cosmology as a result of a better appreciation of the orders of magnitude. The singularity of our Earth does not result from a fundamental asymmetry that would separate our solar system from the rest of the universe as Kepler seems to have believed, but naturally lies in a universe's myriad of local particularities, given that the dimensions of the fixed stars and distances separating them increase inordinately. We can extrapolate that neither the binarism of Lévi-Strauss nor the infinity of archelinguistic play in Derrida prevents these authors from convincingly explaining the production of concepts, phrases and real myths, but rather a misunderstanding of the nature of this binarism and infinity. If binarism were replaced by a much more powerful algebra, indetermination at this level would vanish together with the singularity within its grasp. In the past 30 years, linguistics acquired such powerful models, although the dangers of indetermination remained present at other levels. Just as Olbers's paradox forced cosmology to renounce either the temporal homogeneity of the cosmos or the universality of physical laws, critics of generative-transformational grammar early noted its excessive generality, and recommended either abandoning too powerful a syntax or dividing up the generative algorithm into multiple components which would obey different constraints. As it turns out, not even the straight and narrow path is always the surest.

That the path followed by linguistically inspired French philosophers has been so wide and so poorly marked is a consequence of the indifference with which structural linguistics treated indetermination. The linguist C. E. Bazell who, in 1952, was the first to point out this indifference, gave the name of *the correspondence fallacy* to the structuralist belief that applying two or more sets of criteria to the same phenomena of language would make the results of the analyses isomorphic, indeed, identical. In phonology, for example, it was long believed – and still is – that an analysis based on articulatory criteria will inevitably lead to the same results as an acoustic analysis, so that the translation of one description in terms of the other will be possible, if not automatic. In 1949, Roman Jakobson, Morris Halle and Gunnar Fant made a detailed study of such a translation. The two sets of criteria in this case are theoretically independent of each other, since the acoustic analysis can either precede or follow the articulatory analysis. Bazell argues that sometimes one of the analyses considered as equivalent must be completed before the other. In morphology, a language's declension, for example, is established by criteria such as formal identity and the distribution of units. Regarding the system of cases, the structuralists believe that each case possesses a single global meaning – for example, the dative signifies 'attribution', the genitive 'possession'; that, in other words, a single 'sememe' corresponds to each morpheme without any overlapping. Both Hjelmslev's and Jakobson's descriptions of case systems, as well as Jakobson's descriptions of the Russian verb system, are founded on this belief. Moreover, the fallacy is present not only when a single sememe is attached to every morpheme: description can attribute several meanings to each morpheme, but as long as it excludes the possibility of the overlapping of meaning between morphemes it manifests the correspondence fallacy.

Bazell notes that as a working hypothesis, it is indeed legitimate to think that, in different analyses, any two units will, more often than not, be described in the same way; in addition, either the articulatory criteria can be *directed* towards acoustic results, or the distributional criteria towards the desired semantic results provided that the researcher already has a rough idea of the purpose of the analysis. The correspondence fallacy consists in believing that independent analyses will coincide even if the criteria have not been selected for this purpose. The linguist who is guilty of the fallacy therefore imagines that a unique necessary structural criterion exists which leads to the accurate identification of traditional grammar units or confirms the speaker's linguistic intuitions. This is where an attempt to characterize the notion of word in structural terms comes in, as also the complex definitions of morpho-syntactic distributional classes put forward by Zellig Harris, which generally coincide fairly well with the parts of discourse of ordinary grammars. To find formalisms which correctly represent the intuitions of the speakers was therefore one of the ambitions of structural linguistics well before Chomsky's writings made it the principal means of verifying the validity of formal hypotheses in linguistics. This means that Chomsky also became, a few years later, a victim of the correspondence fallacy.

On a larger scale, the correspondence fallacy is responsible for the practice common to several structuralist schools which requires different levels of language to be treated with the same methods. The glossematic doctrine, for instance, postulates an isomorphism between linguistic content and expression. This doctrine, which has contributed so much to the proliferation of structural semantics, represents a version of the fallacy. Structural semantics, which extends phonological methods to the analysis of meaning, is therefore guilty of the same fallacy.

Bazell's criticism would probably perplex a contemporary linguist: Chomsky's influence has made obsolete even quite recent methodological controversies in linguistics. The interminable disputes concerning discovery procedures are gone, the analytical scruples forgotten, the parsing rules discarded, and the notion of corpus relegated to oblivion. Structural linguists used to see themselves as adventurers among exotic tribes. Surrounded by speakers of an incomprehensible language, they had instantly to deduce its phonology and morphology without referring to the meaning of sentences, since they were not supposed to understand the language whose structures they were carefully describing – thus the importance of the corpus, analysis, methods and criteria. Today, linguists see themselves as theoretical physicists rather than as field anthropologists. They examine the formalisms already existing in the discipline, calculate such-and-such a consequence on paper, and set off to look for bizarre facts, often unobservable to the naked eye, to confirm their hypotheses. Bazell's doubts are hardly taken into consideration.

Pure methodological thinking, entirely free from any theoretical grounding, does not exist however. Insistence on the method of analysis, so typical of structural linguistics, did not eliminate the more substantial theoretical implications or metaphysical echoes as practitioners of the discipline had hoped. Behind the correspondence fallacy, distinct theoretical positions can easily be discerned. The investigator who begins analysing a corpus of data with the conviction that the different approaches will lead to the same results of their own accord and without any effort on his part shows extraordinary confidence in the autonomy and the stability of the object being examined. Two such different methods as articulatory analysis, based on direct observation of the organs producing the sounds, and acoustic analysis, which laboriously examines the ear's behaviour after having mechanically registered the sound spectrum of the spoken word, can produce equivalent descriptions only if the object being studied, namely, the phonological system, already enjoys a remarkable ontological stability. It is as if the right phonological description already awaited: the researchers could not fail to discover such a vein of gold at the heart of the phonetic gangue, no matter the direction they worked from. Likewise, in morphology, we may well wonder why the identification of formal marks through very simple distributional examination would coincide with the analysis of the endless semantic nuances that define grammatical categories. Why would the countless semantic varieties of the use of the Latin genitive or ablative correspond exactly to the morphemes enumerated by distributional analysis, especially since so many verbs automatically require a certain noun case? How do we define, for example, the sememe or sememes of the Latin genitive, given that after the impersonal verb *interest* the name of a living being is put into the genitive, the name of a thing into the accusative with *ad*, and personal pronouns into the feminine ablative (*interest regis, interest ad salutem reipublicae, interest mea*)?

THE MAGIC OF DISTRIBUTION

The belief in the correspondence of meaning and pure distribution was lucidly formulated by Zellig Harris in a remarkable article, 'Distributional Structure', published in a special 1954 issue of *Word*. This issue, which appeared barely a year before Chomsky's doctoral thesis, represented both the triumph of linguistic structuralism and its swan song. Harris expounded what could be called 'extreme Bloomfieldism'. The scientific doctrines of Leonard Bloomfield, father of American structuralism, took shape in the shadow of behavioral psychology and, like it, rejected introspection and intuitive research, which at the time were considered serious symptoms of subjective amateurism. In his influential book *Language* (1933), Bloomfield pointed out that a truly scientific linguistics would have no need to search the backwaters of the mind, since nothing worthwhile could be derived from such a study. The phenomena of signification have nothing to do with the subjective impressions of the listener: the meaning of linguistic utterances proceeds directly from the objective structure of the universe. The meaning of the word *salt* is not a concept but the chemical formula, NaCl; semantics, in order to be complete, must wait for the end – imminent, it seemed in 1933 – of the scientific description of the world. In the meantime, linguists must be content to observe the similarities and differences of meaning, they note, for example, that the same difference separates *male* from *female* as *he* from *she*, *lion* from *lioness*, *gander* from *goose* and *stallion* from *mare*, without necessarily looking for the sense of these terms, which is defined by zoology. In Bloomfield, the theme of semantic differences thus joins with anti-mentalist scruples: linguistics studies differences not because language is mysteriously interwoven with oppositions but because this expedient is the only one that spares it making use of mental notions.

Among Bloomfield's followers, these ideas reappeared with varying fortunes. Kenneth Pike and Eugene Nida – the moderate Bloomfieldians – adopted a more tolerant attitude towards signification; Charles Hockett and Rullon Wells insisted on the formality of procedures and on the exclusion of the mind. Lastly, Zellig Harris, the most consistent of Bloomfield's followers, undertook to reduce all language mechanisms to games of differences only. In morphology, Bloomfield and his followers had already discovered the extent of the difference in the distributional properties of units. The distinction between *lion:lioness*, *goose:gander*, etc., has a homogeneous distribution with the pair *he/she*. Entire grammatical categories, thought the American structuralists, can easily be reduced to similar classes of distribution. And since these linguists found the idea of function intolerable, undoubtedly because of its relationship with intention, they subjected syntactic functions to a similar kind of distributional description. The parts of discourse – nouns, verbs, adjectives, etc. – which are capable of characterization in terms of reciprocal position without too much difficulty served as a point of departure for the distributional description of elements in the sentence: subject, verb, complement, etc. This generalization lead to an obliteration of the boundaries between morphology and syntax, these parts of grammar having both become studies of the formal sequence of units. Functional notions, such as the subject of a sentence, were replaced by complex classes of distribution having the same character as the classes defining the parts of discourse: in 1946, Zellig Harris circumvented the notion of grammatical subject by proposing in its place N^4, a special class of nominal distribution. All structuralisms, therefore, not just the speculative varieties, are in league against the use of intentional concepts. The reduction of syntax to distribution was handed down intact to the syntactic models produced by Chomsky, which in their turn manipulated the units defined by their formal place in the spoken chain. Syntactic functions occupy an unimportant place in Chomsky's grammars, being characterized in terms of structures of constituents. They did not receive the attention they deserved until the end of the 1960s, in Charles Fillmore's case grammar, and later in Joan Bresnan's lexico-functional models.

The elimination of syntactic functions with the help of distributional definitions represented a memorable feat for the radical Bloomfield wing, for it reduced the mental to the very marginal domain of vocabulary. Harris's 1954 article, 'Distribution Structure' extended the distributional principle to lexical meaning. Meaning is only an effect of difference, asserted Harris, and the difference in meaning between unit A and unit B comes down to the difference in distribution between A and B. If, therefore, the word *mare* signifies something other than *lioness*, it is because, in the finished sequence of sentences forming the corpus, the distribution of *mare* does not coincide with that of *lioness*: the noncoincidence itself produces the difference in meaning between the two lexical units. But how does one compare things as incommensurable as meaning and distribution? The answer: by *resorting to the totality*, one of the structuralists' favourite manoeuvres, whereby the details of particularly hazardous descriptions can be avoided. Words acquire their meaning, according to Harris, not individually but as a whole by virtue of the differences in distribution across the whole surface of the language; if it were in some way possible to measure the positions that the 138,000 words contained in the *Chambers 20th Century Dictionary* occupy in billions of phrases (a modest part of the English corpus), these positions would lead to the meaning of these words, or rather *would be nothing but* their meaning. When speaking, we wrongly think that we are referring to the actual state of affairs, that we are working out concepts. What we take for words endowed with meaning are, in Harris's view, linguistic configurations with a well-defined distribution.

The appeal to totality is, however, a purely verbal solution. Harris's distributionism illustrates the fullest consequences of the correspondence fallacy better than any other structural doctrine. A perfectly regulated methodology which saves the researcher from dangerously resorting to subjective intuition strikes an alliance with behaviourism, in whose name the problem of meaning in semantics is eliminated without hesitation. It is hard to imagine how one could be more devoted to empiricist doctrines, how one could more effectively destroy the philological and hermeneutical paradigm, and how, ignoring the remnants of the paradigm, one could better secure the *tabula rasa* required for the absolute beginning. All the same, there is actually no absolute beginning, given that all these intellectual acrobatics in linguistics depend on an invisible safety net. In applying the perfectly empirical, behaviourist and anti-intuitive procedure, the analyst perseveres in his research carried along by the conviction that at the end of his work he will obtain an equivalent description, perhaps slightly different in this or that detail, but nevertheless equivalent to that of non-empirical, mental and intuitive old grammars and dictionaries. How can he be sure of this? According to which empirical, behaviourist and anti-intuitive principle does he know in advance that the analysis will lead to just that point where, without admitting it, he wants it to lead? There are two choices: either the researcher surreptitiously introduces a teleological element into his method, an indication of finality thanks to which the direction of his work is corrected with respect to the expected conclusion. Or the linguist relies on his method without giving it a second thought; but in this case he must have an unshakeable belief that the structure of the object studied, drawing on formidable ontological energy, imposes the same descriptive pattern on all researchers whatever their persuasion. For pure empirism to work in the human sciences, it must incorporate a tacit belief in either finality or pre-established harmony.

Moreover, the notion of distribution, like that of difference, remains intelligible only as long as it is applied to a strictly limited number of linguistic objects. The distribution of the article can always be described in relation to the noun, just as a difference in meaning can always be sought between definite and indefinite articles. But the application of these notions to an indefinite number of categories and occurrences raises difficulties like those which troubled Kepler. If the reciprocal distribution of linguistic units is *the only* principle regulating meaning and usage, it is clear that in going from a small number of phrases to a greater and greater number of statements, the distributions of the elements *would gradually lose definition* and lead to the perfect equalization of distributions as the number of phrases becomes infinite. With samplings of immense or infinite size, what other explicit principle would prevent distribution from becoming random? Faced with this difficulty, we understand why the distributionists have put such emphasis on the finite nature of the linguistic corpus. Infinity, even a potential one, was as distasteful to them as to Kepler, since it made the explanation of visible singularities impossible. What was later called the 'principle of projection' in generative and transformational grammar finally provided a satisfactory solution to this difficulty, but at the expense of a major theoretical conversion. The notions of distribution and difference lost their original status and were henceforth explained in terms of more fundamental mechanisms. To prevent singularities from becoming random when the corpus is infinite, generative grammarians abandoned the idea of language as a simple manifestation of distributions/differences in favour of a more costly but more productive conception, according to which sentences derive (1) from a highly idiosyncratic grammar which generates a finite number of structures, thus saving the singularity of observable languages; (2) from a principle of projection which multiplies the occurrences of these and only these structures *ad infinitum*, thereby gaining infinity without sacrificing the definition of observed facts.

I am by no means claiming that a gulf separates generative-transformational grammar and the distributionism of Harris. On the contrary, without Harris's meticulous distributional studies, his pupil, Chomsky, would undoubtedly not have found a terrain ready for his formal generalizations, just as Kepler might not have been able to formulate his three famous laws without the mass of astronomical observations by Tycho Brahe and his disciples. The notion of transformation itself was created by Harris in order to account for distributional regularities beyond the confines of the sentence. But the distributionists, however scrupulously precise their work may have been, remained deliberately silent about the real norms governing it: the special attention given to the finality of description, the incessant use of linguistic intuition, and the tacit respect for traditional grammars. These norms, running contrary to anti-mentalist ideology, guaranteed the validity of the results. Chomsky, in announcing that linguistics must use these norms, made public what his predecessors had already been silently doing.

These hidden norms made themselves felt in Harris's 1946 article 'From Morpheme to Utterance'. There Harris claimed that classes of morphemes, supposedly established by pure contextual substitution, include all expressions which can be found in the same linguistic environment. If expression B replaces expression A in context C . . . D and, as a result, both CAD and CBD are expressions of the language in question, A and B belong to the same class of substitution. But in order to obtain classes of morphemes from classes of substitution, it is necessary to find the *right* contexts. Thus, in the context *I'm writing a whole . . . this time*, one can insert *poem* but not *house*. On the other hand, both items appear in the context *That's a beautiful . . .* The question is: do they belong to the same class of substitution or not? The answer is yes, given that the minimal difference between their distributions corresponds to the distributional differences between their contexts. Since one can say *I'm wiring a whole house this time*, but *poem* is excluded from this context, *poem* and *house* can be placed in the same N class provided that the words *write* and *wire*, whose contexts are parallel to those of *poem* and *house*, fall into class V.

The sleight of hand is quite obvious. An explicit rule of procedure – the establishment of substitution classes without any prior restriction – is contradicted by the appeal to totality – the introduction of parallel contexts. Under cover of this manoeuvre, the tacit norms listed above are applied: the contexts are not *found* in an inspection of the corpus, but are *proposed* with a view to working towards the end, which in this case consists in distributionally justifying the existence of the *noun* class; the research tool is nothing more than the scholar's linguistic intuition, and the model imitated is nothing more than categories of traditional grammar.

To summarize, briskly dismissing the discipline's past, an anti-mentalist ideology recommends that linguistic phenomena be approached in the pure manifestation of their dispersion. A single operation, the comparison of apparent contexts separated from their mental meaning, suffices to reveal the field's laws of organization. Behind this ideology, one perceives at work both the neglect of singularities and the correspondence fallacy. How could it be otherwise? The break with traditional knowledge having led extremist structuralism to reject all previous research, linguists who embrace this point of view have to derive all their knowledge from the meagre methodological resources to which their scientific choices restrict them. But these choices, despite their rigorousness, do not bring any real autonomy. The new science, born of refusal and revolt, while obliging the researchers to define themselves polemically against the old paradigm and to oppose the so-called sure methods of analysis against philological scholarship and antimentalist dogma against the hermaneutic attention for meaning and nuance, makes it no easier to gain new perspectives of the object of research. As a result, it is necessary to resort to knowledge already acquired. But because this extremist approach prevents an open continuation of the dialogue with linguistic predecessors, the relationship with the disciplinary tradition becomes one of the shameful parasitism. Behind the incorruptible discourse of radical ideology, the old norms and practices, condemned and forbidden, remained the only valid sources of research.

The extreme scientism of the linguistics of the 1940s was productive in some ways. Even though distributionist research seldomly resulted in the discovery of new material, since research clandestinely reverted to intuition, to the principle of finality and to tradition, passing the data through the homogeneous filter of distribution was methodologically interesting. It showed that simple, coherent models could be imposed on phenomena of meaning. The principle of uniformity was thus applied to the internal structure of languages. Lévi-Strauss's enthusiasm for the linguistics of his time was not therefore entirely without foundation. Whether the success of structural linguistics was the result only of the smallness of its field and of language's instrumental character is difficult to decide. At all events, similar epistomological strategies define a much wider-ranging project in Foucault's early writings. Although Foucault repudiated the label 'structuralist', his thoughtless application of the principle of uniformity – a typical structuralist manoeuvre – involved him in the same difficulties as those encountered by the distributionists.

DISCURSIVE DISPERSION, TRANSCENDENTAL CUSTOMS

The philological and hermeneutic paradigm requires factual support from each interpretative construction and a methodological base from each theoretical development. In the 1950s, innovators in the human sciences considered such a paradigm uninspired, too concerned with the concrete, the individual and the singular. Pronouncing the paradigm atomistic, even positivistic, they dismantled it, divorcing the concern for content from method. Foucault's 'discourse on method', *The Archaeology of Knowledge* (1972) exemplifies this divorce. Though certainly not Foucault's best or most characteristic work, it demonstrates, better than any other, the predicaments of French thinkers who attempted to revolutionize epistemology in the 1960s.

Questioning the traditional boundaries between disciplines. Foucault's early work explicitly opposes the accepted disciplinary norms. We have already noted above the 'empirico-transcendental sidestepping', which consists in conducting arguments on two levels at the same time without a system of transitions. If historical proof is missing in such a demonstration, the author will borrow from the language of metaphysics; when philosophical coherence is wanting, he will claim that the subject matter is only history.

In *The Order of Things* (1966), for example, the description of the pre-classical episteme – at the end of the sixteenth and beginning of the seventeenth century – is based on marginal texts which had practically no audience either at the time they were written or afterwards. It emphasizes the philosophical contrast between the sixteenth century paradigm of resemblance and the seventeenth century logic of representation. By the very nature of his argument, indefinite concepts such as resemblance, discontinuity, order, sign, etc. dispense Foucault from producing atomist proofs of philological or historical origin. The following passage (ibid., p. 54) describes the discontinuity introduced in the eighteenth century by the work of Francis Bacon and Descartes:

> All this was of the greatest consequence to Western thought. Resemblance, which had for long been the fundamental category of knowledge – both the form and the content of what we know – became dissociated in an analysis based on terms of identity and difference; moreover, whether indirectly by the intermediary of measurement, or directly and, as it were, on the same footing, comparison became a function of order; and, lastly, comparison ceased to fulfil the function of revealing how the world is ordered, since it was now accomplished according to the order laid down by thought, progressing naturally from the simple to the complex.

In fact the change described here had already taken place with the anti-Sophist reaction of Socrates, Plato and Aristotle, and had led to the creation of Greek logic and science. Descartes, being in part an heir to scholasticism, made few innovations in logic and the cornerstone of his philosophy consisted, notably, of separating Greek logic and mathematics, both judged universally valid, from an outdated cosmology and physics.

Reciprocally, astounding philosophical transitions are considered to be true by virtue of historical justification. Regarding the 'epistemological break' which supposedly revolutionized the structures of knowledge at the end of the eighteenth century, Foucault asserts that it was not 'some progress made in rationality' (*horribile dictu*) but

> a minuscule but absolutely essential displacement which toppled the whole of Western thought: representation has lost the power to provide a foundation – with its own being, its own deployment and its power of doubling over on itself – for the links that can join its various elements together. (ibid., p. 238–9)

And, a few lines further on:

> The condition of these links resides henceforth outside representation, beyond its immediate visibility, in a sort of behind-the-scenes world even deeper and more dense than representation itself. In order to find a way back to the point where the visible forms of beings are joined – the structure of living beings, the value of wealth, the syntax of words – we must direct our search towards the peak, that necessary but always inaccessible point, which drives down, beyond our gaze, towards the very heart of things.

Foucault's reader might object here the discontinuity is perhaps open to a more subtle explanation, that necessary or at least probable passages exist between taxonomic and causal models and vice versa, or even to object that structures as complex as scientific projects – not to mention the whole of Western thought – could not 'topple' because of the 'miniscule displacement' in a single area, be it as important as the relations between representation and causality. These, Foucault's text suggests, are simple historical events which are described without any speculation.

Other critics have already questioned both the value of the historical hypotheses developed in Foucault's early works and their underlying philosophy. These hypotheses and the manner in which they operate are admittedly fascinating. Foucault's epistemological anarchism illustrates an important moment in the dialectic of the Enlightenment, accentuating in its own fashion the preponderance of destiny in the movement of knowledge. In all philosophies radically opposed to that of the Enlightenment, the theme of blind destiny checks that of rational progress. Beleaguered by a world which is infinitely beyond him, the individual loses the essential role which had been his in optimistic eighteenth-century thought. The hope of ever seeing the human mind go beyond the sedimentation of the *nomos* and understand nature and himself dies. This anti-rationalism accurately grasps the extraordinary breadth of modern knowledge, which far exceeds the scope of individual power. Hence the identical manoeuvre of conservatives and revolutionists, who both set off in search of the lost *nomos*, denying the possibility of a purely rational knowledge of nature and man. Edmund Burke and Joseph de Maistre on one side, Marx, Nietzsche and, later, Heidegger and Adorno on the other, react in a fundamentally like manner, even though one side is aiming at re-establishing the old order, while the others are looking beyond the advance of reason, hoping to find the hidden *nomos* which determines its progress and setbacks.

Foucault, like his critics, acknowledged how akin his thinking was to that of Nietzsche. But the invisible driving force to which Nietzsche subordinated the apparent working of reason belonged to an ontological level completely different from that of the mind. By attributing the birth of values to biological energy, Nietzsche thought he had eluded the surface of *intellectual* creation by finding its roots in *life*. In Foucault, the *nomos* to which the illusory work of reason can be reduced, itself belongs to epistemology. It is defined in the 'depths' of the episteme by a covert action involving the mechanisms of representation, an action completed at the perceptible surface of knowledge by the pressure exerted upon it by discursive customs. Nothing outside epistemology can explain the mutations of knowledge. Separated from a more fundamental level but, with the rejection of rational progress, equally devoid of an apparent teleological trajectory, epistemological behaviour in Foucault takes on the traits of customary systems which have to be described in detail before their meaning can be understood. Custom is not rational; hence, Foucault's lack of interest in the causes of the mutations, his insistence on the discursive and not the rational organization of knowledge, and the attention to power networks which fuel this organization. We are a long way from the classical approach against the opacity of customs, yet Nietzsche's biological reductionism has also been avoided.

Once the classical approach has been rejected, the discursive custom is hardly the only choice left, since to look at the work of reason as subjected to the rule of custom can just as easily lead to a sociology of knowledge in the tradition of Tocqueville, Marx, Durkheim and Max Weber. The advantage of this latter option is to approach custom in the privileged place of its manifestation, society, and to follow its consequences in the domain of knowledge. Thanks to this type of examination, knowledge retains a certain independence from the *nomos* which surrounds, influences and partially determines it. Radically to reduce reason to custom – though, again, there is no reason compelling the reduction to be radical – there is no better way than to postulate, as Foucault did, that knowledge, in itself and independently of any activity external to it, unknowingly organizes itself as a system of customs.

This stance comes out clearly in Foucault's use of linguistic notions. Unlike Lévi-Strauss, for whom the laws of linguistic structure open the way to general laws of thought, and unlike Derrida, who is looking for the source of a non-metaphysical ideality in language, Foucault envisages language neither as a model of formal organization nor as the basis of all ideality, but as a restraining set of transcendental customs. This attitude is strikingly similar to philosophical behaviourism in regard to natural languages. Quine, for example, raised doubts about the conventionalist conception of language in 1936. How could language be the object of an agreement between humans, he wondered, while any agreement, to become established, presupposes a language in which its terms can be defined? Should we not look instead towards the distinction between voluntary agreements and inherited customs? If this last distinction has any validity, does language then not place itself alongside customs? And if so, wouldn't the task of the linguist be to describe its empirical characteristics and only these characteristics, since it is useless to look for any system in customs other than their observable regularity? By insisting on the descriptive tasks of their science, linguists of the Bloomfield school agreed with this programme's excessive empiricism. They isolated only the discernible recurrences of the structure of languages strongly doubting the existence of more general traits. As the famous formula of Martin Joos emphasized, 'languages can go through undefined variations as much from the quantitative point of view as from the orientation of the differences'.

Quine and the Bloomfieldian linguists worked on natural languages whose customary and disorderly character has no epistemological consequence, since the linguist describing them has access to scientific metalanguages. Foucault in talking about language certainly did not refer to natural languages but used the concept in its most general sense. In the interest of proving his thesis, he avoided the hidden systematic aspects of language, instead examining apparent language practices, which he regarded as the undefined display of a customary norm. The Foucaldian notion of *discourse* includes this dispersion and passivity at the same time.

Thus, *The Archaeology of Knowledge* proceeds to reconstruct some central notions in the history of sciences – discipline, object and methods – in terms of discursive customs, which results in a conceptual system astoundingly similar to that of the distributionists. The resemblances are particularly apparent in the rejection of mentalist – or intentional – notions; in the programme of objective analysis leading to the application of the principle of uniformity and therefore to the loss of singularities; and finally, based on the correspondence fallacy, in the establishment of a set of notions which closely match traditional ones.

The intentional notions include tradition, disciplines, influence, evolution, mentality – in short, all the historical forms of coherence and continuity. For Foucault, the notion of continuity is a sure symptom of (Hegelian?) humanism, whose principal doctrine proclaims the sovereignity of the subject: 'making historical analysis the discourse of the continuous and making human consciousness the original subject of all historical development and all action ... the two sides of the same system of thought' (ibid., p. 12). Intentionality must disappear, together with anthropologism (i.e. mentalism), to make place for a dispassionate historical analysis; at the same time, teleology, which is an effect of totalization, will yield to the concepts of discontinuity, rupture, threshold, limit, series and transformation (ibid. p. 21).

The reasoning corresponds point by point to that of the behaviourist linguists: fertile in idle fancies, traditional linguistics, the intellectual history of which can be traced back to Humboldt (just as the history of the complicity between humanism and teleological continuity goes back to Hegel), has produced only useless notions. It is therefore necessary to rid it of mentalist prejudices and start anew with facts: 'We must question', writes Foucault, though this could also be Bloomfield or Quine, 'those ready-made syntheses, those groupings that we normally accept before any examination ... And instead of according them unqualified, spontaneous value, we must accept, in the name of methodological rigor, that, in the first instance, they concern only a population of dispersed events' (ibid., p. 22).

Having set aside anthropological notions, the analyst must confront an immense field 'made up of the totality of all effective statements' (ibid., p. 29), a field that has to be dealt with 'in its raw, neutral state' (ibid., p. 27) by the 'pure description of discursive events' (ibid., p. 29). The 'raw, neutral state' of the statements brings to mind the lack of meaning of linguistic units of the distributionists, who also believed they had to set aside all presuppositions and devote themselves to the pure description of linguistic corpuses. The description of regularities perceived in the material's raw, neutral state led the distributionists to discover perfectly singular grammars of each of the languages studied; in the same way, thinks Foucault, the analysis of discursive fields, while excluding the search for meaning or the hidden system ('We do not seek below what is manifest the half silent murmur of another discourse' (ibid., p. 28) will stumble, without exactly knowing how, upon 'the exact specificity' (ibid.) of the discursive sets. Before beginning their harsh descriptive task, the distributionists vaguely knew that the distribution of linguistic units will always exhibit some particularity which will enable the analysis to get under way. Likewise, the analyst of the discourse had to tell himself that, as raw and as neutral as the state of his material was, it was not equivalent to a hopeless 'dust of facts' (ibid.).

The statements in a discourse, we already know – for how could it be otherwise – maintain relations between themselves and form groups which, in their turn, determine themselves reciprocally and enter into relation with 'events of a quite different kind (technical, economic, social, political)' (ibid., p. 29). These relations are supposed to be barely perceptible, since any return to the old coherence is prohibited: far from coinciding with the traditional notions that defined a science – that is, the domain of objects, the disciplinary logic, the conceptual inventory and the subject matter – the study of statements seems to privilege dispersion over cohesion. When the distribution of these dispersed statements displays certain (non-specified) regularities a system of dispersion or a discursive formation is established (ibid., pp. 37–8). As *systems* – this is the word Foucault uses despite the oxymoron in joining it with 'dispersion' – these formations make the constellation of statements spin around some galactic nuclei which, though they may not give cohesion to these constellations, at least give them some kind of inclination to revolve in harmony. In these nuclei we find notions identical to those that have just been obliterated: objects, logic, concepts and subject matter. The object, however, no longer precedes the discourse; logic changes completely into 'enunciative modality' (ibid., p. 50); the population of concepts arranges itself not so much in accordance with system and adequacy but with coexistence and approximation; lastly, the subject matter, affected to a greater extent, becomes a 'discursive economy' characterized by diffraction and by what Foucault, undoubtedly to hide the re-emergence of coherence, delicately calls 'link points of systematization' (ibid., p. 66).

In accordance with the analysis and to reward the researcher's anti-anthropomorphic objectivity, a miracle takes place. Just as in Harris, where the purely asemantic and contextual distribution of units leads to the discovery of the N and V categories, which, taking the linguist by surprise, happily coincide with the obsolete mentalist categories of *noun* and *verb*, Foucault's discursive formations, these pure bodies of dispersion, finally reveal themselves as wonderfully similar, down to the smallest detail, to the old spurned disciplines and to their conceptual articulations.

Despite the impressive appeal to infinity and conceptual indetermination, the failure of the revolt against the notion of discipline is particularly visible in the passage on the formation of objects (ibid., pp. 55–6). As specialists in the history of sciences, we are therefore supposed to have already abandoned all 'ready-made syntheses' to tackle a dispersed population of statements 'in its raw, neutral state'; we have called the totality of statements which react on one another, especially in synchrony, 'discursive formations' or 'systems of dispersion', and we are preparing to map out this shifting multiplicity. Are the objects of science, in particular, anything more than discursive effects? To convince us that the answer is no, Foucault, relying on medical examples, suggests 'First we must map the first *surfaces* of their *emergence*: show where these individual differences, which, according to the degrees of rationalization, conceptual codes and types of theory, will be accorded the status of disease, alienation, anomaly, dementia' (ibid., p. 41). We must then 'describe the authorities of delimitation: in the nineteenth century, medicine ... became the major authority in society that delimited, designated, named and established madness as a object' (ibid., p. 41–2), in order to analyse finally 'the *grids of specification*: these are the systems according to which the different "kinds of madness" are divided, contrasted, related, regrouped, classified, derived from one another as objects of psychiatric discourse' (ibid., pp. 41–2). Behind this rhetoric lurks the empirical field of medicine rebaptized as an authority of emergence, the discipline, which has become an authority of delimitation, and its methods, which have been raised to authorities of specification.

In this manner and like the linguists of the 1940s, Foucault leaves unanswered two essential questions concerning the efficacy of the approach. One is Kepler's problem: how to reconcile the infinity of dispersion with the singularity of perceptible phenomena, or, expressed another way, once the ideal of coherence has been abandoned in favour of a logic of dispersion, how can the regularities be grasped? The other involves the correspondence fallacy: if the regularities have been grasped, how can we be sure that it did not result from a hidden realist prejudice similar to that in structural linguistics? Regarding the danger of indetermination and without overstressing its importance, Foucault, just like Kepler and the distributionists, insists on the finite character of the set of statements which are subjected to analysis (ibid., p. 27). The finitude guarantees the possible appearance of singularities; the definition of the statements and their functioning (ibid., pp. 79–105) gradually limits the number of descriptive choices. But for the effective singularities to be described, the structure attributed to them has to come from somewhere, either from the gaze that examines them or from the very nature of the objects studied. On that point, the methodology developed in *The Archaeology of Knowledge* entirely depends on the behaviour of its objects. And it is precisely this ambiguity that signals the correspondence fallacy.

The statements acquire their signifying energy, we are told, by virtue of their participation in an 'associated field', which defines a 'field of coexistences' (ibid., p. 99) between statements. In this, compared with the sentences of the natural language, which are simply generated one after the other by the linguistic grammar, the statements analysed exhibit an additional property. The enunciative field does not, however, owe its existence to the research which reveals it: in Foucault's formulation, this field presents itself as a totality of discursive events coming to meet the researcher. If this is so, and if the interplay of the 'associated field' or the 'field of coexistences' determines the meaning of a particular statement, then the field in question must be crossed by some minimal gravitational force securing the statement's place in the field's nebula, and this interplay must be inflected by some silent rule which allots each statement its share of singularity. But since these discursive galaxies obviously do not belong to the physical universe, what name can we give to these gravitational fluxes which congeal the enunciative dust, to these imperceptible rules which conduct play, other than a predicate with teleological resonance: project, approach, development; or a name which connotes history and continuity: tradition, discipline, mentality?

There are two possible answers to these objections, coming from the two extremes of empirico-transcendentalism. Before making any judgement, let us wait for the research to advance further, the empiricists will argue; the study of discursive formations is a vast project that new research enriches and defines more accurately every year. Even if some traces of the abandoned paradigm or some concepts marginally affected by teleology and humanism could be detected at the beginning of the project, the progress of the undertaking will sooner or later have done with these remains, just like the epicycles which weighed down Copernicus's system disappeared with Galileo and Kepler a half-century later. But such temporizing, perfectly acceptable in so many circumstances, cannot apply here, for the good reason that the study of discursive formations coincides elsewhere on the map of knowledge with the slowdown in the great reductionist attempts initiated a generation earlier. Temporization had long been the response strategy practised in behaviourist psychology and in linguistics, or by physicalism in the philosophy of the mind. The exclusion of the mental, of the intentional, of teleology and anthropologism was applied with the same intransigence as in Foucault's later work; the effacement of the researcher, objectivism, asemanticism, the faith in simple observations of surface regularities, the appeal to totality, and so forth had already been invented and established. In the 1960s, all these projects were vigorously contested in the disciplines in which they were born: philosophy of science, linguistics and psychology. The functionalism of Hilary Putnam put physicalism into question, Chomsky disputed the validity of behaviourism, and research into psychology rediscovered mentalism. At that very moment when, awakening from the behaviourist slumber, psychology, linguistics and philosophy of science found a new anthropocentrism, Foucault's archaeology – in its empirical interpretation – had just enjoined history to fall into such a slumber. (Note the irony of the situation: a doctrine which postulates the secret existence of uniform epistemes animating the entire knowledge of an epoch finds itself separated from dominant theoretical concerns by a delay of a generation at the moment it appears. Is there a better refutation of the thesis, whether we interpret this dyschrony in the traditional spirit as a sign of progress, or quite simply note the profound heterogeneity of coexisting theoretical paradigms? In both cases, the study of 'discursive formations' remains without an object.)

The transcendentalists, on the other hand, will neglect facts and emphasize the relationship between the study of discursive formations and philosophical thinking on the conditions of possibility of the activities of the mind. Seen this way, Foucault's work would resemble *The Critique of Judgment*, *The Phenomenology of the Spirit* and *Of Grammatology* rather than the works of Pierre Duhem, Karl Popper, Imre Lakatos, Thomas Kuhn, or L. L. Laudan. The categories of episteme, representation, statement, discursive formation, field of coexistence, etc., would not in this case simply have theoretical signification like the notions of representation and explanation in Duhem, empirical content and refutation in Popper, paradigm in Kuhn, or programme of research in Lakatos, but would more closely resemble the historical and transcendental notions of *The Phenomenology of the Spirit* or Derrida's quasi-transcendental notions: arche, trace, text, writing.

Such a point of view has the advantage of neutralizing the historical criticism of Foucauldian constructions. So long as these constructions claim to have some empirical pertinence, research like that conducted by M. Gauchet and G. Swain and critiques like those of Georges Huppert and J. G. Merquior cast serious doubts on the validity of Foucault's theses. But as soon as the statements, the discursive formations, the epistemes, etc., desert the empirically based family of concepts, historical critiques lose all hold. If *Madness and Civilization* and *The Order of Things* use quasi-transcendental discourse, that is, a discourse on the conditions of possibility of historical concepts, it makes as much sense to blame them for empirical ineptness as it does to accuse *The Phenomenology of the Spirit* of purposely falsifying world history.

Such an interpretation of these works, though it diminishes the scope of the historical blunders, also reveals an exemplary difficulty of quasi-transcendental thought. As defined by R. Gasché (1986), quasitranscendentals are concepts referring to the condition of possibility of relations between facts and discourses which take charge of them. In Foucault, for example, the term 'statement', in a quasi-transcendental interpretation, does not refer to the concrete propositions of such-and-such a scientific discipline, but to what makes the articulation of a fact and a proposition possible prior to the constitution of disciplines. In the same way, 'discursive formation' refers to the ideal dispersion at the centre of which fields of knowledge are born and dissolve, objects crystallize and disperse, disciplines are drawn and erased. Far beyond the historicity of the

Zeitgeist, the episteme would therefore define the space where facts, discourses, and the representation which holds them together emerge simultaneously.

In Derrida's thinking, the quasi-transcendentals – writing, trace, metaphor, sign, etc. – develop from a regional concept of linguistic or rhetorical origin to which a radical reversal assigns a function in the general economy of the ideality. It is perhaps the very radicalism of this transfiguration that gives the Derridian notions their resilience and resistance, despite the misunderstandings occasioned by the homonymy with the concepts of departure. Derrida has misunderstood Saussure regarding the notion of writing, because the 'writing' referred to by Derrida is completely different from the notion preoccupying Saussure, and it is this difference that Derrida problematizes in his writings of the 1960s. In other words, despite Derrida's occasional clumsy handling of particular areas whence he draws his concepts, once these are transmuted into transcendental notions, Derrida's thinking finds a natural terrain in which his concepts successfully acclimate themselves. It is much more difficult, on the other hand, to produce transcendentals or quasitranscendentals that keep a regional pertinence after metamorphosis; for, in stripping the concepts of departure of their empirical definition, how can we make sure that the generality thus obtained will subsequently be able to find applications in the very region of origin? The fact that the transcendental approach erases the origin of its concepts is evidenced by the insistence of so many philosophers that their notions have nothing to do with the 'common' usage of the terms they employ. The force of this erasure becomes particularly clear when the practitioners incautiously 'apply' the transcendentals or quasi-transcendentals to their territory of origin: the psychiatric naturalization of *Angst* and the use of difference in literary criticism provide typical examples of such zeal.

In Foucault's work, concepts of linguistic or rhetorical origin are in turn purged of their 'indigenous' content, but the extraordinary generality subsequently lavished on them, rather than being put to good use by truly transcendental reflection, is applied to empirical material. Transcendental discourse surreptitiously takes charge of an empirical domain. The excessive indetermination inherent in the quasi-transcendentals leads to mistreatment of facts, which because they are innumerable and precise need completely different types of categories. How can we hope to succeed in determining the abundance of empirical domains using a handful of under-determined notions such as discourse, episteme, representation, resemblance?

Once the infinity of indetermination has been unleashed, once respect for singularities has been abolished, the correspondence fallacy alone entitles the scholar to feel certain that the nature of his objects is so strongly specified before his intervention and so saturated with *epistemological magnetism* that its description, whatever conceptual tools are used, cannot escape its influence and fail in its purpose. Therefore, only tacit faith in the visibility of the domain of application allows for recourse to transcendental notions. Assured that a tenacious, vigorous and enduring reality will always lay itself open to observation, the philosopher–scholar gives himself over to his feverish speculations.

5 On Conventionalism in Poetics

In *La Troisième République des lettres* (1983), Antoine Compagnon describes how, in a series of rapid, decisive moves, the positivist historians took over French academia at the beginning of the century. Following the Dreyfus affair, university teaching in the humanities fell under the sway of the literary historians – Gustave Lanson, Rudler and their followers. An anti-academic reaction in the literary journals, led by Albert Thibaudet, Paul Souday, Henri Brémond and Charles Maurras then attempted to relegitimate aesthetic criticism. In 'Le débat du *Débat*' (1984), Compagnon interpreted this rivalry as the modern form of the seventeenth-century conflict between the 'historical and erudite tradition of the Benedictine abbeys and the eloquent and rhetorical tradition of the Jesuit colleges'. In this conflict, the *nouvelle critique* of the 1950s and 1960s and especially the work of Barthes would have sided with the rhetorical party. In 1965, Raymond Picard's attack against Barthes was led in the name of erudition. In Compagnon's view, Barthes's work, addressing itself to specialists and to the cultivated public alike, goes beyond the conflict between the teaching profession and literary life, even between theory and history, and proposes an exemplary synthesis of all these tendencies.

Early in the 1960s, it became apparent that many practitioners of the *nouvelle critique* were challenging the atomism of literary historians by constructing holistic literary models deriving from phenomenology (Serge Doubrovski), sociology (Lucien Goldmann), or psychoanalysis (Charles Mauron, Jean-Pierre Richard). As the decade went on, structuralists gradually seceded from the *nouvelle critique* and challenged scholarly empiricism of literary history through methodological one-upmanship. The desire to modernize occurs periodically in literary studies: literary history itself developed in the name of a scientific ideal. Whereas the literary historians had based their science on the historical and philological rigour of the nineteenth century, the structuralist branch of *nouvelle critique* emulated more recent models of scientificity: anthropology and linguistics. But both sought to make up lost ground in the humanities and to unify science and the humanities into a single epistemological order, and both chose models of modernization that were already passing into obsolescence. When, at the beginning of the century, Lanson was establishing history's predominance in literature, history as the universal paradigm in the humanities was being forcefully challenged by the rise of anthropology, theoretical sociology and the new descriptive linguistics; and just when literary critics discovered linguistic structuralism, with its echoes of behaviourism and the project of the unity of science, both these trends quite rightly disappeared from the sciences.

While the theories of *Zeitgeist* depend on the perfect transparency of the intellectual medium of diffusion, the world of culture is subjected as much to contingency and dyschrony as the world of action. Before new ideas which are born into a certain discipline can develop and spread through other disciplines, they have to overcome inertia, hazards and their own depletion. Like the Lansonian literary historians, the theories challengers in the 1960s aspired to rejuvenate literary studies by using sources which had meanwhile been superseded in their original domain. But the structuralist claim to objective and scientific modernity has provoked more radical dissatisfaction than the earlier aesthetic revolt against Lansonism. Even its critics had to admit that Lansonism had at least produced some respected philological and historical results. The adversaries of structuralism today, however, blame it for the very destruction of the literary spirit in France. Consider the following commentary on Racine's *Phaedra*:

There is no substitution of one implication for another, but two identical implications added together, the conjunctive sum of which produces the tragedy. The tragedy is not just the result of a reversibility, of a radical change between before the father's return and after; it would be mechanistic to think that the death of the father would open a space which would just as quickly be swept away and made tragic in its futility by the unforeseen return of the omnipotent father. The textual development is the result of a conjunctive sum, though a reversal does take place at a certain point in the text, which turns around certain implications, yet does not reverse the basic structure of meaning overall. (Kaisergruber, Kaisergruber and Lempert, 1972, p. 181)

(Il n'y a pas de substitution d'une implication à une autre, mais addition de deux implications identiques: somme conjonctive dont la tragédie est le produit. La tragédie n'est pas seulement le produit d'une réversibilité, d'un changement radical entre l'avant-le-retour-du-père et l'après; il serait mécaniste de penser que la mort du père ouvrait un espace qui serait tout à coup balayé, et rendu tragique dans sa vanité meme par le retour imprévu du père tout-puissant. Le développement textuel est bien le résultat d'un somme conjonctive, bien que s'effectue à un certain point du texte un renversement,

renversement de certaines implications, mais non de la structure élémentaire de signification dans son ensemble.)

Taken together, the two implications spoken of here form what the semiologists call the elementary structure of meaning – death and the departure on the one hand, return and life on the other. Clearly, Racine's work is not the main consideration here. The commentary is concerned more with the arrangement of general semiotic mechanisms than with reading a particular text, just as 60 years earlier the Lansonians put literature on a back burner and gave precedence to its historical background. Such approaches always indefinitely postpone contact with the text.

Too bad, one could retort, and quite rightly – too bad for the text, for literature, since these ready-made syntheses, these groupings, according to Foucault's formula, are usually accepted without scrutiny. And since all science is concerned with generality, the study of literary phenomena, in neglecting aesthetic and humanist caprices, has no choice but to accept its natural place, that is, as part of the theory of linguistic and discursive mechanisms. Consequently, the linguistic bias of literary structuralism can be better justified than the phonological forays of a Lévi-Strauss, since poetics, stylistics and rhetoric have always been thought of as an extension of grammar.

In literature, however, as in astrophysics, singularity, jealous of its rights, is not so easily suppressed. Even if all linguistic and discursive rules were known down to their smallest details (and such knowledge remains perfectly unimaginable for now), readers of *Phaedra* would nevertheless have the right to simply exclaim before act 2, scene 5 'How beautiful!' independently of any analysis of the textual mechanisms, however correct it may be. The structure does not suppress the exclamation.

Structural analysis at least tries to suppress the source of exclamation, which is also that of intentional concepts. When, in *Phaedra*, the semiologist discovers the double implication departure versus death, return versus life; when Barthes (*On Racine*, 1963), finds the image of the primitive horde in Racine's tragedies, these notions, logical or evocative, are discovered in the theatre of Racine, despite the layers of aesthetic varnish which conceal abstraction or primitivism. Hidden games of meanings and forms inaccessible to the author and his public in literary texts are the target not only of the *nouvelle critique* – and of its structuralist branch – but also of hermeneutists and poststructuralists. Like the psychoanalytical schema of a Charles Mauron, like the semio-narrative structures of Barthes and Greimas, the fusion of horizons (one of Gadamer's themes) and the contradictions of the text (in the view of the American deconstructionists) produce effects the origin and end of which escape the vigilance of the writer as well as the perspicacity of the readers. The whole of this critique, of course, disputes the validity of the classical notion of the artist-artisan who, applying the traditional rules of his art with perfect aplomb, carefully imitates nature or past masters; but the Romantic image of the artist in communion with nature, which expresses itself in him without mediation or rules, is equally foreign to recent criticism, since the primitive forces which supposedly animate romantic art need the artist as a master of cermonies to supervise their advance. The new critiques want nothing to do with the artist. They distrust him, they wish to annihilate him (in 1968, Barthes wrote a remarkable article 'The Death of the Author'), and see in him the product of *intentional dogmatism* – the doctrine which traces the determinations of works of art back to conscious decisions taken by the authors. The most often-cited example is the thesis according to which the meaning of the work of art coincides with the meaning that the author deliberately suggests for it; as a result, the chief, if not the sole, task of interpretative art criticism lies in recovering an original intention. As with Husserl's vision of geometry, the ideality of the work of art can be repeated *ad infinitum* by reactivation of the founding act, which contains both the end of the work and the rules for its continued existence. The history of the work's reception, as it imperceptibly moves away from the purity of the founding act, cannot but include incidental if not even erroneous elements. Against this degradation, endless criticism seizes upon and reaffirms the original intention providing meaning.

Intentional dogmatism sets forth several theoretical propositions. One affirms the primacy of the subject's conscious activity in the production of works of art; another insists on the conflict between the creative force of the artist and the aesthetic norms prevalent in his day; a third emphasizes the tension, controlled by individual genius, between the representational ends and the style of the work. Among the numerous reactions to intentional dogmatism, the psychoanalytical trends in aesthetics question the primacy of the conscience; conventionalist currents favour the artistic systems in place and minimize the role of the individual creator; anti-mimetic trends claim that the representation of real or fictive worlds does not constitute an irreducible aim of art. There are obvious affinities between conventionalism and anti-mimetism: the two often go together. Moreover, while conventionalism can take a moderate or extreme form, anti-mimetic doctrines have the choice, to the detriment of representation, of studying style or asserting the self-referentiality of literature (by stating that, beyond its superficial thematics, each text speaks only of literature itself); finally, psychoanalytically inspired criticism can probe the work, the psyche of the author, or even that of the reader. Literary structuralism has produced countless combinations from these options. The most lasting have been generated in poetics, especially in narrative poetics. It is natural, moreover, for a trend informed with anti-intentionalism and conventionalism to rediscover, beyond Romantic and modernist aesthetics, the classicist interest for formal devices. Besides poetics, a wealth of research, too rich and diversified to be reviewed here, has developed the anti-intentional and anti-individual programmes with varying success. Nor do these two programmes necessarily coincide. From Hegel to Dilthey, from Riegl to Panovski, critical history of art often relegates artistic individuality to a position of lesser importance. But the emphasis on artistic schools and period-styles does not underestimate artistic intentionality: the formal will, even when attributed to historical periods rather than to individuals, keeps its teleological properties.

Literary structuralism tried to join anti-intentional and conventionalist themes with the anti-mimetic stand. The recourse to linguistics, as well as the rejection of intentional dogmatism, served conventionalist ends well. In addition, Saussurian semiology reinforced the anti-referential point of view, for since, as Saussure anticipated, natural language is not an inventory, the literary text cannot be reduced to a descriptive repertory of the real universe either. Based on these stances, it has been possible to constitute on the one hand a dogmatic semiotics which reduces literary meaning to the formal work of signs and, on the other hand, a narrative poetics which, without explicitly disavowing interest in hermeneutic techniques, limits itself to the purely structural properties of the story and the discourse which relates it.

GENERATIVE SEMIOTICS

In *Structural Semantics* (1966) and *On Meaning* (1970), A. J. Greimas laid the foundations of the richest and most coherent linguistically based semiotic system. Supposedly applicable to all meaningful phenomena, be they linguistic or cultural, Greimas' semiotics demonstrates its literary relevance in his book *Maupassant, la sémiotique du texte* (1976). This system, sometimes called semio-linguistics, is built around two crucial notions: the elementary unit of meaning called the *semiotic square*, and the operation of the *semiotic generation* of meaningful objects.

The semiotic square is presumed to represent the most fundamental articulation of semantic categories. Being binary – that is, based on oppositions – such categories include, according to Greimas, a set of relations of contradiction (A and $\overline{A}$), of contrariety (A and non-A) and of presupposition ($\overline{\text{non-A}}$ and A). Arranged in a square, these relations take the following form:

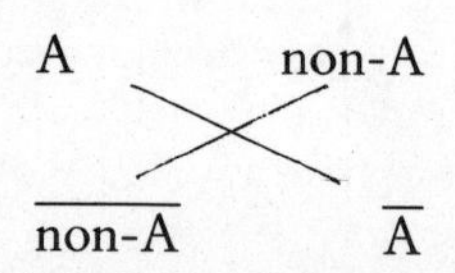

The semantic category 'being', for instance, is articulated by the following square:

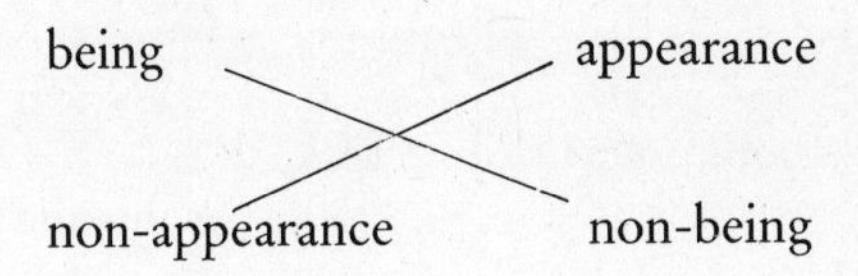

These structures, semio-linguistics claims, lie at the core of any meaningful object or event, at the core of any sentence, sequence of sentences, theorem, scientific treatise, newspaper article, penal code, sacred text, myth, story, novel, poem, painting, theatrical performance, musical work, architectural monument, city, landscape, passion, game, war, epidemic, famine and disaster, and, in each case, the corresponding square *fully captures* the meaning of the object. The doctrine clearly has an anti-referential bias, since the meaning of each semiotic object derives from an immanent structure. This bias is particularly visible in the applications of the theory to narratives.

Like any other semiotic object, each story unfolds around a semiotic square. The example above derives from a semio-linguistic analysis of *Cinderella*. And Clément Légaré, a Canadian disciple of semio-linguistics, argued in 1981 that the French-Canadian story *Pierre la fève* develops from the square:

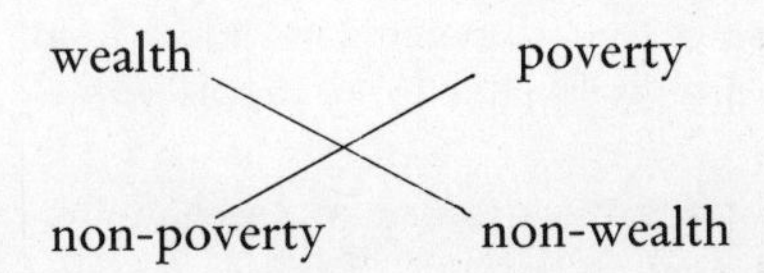

A large gap evidently exists between the semiotic square and the text of the story, which semio-linguistics fills with what it calls the *generative trajectory*, that is, an ordered sequence of formal operations meant to transform the square (also called the deep or fundamental level) into a surface or narrative level, then to deduce the discourse of the story from the narrative level. Ideally, if all these operations were well defined and performed, the last two squares above would lead without any problem to the texts of *Cinderella* and *Pierre la fève*, respectively.

This momentous doctrine raises questions concerning the relevance of formal methods in the study of cultural phenomena. In this particular case, the formal method is narrative semiotics, but similar concerns have been raised by the use of mathematics in linguistics and literary studies, logical research in ethics and game theory in economics. Although some methods have achieved a greater degree of explicitness and formal sophistication than narrative semiotics, they have not been exempt from criticism related to the appropriateness of the chosen formalism and their inner structure.

There are several ways to challenge the relevance of formal methods in the humanities and social sciences. One widely accepted approach rejects formal methods in principle because of what it regards as the radical specificity of the humanities; examples include Hans Gadamer's philosophical hermeneutics and the deconstructionists's literary criticism. Counter-arguments to this approach are provided by epistemological monists in philosophy (Karl Popper, for instance, and Stephen Toulmin) and literary critics such as Jonathan Culler, Shlomith Rimmon-Kenan and Wlad Godzich who accept formal research as one among many rational strategies in literary studies, without rejecting the legitimacy of hermeneutic approaches to literary texts.

Other thinkers attack formalisms by arguing that, without necessarily being inadequate in principle, they are just impractical in most cases involving the social and human sciences. There certainly would have been no progress in astronomy or theoretical physics without the contribution of mathematical models, yet in linguistics such models require excessive formal investments, usually leading to only minimal yield. Traditional grammar, as written by Otto Jespersen for instance, described the subtleties of English syntax as precisely as, if not more precisely than transformational grammar does today; yet Jespersen's argumentation avoided any mathematical formalism. One can obviously counter that, despite the wealth of information it yielded, Jespersen's grammar failed to satisfy the criteria of scientific rigour. But adversaries of formal methods would argue that the scientific ideal inspired by mathematical physics or astronomy is itself too costly for the genuine needs of the social sciences.

A final argument against the use of formalisms in the social sciences and humanities is that, although there is no good reason to exclude formalisms in principle and despite the fact that economy may not even be a decisive consideration, formal methods often fail to produce interesting results, since they do not stress the rapport between new research and the traditional problems in each field. It can be said, for instance, that the use of axiomatic methods in ethics, though shedding new light on the coherence of normative systems, brings nothing new to the central questions regarding the nature of good or responsibility and the tension between facts and values. To this kind of objection, the readiest answer would be to claim that over the years the problems of each discipline changes, so that new scientific paradigms (in Thomas Kuhn's sense) should concentrate on their own problematics and leave aside outmoded concerns. But wouldn't this postulate quite an improbable homogeneity between the evolution of the exact sciences and that of the humanities? Moreover, supposing that such homogeneity may be found, could we dogmatically claim that new paradigms need not care about any of the old problems? Has not astronomy – Ptolemaic or Keplerian – always paid some attention to the movement of the planets?

Clearly, each of these three kinds of objection can be addressed to the formalisms of narrative semiotics. Yet to argue that narratives cannot in principle be examined with semio-narrative tools, or that the formal expenditure is excessive, or that its results may lack literary interest since they fail to relate to more traditional concerns about narratives and their authors, entails a reluctance to address specific questions related to the inner organization of semio-linguistic formalism. But such reluctance is unwarranted. We can go one step further and judge the construction of a formalism, its consistency, power and range of applicability. Thus, in 1961 Hilary Putnam showed that Chomsky's transformational grammar generated all recursively enumerable sets, and thus that the generative power of the grammar had not been successfully limited to the class of natural languages. This severe criticism suggested that the efforts of Chomsky and his disciples since 1957 had been wasted; as a result, the Chomskian model underwent a long series of modifications leading to several new hypotheses and projects. Naturally, such a development was possible because of Chomsky's willingness, from the very beginning of his work, to base his conclusions on fully developed mathematical formalisms.

Semio-linguistics, its conceptual richness notwithstanding, avoids all current formalisms – formal languages, classical or modal logic, game theory, etc. It proposes instead an idiosyncratic construction, not yet completed. How then should it be judged? Following Paul Ricoeur's (1984) example and leaving formalism aside as if it were but a rhetorical device without much consequence, we may discuss the more interesting side of semiotics, namely its conceptual nodes, by treating them as hermeneutic notions. Greimas' semiotics would thus tell a story similar to those narrated by Saint Augustine, Hegel or Dilthey. Indeed, shouldn't the fact that Greimas' notions have been exploited as heuristic tools by literary critics who entirely ignored the formalisms involved (Fred Jameson and Hayden White) intimate that the scientistic programme of semio-linguistics is, after all, less important than the practical results achieved by its application? And yet heuristic value alone is a weak argument in favour of using a formal system in the humanities. Cultural products are so richly textured that the application of any formal grid, from the simplest to the most elaborate, would lead to some 'results'. But, in addition to 'results', we should be able to produce a coherent way of legitimating them. Since semio-linguistics conspicuously lacks the means or the desire to legitimate its results, the best way to approach it is through an analysis of the intellectual origin of its core notions: the square and the generative process.

The semiotic square represents a tentative synthesis of three theoretical sources: Ferdinand de Saussure's ideas on the linguistic sign, Lévi-Strauss's analysis of myth and Propp's morphology of the folktale. These three components are used unquestioningly as if they were well-established truths whose compatibility with one another were given in advance. In fact, however, it is possible to show not only that each of these models suffers from considerable inner tensions that would certainly have justified a severe preliminary evaluation, but also that Greimas' proposed synthesis makes things worse by aggravating already existing problems.

The doctrine of the semiotic square postulates that all perceptible semiotic objects owe their wealth of meaning to the existence of a deep, invisible core which is both founded on a semantic opposition and independent of empirical reality. The two theses of Saussurian linguistics included here are the anti-referential point of view (language is no list of names) and the doctrine of binary oppositions (language is made up only of differences displaying no positive terms). These theses may be indispensable for linguistic research oriented to the inner organization of the language system. To posit that language is something other than a list of names is a commonplace which allowed philology and linguistics to defend their specificity against, say, applied lexicology. Also, linguistic categories are often organized as oppositions simply because binary systems are the most economic way of arranging signs. But can we legitimately progress from an immanent theory of language to an immanent theory of meaning? From the binary character of *signs* should we infer that *meaning* is binary as well? Such a transition, already suggested by Saussure's *Course in General Linguistics*, is all but obligatory. In fact Saussure's *Course* contains the opposite point of view as well, emphasizing that natural languages serve as semiotic *media* to meaningful activities relatively independent of them. Saussure sharply distinguished between *langue*, which is a sign system, and *langage*, which designates the more general human linguistic capacity manifested by various *langues*, without ever saying that the structure of the *langue* is identical to that of *language*, that a theory of signs can serve as theory of meaning, or that a semiotics based on linguistic notions is sufficient for the construction of a general semantics. In the wake of Saussure, Wittgenstein, Nelson Goodman and W. V. O. Quine, modern language theory recognizes that the medium has a certain density of its own; moreover, today we are more sensitive to the interaction between signs and meaning; yet it does not follow that these two distinct levels should be confused.

A brief glance at contemporary linguistic practices demonstrates the limits of the anti-referential and binary theses. Having served in classical phonology, these doctrines have also led to interesting descriptions of morphological categories (the case studied by Hjelmslev, and verbal categories by Jakobson). With Chomsky's research, however, it became obvious that syntax is governed by other principles. In linguistic semantics, the anti-referential and binary approach made various useful descriptions of semantic fields possible without leading to the birth of a linguistic semantics which would cover all meaningful phenomena in natural language. The anti-referential thesis, for instance, unnecessarily complicates the description of deictic elements. The relevance of binary oppositions, obvious in phonology and morphology, disappears when we deal with lexical meaning, since, besides discriminatory opposition, vocabulary displays numerous instances of gradual or continuous relations, idiosyncratic configurations and sheer absence of structure. Rather than from these two Saussurian theses, contemporary semantics of natural languages stems from transformational syntax and the referential and pragmatic trends in the philosophy of language. But if the Saussurian anti-referential and binary points of view fail to command the allegiance of *linguistic* semantics, how can we justify their use in a *general* theory of meaning? True, the semiotic oppositions on which the constitutive model is founded may be of use for grammatical semantics, since grammatical categories often have an oppositional structure. But a general theory of meaning certainly exceeds these narrow limits.

As I noted earlier, Lévi-Strauss's analysis of myth, the second theoretical source of the semiotic square, displays an energetic movement towards abstraction resulting in the elimination of temporality from the set of relevant elements of myth. An achronic formula which looks like 'A is to non-A what B is to non-B' is supposed to underlie all myths and assign an invisible meaning to them. Thus from the Oedipus myth Lévi-Strauss extracts an equation asserting that the overrating of family bonds stands in the same proportion to their underrating as the affirmation of man's autochthonous origin stands to its negation. In reducing the multiplicity of narrative elements to a four-term scheme, Lévi-Strauss fails to take a minimum of methodological precautions: on the one hand, his analysis does not make explicit the criteria according to which certain elements of the myth are excluded from the scheme; on the other hand it fails to keep track of the excluded elements. In Chomskian terms, the analysis lacks the provisions to recuperate the deleted items. Since, however, Lévi-Strauss does not aim at constructing a rigorously formal system, the absence of these precautions only marginally affects the credibility of his discourse. We may accept the disappearance of a number of elements felt to be essential in the Oedipus myth (the hero's guilt, the self-punishment, Jocasta's suicide, etc.) as long as Lévi-Strauss's representation does not claim to *generate* the myth. Greimas' semiotic square, though being as independent as Lévi-Strauss's equation from the details of the text, is set the additional task of producing all that has been irreversibly cut from it.

The problems deriving from Propp's legacy are no less striking or better resolved. *In Structural Semantics*, Greimas successively reduced the thirty-one functions of Propp's narrative model to an equation close to Lévi-Strauss's formula for myths and to the semiotic square as well. In the eyes of semio-linguists, this achievement proves the universality of the semiotic square, equally related to the structure of myth and folktale. But the argument depends on the belief that *The Morphology of the Folktale* (1928) proposes a universal model of folktales. In fact, not only did Propp himself complain about the excessive generality of his first book's title (imposed by the publisher) but, as Claude Bremond and Jean Verrier (1982) showed by confronting Propp's analyses with the tales he is said to have studied, the *one hundred* tales to which Propp's model claims to apply amount in fact to only *one* type of tale, namely number 300 of the Aarne–Thompson classification – *The Dragon Slayer*. The morphology of only one tale has thus served as the foundation of narrative semiotics of all stories, indeed of all meaningful phenomena. Such a generalization is extraordinary.

Moreover, by simplifying the thirty-one functions of Propp's model through successive reductions, Greimas replaced Propp's sequence of functions by a four-term equation similar to that proposed by Lévi-Strauss, which in turn became the four-corner semiotic square. The story of the dragon slayer – the only one that completely satisfies Propp's model – would, read by Greimas, consist of a breach of contract followed by the establishment of a new social contract. The marriage of the hero at the end of the tale signifies the new social contract as well as the restoration of the value system; it retrospectively confers meaning on the story and determines the choice of the semiotic square.

It should be noted, however, that in *The Morphology of the Folktale* Propp does not give the formalism an explicit interpretation. The abrupt ending of the *Morphology* does not allow the reader to grasp either Propp's ulterior intentions or the purpose of his formalism. The question is, therefore, whether Greimas' way of simplifying the model of Propp's *Morphology* is coherent with Propp's theoretical aims. In other words, does the four-term equation that should account for the meaning of every possible story at least describe the meaning of the only tale analysed by the *Morphology*?

To put this question into perspective, it may be useful to recall that for a long time narratologists and semioticians believed that the *Morphology* included everything essential in Propp's teachings. A second book by the famous folklorist, published in 1946, was rumoured to be merely a cowardly recantation of his earlier ideas, required by the official ideology then prevailing in Russia. Fortunately, *The Historical Roots of the Fairy Tale*, still difficult to find in Russian, is now available in Italian, French and, although not in its entirety, in English. In it, beyond a few stereotyped Stalinist formulas, Propp tells a fascinating story intimately related to the system proposed in the *Morphology*. In

Voltaire's *Zadig*, a courtier discovers a torn-up piece of paper containing a stanza written by the hero which seemingly denigrates the monarch. Imprisoned, Zadig is released only when another piece of the paper is found containing the second hemistichs of the stanza: put together, the verses prove flattering to the sultan. Likewise, by itself *The Morphology of the Folktale* looks like a proposal for a rather complex and sometimes awkward formalism which has been established independently of any thematological and historical concerns. But considered together with *The Historical Roots*, Propp's formalism acquires new meaning, its obvious function having been to prepare and support the historical and thematological thesis of *Roots*. If the methodology of narrative semiotics has any relevance, this unexpected turn of events should confirm the reduction proposed by Greimas. Since the semiotic square is supposed to extract the meaning dispersed through the formalism of the *Morphology*, Propp's own later interpretations should coincide with the semiotic simplification. Yet the conclusion of *The Historical Roots* refutes Greimas' reduction. According to Propp, the fairy tale synthesizes two series of motifs: the initiation cycle and the cycle of the journey to the underworld. To this complex core other motifs are then added (the hero's marriage and his accession to the throne), motifs that belong to the third and less important cycle of dynastic succession. Marriage, which in the semio-narrative analysis rectroactively determines the meaning of the tale of the dragon slayer, is in Propp's mind only a secondary element added as a coda to the initiatory and ritual core of the tale. This core, moreover, goes back to archaic religious practices which cannot be reduced to the opposition between breach and re-establishment of contract, or destruction and restoration of values. Greimas' reduction eliminates from Propp's model precisely what makes it genuinely interesting.

The semiotic square thus originates in a theoretical mixture whose components are insufficiently elaborated and whose reciprocal compatibility is taken for granted without further questioning. But should one expect a differential theory of signs to shed new light on the historical and mythical contents of stories? Can one base a generative model on reductive practices that lack explicit constraints? Is one authorized to mix a strong will to abstraction with a morphology particularly attentive to the meanders and physiognomy of texts? Moreover, can one accept the very notion of the semiotic square when there is little proof in its favour in preference to another structure? Why a square and not, say, a triangle or a pentagram? In addition, the gap between the simplicity of the chosen structure and the diversity of semiotic objects is so wide that each object can accept an indefinite number of equally probable candidates to the semantic core position.

To counter this situation, partisans of semio-narratology had to constrain the relations between the text and its postulated semantic core. With this in mind, Greimas and his followers introduced a variable number of intermediary levels between the invisible semiotic square and the visible text. The structure of these levels becomes simpler as one moves towards the 'depths' of the system but more complex as one approaches the text. The narrative is said to be generated from the invisible core by passing through each of the intermediate levels (which are themselves invisible yet become more concrete with each step) until, at the last stage, the text itself becomes available. This process is called the generative trajectory. But how can we 'transform' a couple of fundamental terms into a complex narrative, full of suspense and surprising twists, especially since the 'formal' nature of the generative trajectory does not resist analysis any better than the square presumed to lie at its origin?

Undoubtedly encouraged by the success of formal linguistic grammars, especially the transformational-generative kind, narrative semioticians liberally use terms with a mathematical flavour connoting rigour: 'algorithm of procedures', 'rules of conversion of narrative contents onto discursive contents', 'rules of lexicalization of the discursive figures in the production of linguistic messages', etc. Yet none of these 'algorithms', none of these 'rules', has ever been outlined; and it may be safely assumed that no one has the slightest idea what form they would take. True, semio-linguists have drawn up a list of levels: the semiotic square, the fundamental syntax, the discursive syntax, each endowed with its own semantics. But the form of each level or the relationship between them is left in the dark. Far from remedying the lack of explanation of the semiotic square, the generative trajectory aggravates it, since in the absence of explicit constraints limiting the generative power of the system, any story or text could be generated from the most improbable semantic cores.

We must therefore question the meaning of terms such as *generate* or *generative* in the writings of the semio-narrative school. Generation of the complex from the simple may be considered as a meta-mathematical operation. To generate a set of theorems means to enumerate them according to a method consisting of a finite number of steps. To generate an infinite set, it is worthwhile to build an explicit axiomatic system that specifies all the elements of the set (and only these elements) with the help of a finite vocabulary and a finite set of rules. The generation of a finite set may simply proceed from the enumeration of its elements. In the generation of infinite sets of theorems, we recognize the source of Chomsky's arguments regarding the grammars of natural languages. Obviously semio-narrative generation does not fit this category: first, because it deals with finite sets of cultural objects; second, because even if we argue that semiotics envisages its objects from the point of view of their potential infinity, still no formal detail of the generation has ever been provided. Does then the term *generation* have a biological connotation? The metamorphosis of a fertilized egg into a mature organism may well resemble the adventures of the semiotic square in its journey towards the visible text. Yet the resemblance is superficial: whereas the fertilized egg already possesses all the genetic and topological information that will lead to the growth of the organism, in narrative semiotics the constitutive model is limited to just a couple of semes. In fact the only meaning of the term *generation* which resembles semio-narrative practices is the gnostic acceptance of the term. As in Lévi-Strauss's work, there is a disturbing resemblance to doctrines and modes of thinking that everyone (wrongly) assumed to be long dead.

Like universal generation in gnostic systems, the generative trajectory proceeds from a hidden maximum of simplicity towards a visible maximum of diversity; in both, the hierarchy of steps whose numbers can be increased at will expresses essences arranged according to their descending order of abstraction. As in gnostic systems, the stages of the generative trajectory are discovered by purely intellectual intuition without the help of any logical or experimental disciplines. And as in gnosis the trajectory goes both ways: from the semiotic square through successive emanations narrative levels proceed forth leading to the text, not unlike the hidden God who expresses himself through hierarchical stages until the birth of the visible universe; conversely, the human soul may, under gnostic guidance, renegotiate these numerous levels to return to its maker, while the narrative semiotician, guided by the doctrine, can select the ascending approach that will bring him back from textual multiplicity to the unity of the depth.

These features are not typical only of narrative semiotics. If we call gnoses those doctrines that combine a strong desire of systematization with a purely intuitive, even imaginative, method while stubbornly rejecting logical constraints and confrontation with facts, many modern theories would have to be included, since all messianic sociologies of our century and most psychoanalytical trends developed gnostic branches at various degrees of esoteric intolerance. Given that this type of thought remains vigorous and ready to proliferate, especially with the help of radical modernization, it is difficult to avoid feeling that, in the contemporary human sciences, epistemological criticism still has a few things to say.

NARRATIVE POETICS AND THE PUZZLES OF REPRESENTATION

French research in poetics has rarely entertained such extreme formal ambitions. The poeticians of the 1960s and 1970s most often sided with what I have called *moderate* structuralism, and embraced formalism not so much for its method but for its applications to a variety of literary artifacts. Yet even moderate formalism tended to avoid intentional notions, in particular, representation.

At the abstract level of narrative structures, poeticians carefully stressed that sequences of functions, narrative programmes, motifs, or moves were all only syntax, indifferent by nature to the representation of real conflicts. As for the analysis of narrative discourse, interested in such topics as the play of tenses, voices and points of view, it had neither the means nor the desire to confront mimesis and representation. Under the attentive eye of the modern narratologist, a novel such as Flaubert's *Madame Bovary* ceases to describe provincial boredom in nineteenth-century France and becomes a double structure combining an abstract sequence of universal narrative programmes and a subtle texture of voices, modes, durations and frequencies.

Such an approach would undoubtedly have helped the defence at Flaubert's trial in 1857; Flaubert's lawyer could have argued, why look for outrages to public decency in a text composed merely of conventional discursive effects which does not go beyond the universal narrative grammar? A judge versed in semiotics could then have answered that the trial itself being but a narrative structure, Flaubert's transgression would have to be punished or aquitted in accordance with the same universal grammar! The accusations against *Madame Bovary* nevertheless had more muscle, and literary theory must account for their possibility.

We can of course dismiss the question and stipulate that judges, as well as critics and the public, allowed themselves to be deceived by the *referential illusion* (Riffaterre, 1978) and naively believed that the sentences of the novel enjoyed some form of a link with an extratextual reality. To condemn the episode of the adulterous cab ride would amount to assigning it a referential value comparable to that of a description of a real object, the city of Rouen for instance. The text in front of us, however, does not contain any cab or any guilty love, but only a fiction dangerously playing with lexical items. The famous description of Rouen may, after all, be no more than a textual arrangement without any referential value. In an important article, 'The Reality Effect' (1968), Roland Barthes claimed that descriptive passages lack any narrative significance and that therefore their only role is to interrupt the advance of the plot, and to connote the amorphous presence of reality. The details of a description can be indefinitely multiplied or changed:

What does it matter that a detail has no function in the account as long as it denotes 'what took place'? 'Concrete reality' becomes a sufficient justification for what is said.

And later (p. 16):

Eliminated from the realist utterance as a signified of denotation, the 'real' slips back in as a signified of connotation; for, at the very moment when these details are supposed to denote reality directly, all they do is to tacitly signify it. Flaubert's barometer, Michelet's little door, in the last analysis, says only this: *we are the real.*

Realist details hide the narrative scheme under a layer of referential illusions superimposed on it. Just as Hjelmslev considered the universe to be a peripheral component of language, Barthes reduces the referential links of literary texts to intratextual effects subordinated to the narrative structure and lacking any independent function.

Realism, a referential project *par excellence*, was soon to be described as a set of stylistic and textual conventions. Dismissed as 'ritualistic and quasi-obsessional' (Hamon, 1973, p. 119), interest in the real was identified with 'a certain number of structural features, mimesis-connotators, and particular narrative or rhetorical schemata' (ibid., p. 131). The list of realist features, established by Philippe Hamon and rearranged by Christine Brooke-Rose (1980), conjured away the referential project of realist texts and claimed to have reduced these texts to a combination of purely formal characteristics.

Because of its anti-teleological bias, one of the difficulties of Barthes's thesis stems from the separation it postulates between realist detail and narrative development. Various researchers have shown, to the contrary, that details and descriptions do fulfil precise functions in the macro-structure of *Madame Bovary*: far from being secondary, non-functional passages, descriptions generate narrative significance (Duchet, 1969). Menahem Brinker (1983) makes a similar argument with regard to supposedly insignificant details in *Anna Karenina*. Barthes's difficulties arise from the fact that, in a conventionalist and anti-mimetic perspective, narrative poetics grants a certain theoretical priority to narrative regularities. But mythocentrism, the belief in the centrality of narrative aspects, is not the only conceivable approach. By reversing the perspective, we can also start out from the primacy of reference and representation to which narrative structures and discourse techniques are subordinate. And while in recent literary and semiotic discussions, mimesis has been approached – distrustfully – from a diegetic point of view, theoreticians of the visual arts, less constrained by narrative concerns, have developed an important debate on the nature of artistic representation. Does it depend on resemblance? What are its relations with reference and denotation? What is the role of convention in artistic representation?

DENOTATION AND ILLUSION

Mimetic theories of art do acknowledge the role of conventions in artistic activities. Ernst Gombrich (1960) frequently insisted that spectators of a painting bring with them a set of conventional expectations. There is no innocent eye. Nevertheless, far from being entirely arbitrary, artistic conventions are largely determined by the psychological constraints of visual perception. Resemblance therefore constitutes a condition of representation; moreover, in certain cultures at certain moments, such as 600–500 BC in Greece and the fourteenth and fifteenth centuries in Europe, there develops a conscious effort to capture the resemblance between artistic representation and its model. The effort lasts for several generations of artists; its ideal limit is visual illusion, and the optical discoveries it occasions often enjoy the status of genuine scientific knowledge, such as the discovery of the laws of perspective during the Renaissance.

In contrast, Nelson Goodman (1968) though agreeing that there is no innocent eye, argued that resemblance and illusion are not sufficient conditions for representation. In Goodman's view, for a picture to represent an object, it is enough that it denotes the object. But, obviously, resemblance is not sufficient for establishing denotation; Raphael's portrait of Julius II may well resemble my friend Jim without this peculiarity making it a portrait of Jim. In contrast, any clumsy sketch, any abstract portrait of Jim will qualify as a representation of him if the artist says so, despite the lack of resemblance. A picture will become a portrait of Jim as soon as we decide to call it so: the image, though it does not resemble Jim, will denote Jim, and therefore will represent him too. 'Denotation', Goodman writes, 'is the core of representation and is independent of resemblance' (ibid., p. 5). Besides, how can we make sense of the notion of resemblance? Objects offer themselves to us in an infinite number of ways. 'The object before me is a man, a swarm of atoms, a complex of cells, a fiddler, a friend, a fool and much more'. (ibid., p. 6) The choice among these aspects cannot but be arbitrary. Any representation starts out from a point of view; it provides a version, a construal. But construals are not copies: they are feats. How can we still speak about the progress of resemblance? The laws of perspective themselves, Goodman claims, are far from constituting reliable independent criteria of fidelity to the model.

That Goodman's positions are surprisingly similar to those of Roland Barthes confirms the intellectual proximity between French structuralism and those trends in logical positivism that are close to behaviourism. Both Goodman and Barthes reject resemblance, both dismiss the idea that works of art reproduce their models in detail: between the work of art and its model, the relationship is not a one-to-one correspondence but rather a more general and even an arbitrary one. The portrait of Gertrude Stein by Picasso is not a mimetic project, Goodman claims; in Barthes's view, Flaubert's description of Rouen does not depend on conformity with the object but on the cultural rules governing representation. In Barthes's text, the rejection of resemblance is even more radical than Goodman's: the latter thinks that Picasso's portrait denotes Gertrude Stein while, according to Barthes, descriptions do not refer to concrete objects but merely signal 'we are the real'. The fear of singularities surfaces again. Reference to an extratextual universe loses all differentiation; it becomes a permanent abolition of the most essential feature of semiotic systems, namely the power to make distinctions, as if realist description froze us forever in that stage of Hegelian phenomenology at which the 'here' and the 'now' are emptied of their sensory richness and specificity and are left to signify only vacuous universality.

Goodman's distinctions are more elaborate; he separates representations of actual objects which denote in the true sense of the word (e.g., Picasso's portrait denotes Gertrude Stein) from non-denotative rep-sentations of fictional characters or objects, such as unicorns or Mr Pickwick. These are labelled unicorn-representations and Mr Pickwick-representation, the dash reminding us that the object does not exist independently of its representation. Also, Goodman takes into account the representation of an object as belonging to a kind – for instance, the representation of Churchill as a child or of Julius II as a pope. The denotational theory establishes a tiny system of distinctions allowing the critic to account, if not for the resemblance between representations and their objects, at least for the nature of these objects – real or fictional – and the category of representation. The theory authorizes the critic to distinguish between the description *of* Rouen:

Sloping downward like an amphitheatre, drowned in mist, it sprawled out shapelessly beyond its bridges. (*Madame Bovary*, p. 299)

and the Monsieur-Rouault-description:

He was a stocky little man of fifty, fair-skinned, blue-eyed, bald in front and wearing earrings. (ibid., p. 17)

We have the right to add that Flaubert represents Rouen-as-a-city and Monsieur Rouault-as-a-sick-man. The taxonomy remains quite meagre. In particular, it does not offer the means of distinguishing between the first description of Emma in *Madame Bovary*:

Charles was surprised by the whiteness of her fingernails. They were almond-shaped, tapering, as polished and shining as Dieppe ivories. (ibid., p. 17)

and the first description of Ellénore in *Adolphe* by Benjamin Constant:

Ellénore was not a woman of exceptional intelligence; but her ideas were sound and her way of expressing them, which was always simple, was sometimes made striking by the nobility and loftiness of her sentiments. (ibid. p. 10)

In accordance with the denotational theory, we can distinguish between an Emma-as-bodily-detail-representation and an Ellénore-as-speaker-representation. To limit ourselves to this distinction would mean to neglect an essential aspect of Flaubert's realist and metonymic technique. For Goodman, however, realism is only compliance with the artistic conventions in force at some moment. A painting is realist when 'practice has rendered the symbols so transparent that we are not aware of any effort, of any alternatives, or of making any interpretation at all. Just here, I think, lies the touchstone of realism: not in the quantity of information, but in how easily it issues' (1968, p. 36). Realism thus becomes a question of conformism: a Byzantine painter was a realist as long as he followed the canons of Byzantine art; consequently, Andrei Rublev was a lesser realist than his contemporaries since he deviated from the established canon.

Such a view entails that artistic conventions emerge suddenly as organized ensembles of coherent precepts. It thus excludes the search for realism, the partial successes and mixed results such as the hesitation between naturalness of appearance and unperfected perspective in Giotto's painting. Does each painter, perhaps in each stage of his life, obey different sets of conventions? But if this were the case, schools and traditions would be eliminated, as well as their unremitting competition and mutual influence. Or we could keep the schools but grant artists a margin of irrealism which could accurately measure how far they veered from dominant trends. In addition, how would we justify the transition from one convention to another? If all are equally arbitrary, why are some eventually replaced?

Gombrich answers Goodman's critique by linking artistic change with more general cultural purposes; in art as in nature, 'the fitting of form to function follows a process of trial and error, of mutation and the survival of the fittest' (1965, p. 225). The pictographic method used by medieval painters narrates the sacred event 'in clear and simple hieroglyphs which makes us understand rather than visualize it' (ibid., p. 223). To borrow a notion from Goodman which becomes particularly pertinent in this historical context, the purpose of the pictographic method is to denote the event rather than to reproduce its sensory aspects faithfully. When the expectations of the public change and give priority to the representation of sensory appearances, Giotto's innovations can elicit approval and bring about emulation. Once the mechanism of change is triggered, the public becomes more and more aware of the new objectives of visual representation; artists, in turn, invest more and more energy in the improvement of the technique; perspective is discovered, the balance between light and shadow is gradually perfected, textures and facial expression are represented with increasing skill such that effortless cognition of the visual appearance becomes one of the main objectives of painting.

A system which selects ease of access to information as the unique criterion of realism is bound to fail to distinguish between the flow of information and its nature. Within the Byzantine pictorial code, information flowed without difficulty; its nature nevertheless cannot be labelled realist in the same sense as in sixteenth-century Italy. It is always possible to establish pictographic, conceptualist, or essentialist codes which ensure the flow of information. Conversely, realist efforts towards a faithful representation of appearance can sometimes obstruct the passage of information especially when new methods are employed. Such obstructions are rare, since we spontaneously appreciate advances made in the representation of appearance. None the less, the resistance encountered by the impressionists calls attention to this possibility. Moreover, certain realist representations require considerable effort on the part of the spectators because of the quantity of information stored in the painting: Raphael's portrait of Joanna of Aragon calls for a more sustained as well as a more sophisticated visual effort than a piece by Mondrian.

FROM CLASSICAL SHORTCUTS TO REALIST DETOURS

Let us return to the description of Ellénore:

> She had many prejudices; but all of them ran counter to her interest. She attached the greatest importance to regularity of conduct, precisely because hers was not regular according to conventional notions. She was very religious, because religion severely condemned her kind of life. In conversation, she shunned anything which, to other women, would appear innocent jokes, because she was always afraid that someone might, as a result, imagine that remarks in bad taste could be addressed to her on account of her position. (*Adolphe*, p. 10)

This passage offers a sequence of clearly deliminated schematic features. The resemblance between this procedure and the pictographic method is quite striking: the moral properties described here take the form of broad generalizations made from events which the author neglects to narrate. To use Gombrich's terms, such descriptions make us 'understand rather than visualize' the character. They favour a certain mode of apprehending the world, which includes a filtering of narrative episodes through a framework of moral interpretation. From a diegetic point of view the description is perfectly functional: the reader of *Adolphe* would not find any superfluous detail, since the contradictory features of Ellénore are told only in as far as they will help us understand her excessive infatuation with Adolphe. Should we be looking for an 'effect of coherence' here similar to Barthes's 'effect of reality'? Are Ellénore's features narrated not because Constant wanted to represent a certain character but just to connote moral coherence? If the answer is yes, then statements such as 'In conversation, she shunned anything which, to other women, would appear innocent jokes' would not tell us anything about the behaviour of the character, but would rather mean 'we are the coherence' of this character and the guarantors of her credibility. This kind of argument has often tempted theoreticians. But does a reduction of this sort hold any interest?

Perhaps it does, if the purpose of our reading is to unveil the structural mechanisms of the text. We saw that the narrator does not think it fit to present the detailed circumstances that made him conclude that Ellénore rejected the most innocent jokes; also, this kind of description will lead him to higher order generalizations: 'She had many prejudices, but all of them ran counter to her interest.'

The coherence effect indicates semiotic effectiveness and the transparency of signs. The text of *Adolphe* appears to say that these general propositions do not need more elaborate evidence; the assured voice of the narrator implies that the links between external symptoms and personality traits, between narrative signifier and moral signifieds, are entirely determined, and consequently that a judicious presentation will spare us the myriad of significant events and offer only the final product – the description of the character. And yet the effect of coherence accounts only for a part of the representational game. For, while it undoubtedly seems justified to study description as the privileged place where the semiotic mechanisms of *Adolphe* become apparent, the complementary operation – examining the literary and cultural purposes that animate these mechanisms – is of equal interest. Composed just before the disappearance of the classical style of writing, *Adolphe* still makes use of psychological schematism, and if it proposes a transparent representation of the human soul and its passions, it is because this was still the principal task of serious works of fictions. In Goodman's system, such transparence would signal easy access to the object represented, the touchstone of conventional realism. But what is the *criterion* for easy access? Texts such as *Adolphe, Dangerous Liaisons* or *The Princess of Cleves* manifest a certain conception of attention and of its movements which contrasts with the later spirit of realism. An author who refrains from describing physical appearances, costume, setting, idiolects and mannerisms, and eliminates the little incidents that illustrate personality features from the story is addressing remarkably attentive readers, since every detail of such a simplified text becomes essential. This technique of representation proceeds along an opposite path to what will later be called defamiliarization. 'Ellénore was not a woman of exceptional intelligence; but her ideas were sound and her way of expressing them, which was always simple' has a familiar sound: it may just be gossip (to use a notion Patricia Meyer Spacks introduced to critics). But the very absence of more vivid textual procedures presupposes a familiarity with the essential, a particular strength of the attention. To stay alert, attention does not require the support of sensory surfaces nor the incessant change of stimuli. Its training is such that it knows how to home in on moral traits and how to stay there without distraction. Let us call this procedure the *classical shortcut*.

In contrast, the description of Emma uses a technique which could be labelled the *realist detour*. Flaubert's text avoids strong hypotheses on human conduct; the narrator hides behind the objects, allowing them to reveal themselves through his discourse. Of course, the writer cannot disappear altogether: just as Masaccio's realism does not entail the disappearance of the painter's eye, Flaubert's realism does not generate narratorless texts (*pace* Ann Banfield). The code changes, however: instead of effects of coherence we find effects of reality, and at the same time the semiotics of transparency that readily dispenses with details is replaced by a semiotics of relative opacity, which carefully preserves the materiality of appearances in all its concreteness and variety. Thus free indirect discourse may signal the need to create a distance between the act of narrating and the fictional world: whereas the narrator of *Adolphe* calmly speaks for himself and courageously takes the classical shortcut, here, in a typical realist detour, we see only a few bodily details, and only through Charles Bovary's eyes.

These changes in the rules of the game are not mere arbitrary mutations. Starting with Tocqueville, sociologists of knowledge often described modern man's fragmentation of attention, linking it with the development of modern industrial and democratic societies. No wonder that Flaubert's representation techniques respond to the public's new expectations, to these new ways in which the attention has been trained. Such a change did entail certain risks however. We saw that, in painting, realism makes recognition of the represented object easier. To forget, after persistent efforts, what we *know* is before us and to paint instead what we see brings painting closer to the natural movement of the eye.

In Renaissance painting, attention concentrates on a coherent space, which it manages to embrace with just one look, even if it subsequently has to take part in various games and mirror-like effects offered by the space of the painting. Thus, in bringing together easy recognition and the concentration of attention, Renaissance painting is formally close to the classical shortcut. But in linguistic arts the position of realism is quite different. Natural language speaks about the universal, not the particular; it handles conceptual essence, not sensory appearances. Consequently, in literature, schematism of representation does not derive from technical naivety; rather, it results naturally from the schematism of its medium, language. Realism's interest in sensory appearances brings about a major reorientation of our linguistic habits. It is more natural, closer to our everyday technique of gossip to describe a friend by saying that she has many prejudices and that all these prejudices go against her interest, rather than: 'Her hands, however, were not pretty – not pale enough, perhaps a little rough at the knuckles; and they were too long, without softness of line' (*Madame Bovary*, p. 17).

Flaubert's writings also contain a principle of dispersion. Whereas visual illusion acquires its force only after the discovery of the unifying force of perspective, literary realism is related to multiplicity, to plural focalization and to the inexhaustible sensory world, across which the voracious eye of the writer restlessly wanders. Nevertheless, once we contemplate the text from a distance, we can confront the entire fictional universe in a single sweep of our attention. It then appears that the slow, detailed, inexorable advance of Flaubert's representations does not flatly contradict the purpose of the classical shortcut as much as we may expect. The description of Emma continues as follows:

The finest thing about her was her eyes. They were brown, but seemed black under the long eyelashes; and she had an open gaze that met yours with fearless candor. (ibid., p. 17)

This Flaubertian detour brings us back to the familiar path: barely hidden behind physical appearances, moral notions become visible again. Their slow emergence will not be deferred indefinitely; at the end of the detour, an integrating schema will take shape from the mass of details: the moral traits and the passions of the soul will shine forth as limpidly as those of Constant's heroes. In a sense, *Madame Bovary* aims only at covering the vast transparent spaces of classical writing with incomparable meticulousness but without abandoning their fundamental moral schematism. The 'idea behind the book' still follows the classical system, as Flaubert's lawyer correctly assured the judges at the author's trial:

Mr Gustave Flaubert ... maintains before you that the idea behind his book, from the first line until the last, is a moral and religious one ... which can be summed up in these words: the exhortation to virtue through the horror of vice (Gustave Flaubert, *Oeuvres* (Paris: Gallimard, Bibliothèque de la Pléiade, 1951), ed. A. Thibaudet and R. Dumesnil, vol. 1, p. 364)

Adolphe and its shortcuts bring us to exactly the same conclusions. In *Madame Bovary*, however, they are more difficult to discern. Flaubertian realism is therefore not just dependent on readability.

CONVENTION AND REPRESENTATION

Despite its flaws, radical conventionalism does nevertheless capture an important aspect of literary realism. But the notion of convention contains an ambiguity. Traditionally, it is opposed to intention: such-and-such behaviour is conventional in the sense that the individuals who display it obey social rules without examining them and without intentionally adhering to them. Thus used, 'conventional' connotes inauthenticity, arbitrariness, etc. Whether we drive on the right or left side of the road is conventional in this sense of the term. It is also Goodman's and the structuralist way of using the notion.

A different view of convention links it with the implicit rules which co-ordinate our social behaviour. This is Hume's use of the notion as developed by David Lewis (1969). According to Lewis, a given regularity of behaviour is called conventional if every member of the community conforms to it, if everyone expects everyone else to conform to it, and if everyone prefers to obey the regularity on condition that everyone else does the same. In Lewis's conception, convention solves problems of social co-ordination by establishing a flexible yet stable system of mutual expectations. Such a definition does not preclude the possibility that conventional behaviour is aimed at solving non-arbitrary problems. Therefore, conventions include social mechanisms oriented to certain objectives. The contemporary habit of jogging presents all the characteristics of a convention of co-ordination without being arbitrary with respect to its aim, since a population which adopts this convention will be in better physical condition than another population whose conventions require, say, excessive equal consumption of beer and sweets in front of the television. Similarly, we cannot say that realist conventions choose arbitrary aims which could be as easily attained by other conventions. Realist representation is the result of a certain type of co-ordination and can only obtain when the conditions of the game – the dispersion of attention, for instance, as well as the interest in sensory appearances – are met.

If this is true, we are confronted with the task of reconciling mimesis and diegesis, representation and the rules of the co-ordination game. We thus come back to our point of departure: how to account for the fact that *Madame Bovary* is *both* a conventional narrative structure textualized with the help of a set of equally conventional discursive procedures *and* a description of provincial boredom in mid-nineteenth-century France. And how do we also account for the accusations brought against the book, based on mimetic aspects (as an outrage to public decency, for instance), and the acquittal based on diegetic reasons: 'the work appears to have been patiently and seriously prepared from the literary point of view and concerning the study of the characters . . .' (Flaubert, *Oeuvres*, vol. 1, p. 683). To dismiss mimesis leads nowhere; on the other hand, to understand the nature of literary representations requires more than Lewis's notion of convention: an explicit model of the relations between structural properties and mimetic success is needed. Here are two alternative proposals.

The first model directly links structural qualities and their mimetic objective. If all stories contain, say, *prohibitions*, *violations* and *punishments*, this phenomenon is explained by the crucial role of these categories in the organization of social behaviour. If, at the level of discourse, narrative texts use what Genette (1982) calls *anachronies* (*analepses* and *prolepses*), the explanation lies in these texts' obedience of the natural laws of perception and memory. Such a model, which could be called *causal*, aims at explaining the structural properties of narrative texts in terms of their conformity either with the represented objects or with human cognitive mechanisms. Each system of literary conventions is related to perceptual requirements. Changes in the game of representation are governed by the natural constraints that limit the range of our possible interests. For a realist like Flaubert, the physical appearance of a hand or dress offers more *vivid* details than moral characteristics do. Neither Flaubert nor Constant is writing a novel about a deserted planet, covered by darkness, where no event ever breaks the cosmic monotony. Not that such a text would be radically inconceivable: the first act of Chekhov's *The Seagull* is an example to the contrary; it is just that such a text would interest no one.

The difficulties of a causal model come from the fact that, although the appearance of many structural properties can be attributed to representational factors, the grammars of stories and discourse do not always stay attached to these factors. On the contrary, between structural and discursive properties on the one hand and the objectives of representation on the other, a space of freedom and indetermination opens. Here is an example.

The Hamon/Brooke-Rose description of nineteenth-century French realism finds a set of discursive realist traits that depend on two main categories: first, a *plethora of information*, which includes the appeal to memory, the knowledge of the author being circulated through substitutes descriptions, abundant redundancy and predictability, a cyclothymic rhythm and the defocalization of the hero; and, secondly, *readability*, which is obtained through semiological compensation and overcoding, the psychological motivation of the characters, demodalization and transparent writing and the use of parallel stories.

But these discursive categories can be found in texts that visibly lack a realist orientation or even display an anti-realist orientation. Christine Brooke-Rose in 1980 noted that Hamon's list of features quite appropriately fits fantastic texts such as J. R. R. Tolkien's *The Lord of the Rings*. Was this remark a mere confirmation of a well-known fact, namely that fantastic texts include numerous realist elements? A brief examination of *The Quest of the Holy Grail* in the light of Hamon/Brooke-Rose's categories will suggest a different answer.

Without even mentioning the historical distance between *The Quest of the Holy Grail* and modern realist texts, it seems to me that we could hardly find a text more openly oriented to allegory and symbolism, more sincerely indifferent to the world of empirical experience. None the less, the Hamon/Brooke-Rose categories perfectly fit this text. There is frequent appeal to memory (in the episode featuring Lancelot, among many others) and information invades the text from all directions: the hermits, the knights, the king, all possess a mysterious certainty about the future, the origin of which is never revealed:

'Sire, I will not', [said Lancelot], 'for I know that none shall fail in the attempt but he receive some wound.'
'How came you by such knowledge?' [said the king].
'Sire, suffice it that I know. And I will tell you more: I would have you know that this day shall see the beginning of the great adventures and the marvels of the Holy Grail.' (*The Quest of the Holy Grail*, (Harmondsworth: Penguin, 1977), trans. P. M. Matarasso, p. 35)

The knowledge of the author circulates, disguised, as vigorously as in nineteenth-century realist novels in the interventions of substitute characters, in this case, monks and hermits, who are willing to give their allegorical interpretation of various episodes. The descriptions are numerous and detailed:

This sword was very curiously fashioned: for the pommel was formed of a stone combining all the colours that could be found on Earth. And prized even more highly: each of the colours had its own specific virtue. The tale states furthermore that two ribs composed the hilt, and each of these was taken from a most unusual beast. The first belonged to a species of serpent more often found in Caledonia than elsewhere; this snake is called the papalust. (ibid., p. 214)

Seldom do stories make more use of redundancy and predictability: most of the knights' actions are predicted, sometimes in great detail. The cyclothymic rhythm is present everywhere, for instance, in Perceval's and Lancelot's adventures; the defocalization of the hero plays a greater role than in any other medieval romance. Readability also conforms to Hamon/Brooke-Rose's features: the psychological motivation of the characters obeys medieval psychology, with its accent on self-examination and contrition; then there are rapid disambiguation, transparent style, quotations, absence of subjectivity and finally the insertion of the plot into the larger story of universal Redemption.

Should we conclude that the Hamon/Brooke-Rose list of features does not closely enough fit the realist discourse? Yet the description is excellent, and its pertinence to modern realism cannot be doubted. Should we then consider *The Quest of the Holy Grail* a realist text? This is equally unacceptable. We can, of course, get out of this predicament by arguing that the resemblances are superficial and that a simple reading of *The Quest of the Holy Grail* and of the *Sentimental Education* would show that all the noted features play different, even contradictory, roles in medieval and realist texts. But if there *is* a difference it should be accounted for in some way, and preferably not by recourse to the equally superficial stylistic and discursive features. For, if the inventory of structural properties does not adequately identify realist discourse, it may be that realism is not a discursive phenomenon. And if it proves difficult to discard the mimetic project, it may be that the difference between *The Quest of the Holy Grail* and Flaubert's novels originate precisely in this kind of project.

Such perplexities arise not only in relation to realism. All lists of structural traits which attempt an exhaustive description of stylistic or cultural categories have met with similar difficulties. The famous dichotomies proposed by Wölfflin (1915) as criteria for distinguishing between baroque and classical art are hardly any more specific, or less problematic, in their application to particular paintings. In a study on Elizabethan tragedies (Pavel, 1985), I tried to define the baroque plot by starting from a list of structural features. But it soon became apparent that narrative grammars are resistant to this type of enterprise, and that structural features are by nature mobile and universal. Marlowe's *Tamburlaine*, Cleland's *Fanny Hill* and Kafka's *The Castle* display closely related plot structures, while *Tamburlaine* and *King Lear* are completely opposed from the point of view of plot. Yet only these two latter texts truly qualify as baroque. It proves impossible to predict whether a text will be baroque or not by starting from a list of structural features, just as one cannot say in advance whether a text satisfying the Hamon/Brooke-Rose list can be claimed by realism or not.

Aestheticians have long known that the use of aesthetic terms such as *moving*, *coherent*, *delicate*, or *sentimental* is not governed by sets of necessary or even sufficient conditions. Frank Sibley (1959) showed that no list of properties allows us to infer that a work of art possessing all those properties is *delicate*, *moving*, or *tragic* as a result. In the best possible case, we can say that this or that set of structural or stylistic traits *leads us to believe* that this or that aesthetic property will be present, or, in different terms, that the traits in question are more or less characteristic for the aesthetic property. The transition from one level to another does not obey strict rules. Joseph Margolis (1980) has called this phenomenon *emergence*: works of art possess properties which cannot belong to their material media; among those properties, which he calls functional or intentional, Margolis includes expressivity, representation, meaning and style. The discovery of these general properties, among which I would list such stylistic and cultural categories as baroque, classicism and realism, will always entail the risk of going beyond structural certainties, of suggesting an interpretation.

If so, an alternative model of the relations between structural traits and aesthetic properties, including representation, should contain two distinct levels, each having its own independent organization. Such a model, which I would call functional, would distinguish between a set of primary operations and a higher level, that of the intentional project, which enjoys a relative independence with respect to the primary operations. At various moments, the same intentional project can be served by various arrangements at the primary operations level. Conversely, the same primary operations can be related to various intentional projects. The theoretical metaphors used by functionalist philosophers of mind (Putnam, 1975) are immediately recognizable. Formulated as part of the cognitivist project and directed against behaviourism and other varieties of reductionism, functionalism is interested in the complex relation between the intentional aspects of the human mind and its material aspects.

In a functional model, the structural properties of literary texts fill the role of primary operations, which are flexibly related to various mimetic projects. The relative autonomy of mimesis allows for a multiplicity of representational games, from pure pictographic denotation to the illusion of resemblance. The structural means, far from determining the nature of the representational project, are chosen and arranged according to the needs of this project. Therefore, if the sequence *prohibition*, *violation*, *punishment* is put to use differently in the Biblical story of Adam and Eve and in *Madame Bovary*, the dissimilarity must be attributed to the mimetic programme which uses the grammar of plot only indirectly as a set of primary operations. The discursive procedures are also included among these operations, and as such play various roles in the games of representation. Overcoding, for instance, which is found in Balzac's and Flaubert's novels as well as in *The Quest of the Holy Grail*, serves a different purpose each time. In *The Quest*, the spiritual interpretations added after each event belong to a system of representation that aims at spiritual relevance. In Balzac's novels, the innumerable digressions about the economic, legal and moral mechanisms of nineteenth-century France depend on a mimetic project oriented to the representation of society as a coherent system. In a sense, the two programmes resemble each other, since overcoding reveals a truth hidden behind the events in both (the spiritual unseen in *The Quest* and the socially unseen in Balzac). Though it separates intentional from structural properties, functionalism by no means argues that the relations between them are purely arbitrary.

Margolis calls a system which includes physical and intentional properties and can neither work properly outside its physical properties nor be reduced to its physical properties 'emergent and incarnated'. In other words, though the emergent level in such systems may not maintain fully determined relations, it at least maintains *privileged* relations with the matter in which it is manifested and without which it could not exist. Artistic works – including the subclass of literary works – are examples of such emergent configurations whose teleological properties – representation, meaning, style – cannot be reduced to the material or to the structural devices, yet depend on them for their existence. Neither strictly determined nor arbitrary, the links attaching these properties to the structures that manifest them belong both to the orders of nature and freedom. They are equally subject to the pressure of tradition and taste, yet allow individual genius to effect its surprising intervention.

Caught in a functional configuration, overcoding in Balzac and *The Quest* obviously serves some purpose other than to point to its own presence; although in both cases this stylistic device contributes to a similar end (the revelation of an invisible domain), differences still exist, since Balzac's wealth of divergent information surpasses the comparatively meagre allusions to the Holy Scriptures in *The Quest*. Between a structural device and its historical uses, the relation is one of *elective affinity*. Beyond structural regularities, in the study of aesthetic objects, literary texts included, there lies the inescapable horizon of teleology.

6 On Discretionary Intellectual Behaviour

The linguistic model, sometimes an instrument of modernization, sometimes a metaphor for a new transcendence, has served to justify the most diverse intellectual ends. The preceding analyses have tried to show that such flexibility is in large measure akin to the conceptual simplicity of structural linguistics by stressing the underdetermination of notions, such as difference in the case of Saussure and Hjelmslev, and distribution in the case of the American structuralists. The inadequacy of these notional mechanisms has brought about many different effects according to the ends to which they were put, and, despite their common linguistic sources, it is obvious that, between structural anthropology and Derrida's thought, epistemological difficulties have entirely changed in content. On the one hand, scientific optimism hid, perhaps deliberately, the inadequacies of formalism in the hope that any progress made would ultimately be correct; on the other hand, Derrida's grammatology readily thrived on the underdetermination of Hjelmslev's glossematics, which it used as support for the deconstructive method. But, fundamentally, whether some semiotic theory of meaning is fervently being proposed or the indefinite interplay of differences is ironically being demonstrated, they always come down to the identification of meaning with the sign, they always entail the reduction of intelligent activity to linguistic schemata and the replacement of intention by the undetermined play of customs.

ON THE PHILOSOPHY OF LANGUAGE IN FRANCE

It is, however, less urgent to condemn or to absolve such-and-such a tendency of an intellectual movement so fertile in consequences – since the destiny of research programmes is, in any case, played out in the disciplines concerned – than it is to try to understand how and why this tumultuous state of affairs was possible, particularly in France in the 1960s. Why, in other words, did the intellectual modernization project have to borrow forms that at times were so virulent and at other times so erratic? Why too, once language had been chosen as the locus for theoretical change, was there no debate on its nature and functions? Why, lastly, within the movement, did certain branches rapidly degenerate and, simultaneously, speculative trends persist?

These questions can be approached either in relation to the sociological and political environment of the structuralist movement, or through the internal logic of epistemological development in France; in the second case the French tradition of language studies has to be looked at in detail. Whereas socio-political explanations of structuralism are abundant, the attempts to examine its epistemological context have been rare indeed. Promoters of the trend readily provided a mythical picture of their intellectual origins. Some, as in the case of Lévi-Strauss or Lacan, claimed to take their inspiration from the great pioneer, Saussure; others, such as Greimas and Derrida, while recognizing their predecessors' contributions – again Saussure, also Hjelmslev and in Derrida's case, Heidegger – have daringly assumed the role of founder. Furthermore, the search for origins has provided many harbingers: Marx, the first structuralist, forms an impressive triad with Nietzsche and Freud, but also, in reverse chronological order, we have Leibniz, Port-Royal, Raymundus Lullus, Abelard and Stoic logic.

Nevertheless, whatever minds may have at other times and in other places entertained ideas related to those of the structuralists, the movement's intellectual origin only coincided marginally with the historical affinities experienced *a posteriori* by its members. Moreover, the nature of structuralism would not better be explained if, while questioning these imaginary affinities, one were content to replace them with a precise system of filiations. To attempt to exorcise the philosophical singularity of a Derrida or of a Foucault with the help of references to structural linguistics, to Heidegger, or to Nietzsche, or to say that Greimas derived his notions from Hjelmslev, or Lévi-Strauss from Jakobson amounts to no more than acknowledging a debt. The most singular part of the enterprise undoubtedly lies in the nature of the decisions taken. Having noted Derrida's indebtedness to Saussure and Heidegger, or Foucault's to Nietzsche and the distributionists, we must also seek the reason for these affinities. Why of all the philosophical sources possible, have the representatives of speculative structuralism maintained links precisely with those thinkers and with linguistics? Why did French philosophers of this period choose to carry on a dialogue with German thought, and why did this stop at Hegel and Marx, Nietzsche, Husserl and Heidegger, as if these authors exhausted the spectrum of German philosophy? Clearly, these names, far from lending their prestige to the rise of speculative structuralism, had dominated philosophical debates in France since the end of the 1930s, as if an epistemological sorting system at work long before 1960 had ferreted out all those who deserved some credit.

The restrictive nature of this sorting system is perfectly evident: not only did the majority of French thinkers of the period show complete indifference to the questions raised by English and American philosophy – that is well known – but also, important areas within the German and *even French* traditions were marginalized. The anti-idealism of Herbart, Brentano, Frege and Mach had practically no effect in France during the 1960s. Moreover, grouped together under the infamous 'neopositivist' label, the Vienna School's representatives and friends Schlick, Carnap, Neurath, Feigl, Bergmann, Popper and Tarski were ignored. The French philosophy of the sciences and epistemology in the first half of the century scarcely received any better treatment. The once-illustrious names of Henri Poincaré, Pierre Duhem, Emile Meyerson and Léon Brunschvicg are hardly ever mentioned in postwar debates. The contrast between the Gaston Bachelard of the thirties and the author of *The Poetics of Space* is a highly significant one.

To retrace the origins of this situation, it is tempting, following Antoine Compagnon's example, to look for clues at the beginning of the century, when intellectual territories were being redistributed during the Dreyfus affair. Except for Poincaré's intervention, both philosophers and scientists seemed to remain indifferent to the debate around the affair. Raising itself above the fray, philosophy refused to soil its hands in the political clash. In a certain way, avoiding the corrosive effect of struggles for intellectual power was the wisest thing to do: Bergson was never going to experience – and for good reason – the bitterness of a Péguy. French philosophy at the turn of the century remained indifferent both to the intellectual debates in its immediate surroundings and to developments in neighbouring countries. The reception of phenomenology was delayed until it came to serve as a theoretical foundation both to Sartre's brand of humanism and to Derrida's thinking. More significantly, during the years of the Dreyfus affair, in England and in Austria a radical trend was opposing metaphysics in general and Hegelian idealism in particular. This trend led to the rise of a new epistemology uniting empiricism and logic in the same project. In France, such a turn of events remained inconceivable.

At the turn of the century in France, Hegelian idealism was far from enjoying the same influence it had in Germany and England. The great names of the age – Renouvier, Boutroux, Bergson – were anti-Hegelians for different reasons. With no French Bradley or McTaggart – though Ravaisson may, to a certain point, be considered as their equivalent – the presence of a Bertrand Russell was not needed. Was this because the reaction against both German idealism and its French disciples (notably Victor Cousin) had taken place a generation earlier? Was it because the epistemology of the sciences had already been introduced by Claude Bernard? Immune to pure idealism through the tradition of common-sense philosophies, from Descartes to the Scottish philosophers (for example, Thomas Reid, who was so admired by Royer-Collard), French philosophy at the end of the nineteenth century reconciled all too well the demands of a moderate spiritualism with attention to developments in the experimental sciences. Scientific and formal radicalism did not exercise any attraction whatsoever. Bergson's philosophy provides the most striking example of this synthesis of spiritualist common sense and interest in science, but traces of it are found everywhere, even in a dissident such as Pierre Duhem.

Duhem's case is a revealing one: the creator of the conventionalist theory of scientific models who would later experience considerable success among English-speaking philosophers, this great thinker who recognized the reciprocal limits of science and of metaphysics never brought himself to challenge metaphysics as his English and Austrian colleagues had done. He was certainly right not to do so, for, after a long period of radical empiricism, English and American philosophers finally lifted the moratorium on metaphysical thinking; but isn't it sometimes costly to be right too soon, especially when the untimely certainty of being on the right track discourages the exploration of alternatives?

In the same vein, during his polemic against Louis Couturat and Bertrand Russell in *Revue de métaphysique et de morale* (1906–9), Henri Poincaré strongly opposed Russell and Hilbert's attempts to reduce mathematics to logic. Poincaré's arguments, which raised doubts about mathematical induction and actual infinity, were, in a certain sense, proved right 30 years later by Gödel's work. But how heavily Poincaré's refusal to take part in the renewal of mathematics weighed on the future of French logic and epistemology! Despite the difficulties encountered, Hilbert's project not only originated the development of meta-mathematics, a development which led notably to the theory of recursive functions and Turing's work, but also an extensive philosophical discussion developed around the Cambridge, Oxford and Vienna schools on the major issues in logic, language and modern science.

True, the theses of the first logical atomists, of the Vienna School, and of the Unity of Science project too often had an extremist character; demonstrating the non-sense of metaphysics finally proved to be an impossible task; and the project to unite science by using the psychology of perception or theoretical physics as its model is no more than a slightly embarassing memory today. But the debate as a whole generated a deluge of research formal and natural languages which, among its many applications, served to inspire and to correct structural linguistics and its theoretical successor, generative-transformational linguistics. Above all, the radicalism of the logical empiricists had an important influence on the way philosophy was debated: obliged to provide proofs based on mathematical logic and the theory of science, philosophers of this school very early on became accustomed to arguing their theses meticulously, to evaluating objections carefully, and even to yielding when the counter-arguments proved compelling. In this way, attention was paid to language on two accounts: the desire to understand its mechanisms led to a consideration of the formal structures which underlie language (formal theories, but the philosophies of ordinary language too); and the need to control its excesses led to a practice approaching that in the sciences, a practice that is attentive to precision in propounding arguments, to verification and refutation.

Even though most French philosophers had nothing to do with these preoccupations for a long time, despite the efforts of a few thinkers devoted to the epistemology of the sciences, the blame can by no means be attributed to Henri Poincaré or to chance alone (although historians have noted the disappearance of three of the most gifted French philosophers of mathematics and science in their early youth: Jacques Herbrandt, Jean Cavaillés and Albert Lautman). More convincing causes can be found in the institutional organization of philosophy. Authors as diverse as Albert Thibaudet, Jean-François Revel, Pierre Thullier and Vincent Descombes saw the state's control of philosophy as the cause of eclecticism, common-sense hegemony and the excessive influence of a few individuals' choices and preferences. The secure institutional position of philosophy in the first decade of the twentieth century also played a certain role. From its precarious beginnings in Bordeaux, sociology set out to conquer Paris in the enthusiasm of the Dreyfus affair; at the same time, the history of literature profitted from the confusion to displace rhetoric. Philosophy, however, as an entrenched institution, had no need to get caught up in the excitement of the Dreyfus years. At that time, it had good reason to be pleased with itself: having already eluded the absolute idealism of Hegel, it also took pains to avoid Russell's extreme formalism by prudently sticking to the path of neo-Kantian intellectualism, not forgetting, of course, moral imperatives and attention to the concrete. But while anti-psychological formalism was triumphing in logic elsewhere in Europe (whether in mathematical logic or in phenomenology), Goblot chose to bring his work closer to psychology and remain faithful to the concrete. In other words, the reaction against rhetoric by the turn-of-the-century literary historians had no counterpart in philosophy. The different traditional trends continued to exercise their hegemony in philosophy by effectively preventing the pursuit of renewed reflection on language in the name of resistance to positivism.

In the 1920s and 1930s, the balance of forces in French philosophy underwent few modifications. Meyerson, Brunschvicg and Bachelard developed a critical reflection on science, but kept Austrian and Anglo-Saxon concerns in the background. The prestige of Bergsonism was followed by the first contacts with phenomenology (Husserl's lectures *Cartesian Meditations* to the Collège de France), and by secular and Christian forms of existentialism. At the same time, the rise of the

Third Reich in Germany, the annexation of Austria, the occupation of Czechoslovakia and the partition of Poland brought about a profound rupture in central European philosophy: faithful to libertarian values and composed in large part of intellectuals of Jewish extraction, Austrian and German anti-idealist, scientific and positivistic philosophers were forced into exile: Carnap, Reichenbach, Menger, Gödel and Tarski settled in the United States, Waismann and Neurath in England, Popper in New Zealand and later in England. Quine and Nagel in America, with Feigl who had been there since 1931, and Russell and his friend and protégé Wittgenstein in England, had for a long time been supporters of this trend. What postwar French authors persisted in calling 'Anglo-Saxon philosophy' in fact represented an amalgam of the philosophies of science and language practised between the two wars in Austria, Germany, Czechoslovakia, Poland, Scandinavia, England and the United States. That English became the language of this amalgam and England and America its theatre was mostly the result of the contingencies of political history. But the fact that none of these emigrés tried to settle in France also reveals a difference in epistemological outlooks.

With historical events eradicating all positivist resistance in Germany and Austria, the influence that Heidegger – and, through him, Nietzsche – enjoyed during and after the war on both sides of the Rhine is not surprising. As for the rise of Hegelianism in France, it was undoubtedly linked to the strength of postwar Marxism. We should also note that idealism had not been taken seriously in France for very long, so the conditions were right for the stunning success of *The Phenomenology of Spirit*. It was thus at the meeting point of existentialism with Marxism and with the dialectic of the spirit that not only the postwar humanism was constituted but also the lasting philosophical pantheon which was to dominate the French philosophical imagination up to and even beyond the revolt of speculative structuralism. But apart from Husserl, none of the forerunners (Hegel, Marx, Nietzsche, Heidegger), despite the tardy zeal of their interpreters, had accorded more than an incidental place to the problematic of language. When the urgency of this problem began to be felt in France in the fifties, the philosophical apparatus in place was scarcely able to cope.

Linguistics, the other major participant in the structuralist debate, remained equally isolated during the first half of the century. The formalist and innovative aspects in the teaching of Saussure were obscured by Antoine Meillet, whose watered-down version of his master's work retained chiefly those views compatible with the orthodoxy of the New Grammarians. Meanwhile, in Geneva, Prague and New Haven, structural linguists were concentrating on the abstract and systematic aspects of language. Despite the efforts of Emile Benveniste and André Martinet, who founded a vigorous school of linguistics in France, the discrepancy was not immediately noticed, since not all trends in modern linguistics were aligned with the same energy on the side of anti-historicism, just as they did not all adhere to the scientific credo in its most rigorous form. For some time, it seemed easy to bridge the gap between traditional and modern linguistics. As late as the end of the 1940s, W. v. Wartburg and S. Ullmann still believed in the possible synthesis of the past and the present. Linguistics, however, gradually shifted towards modern logic and the new philosophy of science. Its recent history consists in the advance of formalism: the Geneva school was still practising a traditional form of Saussurianism; the Prague linguistic circle was occasionally resorting to set theory and was maintaining contacts with the Vienna School; Hjelmslev was closely following developments in logical positivism; Bloomfield joined the project of unity of science; and, later, Chomsky's research benefited from the results obtained in the theory of recursive functions and formal languages. Influenced by contemporary philosophy of science, Chomsky and his followers proposed a series of theoretical models which quickly signalled the vitality of the enterprise. Starting in 1955 with a formal refutation of linguistic structuralism, the new school advanced with remarkable speed until 1965. And at precisely this moment, structuralism, whose decrepit models were rejected by linguistics, was selected as the starting point for a revolution in French epistemology.

This choice deeply affected all branches of French structuralism. The work of Lévi-Strauss, of the early Barthes and of Lacan to some degree, represented the delayed – and, for this reason, even more noticeable – explosion of the neglected debate on language and epistemology. The urgency of this debate, which had been suppressed for a long time, was further aggravated by the delays. As Frege, Russell and Wittgenstein had realized at the turn of the century, the difficulties of Kantian and post-Kantian epistemology derived in large part from the fact that it took the transparency and malleability of philosophical language for granted. A set of factors, including logical paradoxes, the difficulties of the philosophy of science and the excesses of Hegelian idealism, demonstrated how illusory this transparency was and persuaded the philosophers concerned that the rehabilitation of epistemology, indeed of philosophy in its entirety, had to come from the study and reform of its language.

In France, philosophers were not interested in a discussion on language. Those who, like Brice Parain, had worked on linguistic problems, had not succeeded in capturing their colleague's attention. Philosophy of language and of logic was considered a narrow speciality, and its influence remained limited. The analytical philosophy of language and science had not been developed, and symbolic logic had not maintained contact with philosophy. It was left to the more daring practitioners of anthropology, psychoanalysis and poetics to discover and deal with the problem. They sought a model that was both rigorous and intuitive.

Structural phonology, especially in the version taught by Jakobson, was an excellent candidate. Known in France only to a few specialists, it offered just that dash of formalism necessary to create the impression of scientific rigour; moreover, its simplicity permitted easy universal application and freedom to modify the details at will. Its inventory of general notions (such as binarism, arbitrariness of the sign, universals and aphasia), was small, encouraging its users to speculate. Finally, because Jakobson's interests had always been multi-disciplinary, he had already applied his linguistic ideas to other disciplines, particularly poetics and psychology.

The fact that the debate on language started in anthropology, psychoanalysis and poetics led to the neglect of epistemological precautions. Impatient to modernize anthropology, Lévi-Strauss declared the universal validity of the phonological models without asking questions about the intrinsic value of these models or about the researcher's chances of deriving fruitful applications for the theory of myth. Paradoxically, the absence of a critical attitude showed both the need for a reform in the human sciences and, at the same time, guaranteed the failure of an undertaking conducted with such levity. This was the case, a few years later, with Barthes's narrative syntax: of all the sources available, it based itself on the linguistics of Hjelmslev, an author known for never having developed syntax.

RELATIVE DEPRIVATION AND LOCAL DISPARITIES

Structuralism's epistemological weakness had been noticed at the beginning of the structuralist experience. Specialists immediately denounced the vague use made of linguistic notions (Georges Mounin, Bertil Malmberg), yet their warnings had no visible effect. More significantly, some of the most active authors in the modernization inspired by linguistics, notably Barthes, reversed their opinions around 1970 and recommended renouncing the scientific ideal that seemed to be out of reach.

The contradictions between moderate and speculative structuralism have often puzzled historians of the movement. In 1982, Jonathan Culler noticed the diversity of qualifications – and criticisms – that structuralism has warranted:

> Science or irrationalism, rigidity or permissiveness, destruction of criticism or inflation of criticism – the possibility of such contradictory charges might suggest that the primary quality of 'structuralism' is an indeterminate radical force. (ibid., p. 22)

To account for these antinomies, Culler proposed a chronological explanation: the Socratic variety of structuralism, displaying an optimistic confidence in science and rationality, was followed by a Nietzschean period, characterized by the tragic (and ironic) search for the uncanny. Yet the precise temporal borders between these two stages are difficult to identify. A quite uncanny reading of Saussure was proposed by Derrida as early as 1967. Barthes's *S/Z* (1970), blends a scientistic attitude with its persistent and ironic negation. Speculative structuralism seems to have been concomitant with scientific structuralism from quite early on. It 1968, the gap between the calm advance of moderate structuralism and the febrility of metaphysical structuralism was already discernible.

Since then, the gap has widened to polarization: one tendency actively promotes rigour, thrift, careful and tireless work devoted to the search for truth; the other encourages self-indulgence, excessive behaviour and sceptical, even anti-intellectual attitudes. On one side, the professed ideal was supposed to lead to rational knowledge, to moderation, to the perpetual postponing of theoretical satisfaction. The four volumes of Lévi-Strauss's *Mythologiques*, for instance, develop innumerable empirical and formal analyses, bringing them together in a theoretical conclusion only at the very end. On the other side the style of thought is hedonistic and violent, often degenerating into intellectual acrobatics, and, in the absence of empirical or formal accumulation, into instant theoretical gratification. Deleuze and Guattari's *Anti-Oedipus* stands out as the most successful instance of such a style. Equally symptomatic is Foucault's *The Order of Things*, the last chapter of which consists of a long sequence of theoretical ejaculations devoid of any preparation.

Both the obscurity and the conceptual aggressiveness of speculative structuralism may quite simply be attributed to a theoretical discomfort which the discursive disorder attempted to hide. In accordance with the epistemological background described above, it shouldn't be surprising that a group of authors ill-prepared to confront the philosophical problems of language should affect the least comprehensible style. But sociologists of knowledge, who couldn't content themselves with such psychodramatic interpretations, proposed various other explanations of the structuralist phenomenon based on resilient French cultural traditions, the interaction of intellectual institutions and the immediate political context.

Thus, Sherry Turkle has related the remarkable diffusion of Lacanian psychoanalysis to the traditional French tendency of investing intellectual constructs with an abstract ideological signification, instead of orienting them towards the solution of concrete problems. According to this theory, the seventeenth-century pedantry, so cruelly ridiculed by Molière, the *esprit littéraire* whose pernicious influence Tocqueville deplored in his memoirs, the 'Byzantine' France of Julien Benda, would all instantiate the same pattern that led to Lacan's success and, more generally, to speculative structuralism. Though the keen analyses of Turkle really succeed in stressing the force of cultural recurrences, to a certain extent they miss the specificity of the phenomena under study. For, the *esprit littéraire* indeed flourished between the seventeenth and nineteenth century, as well as before and after each of the numerous French revolutions, 'Byzantine' France indeed adulated Bergson or Paul Valéry, and yet never before in modern France has such an extraordinary philosophical trend managed to get so warm a reception. Turkle's explanation emphasizes the inevitability of the phenomenon, but neglects its excessive and peculiar sides.

Raymond Boudon offers an interpretation more sensitive to the contemporary sociological context. In order to make the success and diffusion of speculative structuralism comprehensible, Boudon uses François Bourricaud's theory of the three-level intellectual market in modern developed countries. Success of scientific and philosophical production in the first market, made up of a community of specialists, rests on the judgement of one's peers. In the wider second market, made up of intellectuals, political decision-makers and leaders of influential organizations, success mainly derives from the work's ideological value to the groups involved. At a third level is a diffuse general public whose taste and opinions in principle depends on the verdicts neither of the specialists nor of the political and ideological groups. Leaving the general public aside, Boudon examines the circulation of scientific and philosophical works between the specialized market and the political and ideological market.

In an ideal situation, he claims, specialized intellectual products reach the second market only after they have gained approval of specialists of the first market. Thus, the influential *A Theory of Justice* by John Rawls and *Anarchy, State and Utopia* by Robert Nozick conquered the second American market, becoming theoretical landmarks for the liberals and the conservatives respectively, only after the professionals of philosophy favourably judged the two books. In contrast, during the late 1960s, the specialist's market in France was suddenly weakened by the implementation of unionism in academic and research institutions through a series of laws enacted after 1968. Since any union, in order to serve its membership better, must obtain personal advantages for as many members as possible, meritocracy could not operate. As a result, numerous scientific and philosophical books were promoted directly in the second market, notably through the media, before peers had a chance to express their opinions. These short-circuitings transformed a few specialists into media stars, rendering them invulnerable to professional evaluation. Natural sciences and the better developed social sciences – history, for instance – suffered only marginally from such circumstances, since either their nature or their maturity effectively maintained quality control. Younger disciplines, however, in which value criteria had not yet had time to consolidate – and this includes interdisciplinary research – became easy victims of the new configuration. In order to bestow some epistemological legitimacy on the lax practices that ensued, researchers felt a quite natural attraction towards anarchist epistemologies

(Feyerabend's, for instance, or Foucault's) and clearly understood that it was in their own interest to select as models the media stars whose confused writings had escaped professional evaluation. Stylistic obscurity became the mark of a scientific status that nobody had either the competence or the courage to doubt.

Boudon's model captures the dynamism of French intellectual institutions during the first decade of the Fifth Republic. It is also valid for linguistics and its interdisciplinary applications. The forceful objections that professional linguists, such as Georges Mounin and Bertil Malmberg, raised against the linguistic speculations of Lévi-Strauss, Lacan or Barthes only reached a limited audience, presumably because the works they incriminated had already conquered the second market with the help of the media.

Yet, despite its sociological sophistication, the model appears to have a critical flaw. In Boudon's view, the disappearance of the strong link between scientific productivity and career success, by subverting the first market, pushed researchers towards the second market governed by the media and by the caprices of Parisian intellectual fashions. If this had actually happened, there would have been two consequences: first, speculative structuralism would have developed fully only after the unionizing reforms in 1968–9; secondly, the intellectual decadence allegedly triggered by the unions would have become more and more severe, while the success of speculative structuralism, relativist epistemology and the intellectual luminaries (*maîtres à penser*) would have increased indefinitely.

In fact, however, when the reforms of 1968–9 were introduced, the major figures of ideological and metaphysical structuralism – Althusser, Lacan, Derrida and Foucault – were already enjoying considerable notoriety outside the professional milieux. Nor did these reforms lead to a progressive decline in the quality of French research. By the end of the 1970s, the influence, if not the species, of *maîtres à penser* was fading away, and the media turned its attention away from the social sciences, thus encouraging a rally in the specialist's market.

The vulnerable point in Boudon's argument is the attempt to establish a causal link between the troubled years of 1968–9 and the rise of speculative structuralism. Boudon is certainly not alone in seeking such links. Both the partisans and the adversaries of the May 1968 rebellion have repeatedly related it to the success of structuralism. As early as the summer of 1968, the authors of *La Brèche*, an intellectual manifesto in favour of the student revolution, and Raymond Aron, who condemned it, shared the conviction that 'the mixture of Lévi-Strauss, Foucault, Althusser and Lacan' (Aron, 1968, p. 136) had, directly or indirectly, led to the student movements. On the other hand, anthropologists and semioticians have maintained that the explosion of May 1968 had prematurely buried structuralism. Almost everyone thus found some linkage: structuralism caused 1968; 1968 caused structuralism; 1968 destroyed structuralism.

But the researcher who, today, tries to clarify the relationship between 1968 and the French intellectual life must acknowledge both the diversity of factors that stimulated the rebellion and the strangeness of its consequences. Consider, for instance, how many political factions were involved: begun by various anarchist groups, by Maoists and other Marxist-Leninists, the movement gradually included the communists, the social-Christians, the socialists and the unions. Consider too the global scope of the seism and the immense diversity of its objectives: the Chinese Cultural Revolution of 1966, attempting to reverse the modernization undertaken by a Marxist bureaucracy; the American student movements of 1965–7 directed against the Vietnam War; the 1968 attempt in Prague to add a human dimension to a communist regime in central Europe; the student and worker's strikes in France; and the Canadian separatist crisis in 1970. To insist on the anti-authoritarian character of all these explosions would be tautological, since by definition every rebellion is directed against authority. Given the amplitude of the tremor and the fact that the French episode was neither the last, nor necessarily the most characteristic, would it not be presumptuous to see in the obscure speculations of a handful of Parisian philosophers anything more than a symptom of the troubled times?

These difficulties suggest that the best strategy would be provisionally to discard the 1968 revolt as an obligatory point of reference for the interpretation of structuralism, leaving it for a later stage of the argument. In fact, the first manifestoes of French structuralism, stressing the need for a scientific revolution based on linguistic models in the social sciences, date from 1945. We should perhaps briefly consider the nature of the structuralist impetus, and since the representatives of this trend all have achieved notoriety as reformers, some even as revolutionaries, it is appropriate to consider their contributions as intellectual *action* and, more specifically, as modernizing action.

It is well known that during a modernization process, the various sectors and regions of any given social unit do not always change at the same pace. This truism, which the sociology of economic development successfully applied on a planetary scale, not only goes for those societies which experience major difficulties during their modernization – crises, demodernizing revolutions, etc. – but also for those cases in which the process develops in an exemplary manner. Under the best circumstances, it is still possible for a certain sector to be locally delayed. Usually, when this happens in societies well on the way to modernization, the means for remedying such delays are in principle available and local pressure suffices for the inadequacy to be corrected. Thus, in spite of considerable successes in other areas of modernization, France, during the 1960s, experienced a delay in the establishment of its communications infrastructure, especially its telephone system. Once the problem was identified and the appropriate measures taken, just 20 years later France possesses the most developed telephone network in Europe. In this example, the reality of the delay was unanimously accepted and its elimination perceived as desirable.

It is, however, conceivable that a given situation is interpreted as a local disparity only by some of the participants. The delay and, correlatively, the desire to eliminate it derive in such cases from a feeling of deprivation that resembles both what Marx called 'relative pauperization' and the influence of the 'reputable standards of expenditure' noted by Veblen. The effects of these feelings are well known regarding consumption in industrial societies, as well as in the interaction between industrial and developing countries. In this last case, for instance, the life-style and expectations of Western society often strongly influence the local elites of developing countries, but since this life-style spreads more quickly than the technological and political innovations that make it possible, the tensions become unbearable between aspirations and reality. The same *demonstrative effect* influences investment. Sociologists of development have shown how, during the nineteenth century, the military expenditures of less developed European powers ran proportionally higher than those of more advanced nations, just as in our time industrial investment for the sake of prestige slows down the economies of many developing countries.

Developing countries are not the only ones affected: as critics of advanced liberal societies have often emphasized, such demonstrative effects can occasionally surface in the healthiest economy. *Real* regional disparities create well-known problems for contemporary societies. *Perceived* disparities generate additional difficulties; these result from demonstrative effects, especially when the perception of these effects is *not* unanimously shared. Imagine that a group of Florentine entrepreneurs, concluding that the leather trade in their city is an undesirable symptom of economic backwardness, decide to finance a new industry which produces the same items in plastic at incomparably lower prices. Clearly, such an initiative, which derives from a misplaced feeling of relative deprivation, would be fiercely opposed by those who think that craftsmanship deserves to be protected and encouraged in modern society.

Similar situations occur quite frequently in the realm of knowledge. The introduction of the scientific ethos, accompanied by logico-mathematical technology, always acted as a powerful factor in modernization. After Galileo demonstrated the advantages of mathematization at the beginning of the seventeenth century, physics abandoned the Aristotelian system, establishing something like 'reputable standards' of scientificity in regard to which other disciplines started to feel 'backward' and to re-evaluate their own epistemological status. Hence, the feeling of relative deprivation so often experienced since then by less fortunate neighbours. In the social sciences and the humanities, this configuration could not fail to generate conflicts, since the partisans of traditional methodologies stubbornly opposed any attempt to modernize these fields. In several disciplines, the debate ended by dividing territories. Modernization encourages disciplinary proliferation: interpretative and quantitative sociology, historical and synchronic linguistics, experimental psychology and psychoanalysis all maintained their legitimacy. Other social sciences, notably anthropology, history and philology, took only marginal advantage of the formal techniques, since these disciplines appeared to depend on empirical inquiry, individual talent and non-formal thought. Preoccupied by these tensions, the theoreticians of the cleavage between the *Natur-* and *Geisteswissenschaften* have on several occasions marked out a kind of no-man's-land in which the human sciences could feel protected from the pressure exerted by the natural and exact sciences. Yet the demonstration effect of epistemological modernization did not simply vanish, and as soon as it had been contained within a new set of borders, the influence of 'hard' sciences again started to threaten the neighbouring disciplines. The most spectacular episode of this protracted advance has been the modernization of epistemology itself, inaugurated by Russell and Wittgenstein and continued by analytical philosophy. By taking part in this operation, synchronic linguistics derived considerable benefits, including a dramatic increase in prestige. Considered from this point of view, Lévi-Strauss's 1945 campaign against traditional techniques in anthropology and his advocacy of linguistics as a model of scientific success represented the attempt to counter a local delay.

Attempts to correct local delays – local backwardness, as it were – be they social or epistemological, may fail on three accounts: if not all participants genuinely feel change to be necessary; if the technological solution is inadequate (imagine, for instance, France rectifying its communications problems in the 1960s by an unprecedented extension of its telegraph network); or if the modernizing movement puts an unbearable pressure on the social – or cognitive – group, thus causing an anti-modernizing reaction. The advance of scientistic structuralism, unlike that of moderate structuralism, has been affected by each of the three errors.

If it openly showed its concern for the backward state of literary theory, moderate structuralism could argue that research into poetics in France was hardly on the leading edge of the discipline at that time. Given the lively development of Russian, Czech, German and American formalism, the French delay was not imaginary. Thanks to a series of wise decisions, moderate structuralists proposed a modest amount of technological investment; they refrained from overusing the gadgets offered by structural linguistics (binarism, distribution and asemanticism), and, more importantly, did not succumb to the temptation of inventing new gadgets of their own. The recent opinions voiced in France, which claim that structuralist poetics contributed to pervasive cultural relativism, clearly fail to do justice to the founders of the discipline. As envisaged by Barthes, the reformation of literary studies ought to model itself on the division of territories in modern linguistics, in which older branches – descriptive and historical grammar, dialectology, the history of language – continued to prosper alongside the new enterprises based on formal theory. Poetics was destined to become a true science of literature which would coexist with literary history and criticism.

This does not mean that moderate structuralism has always been above reproach. Its critics rightly observe that the doctrine of self-reflexivity in literature, that is, the claim that literature primarily speaks about itself, has had a negative influence on literary studies. But this doctrine was only a regulative myth similar to the deterministic triad 'race, period, environment' of historical criticism or the rigorous materialism of nineteenth-century physics. The purely metaphorical character of these normative doctrines in no way affected that validity of the research they inspired and justified. Every regulative myth occasions marginal exaggerations: structuralist poetics was flawed by excessive conventionalism and a failure to examine the referential power of literary texts. Nevertheless, the poeticians associated with moderate structuralism knew how to avoid the ruinous modernizing strategies practised by other branches of the movement.

Scientific structuralists, for their part, dogmatically decided that, compared to structural linguistics, anthropology suffered from underdevelopment. But this delay may well have been imaginary, since the absence of linguistic formalization or logico-mathematical techniques may simply indicate that the rationality of anthropology, like that of all interpretative disciplines, does not depend on formalisms. Secondly, the technology selected – structuralist phonology – was of inferior quality, and by then was already obsolete in its original field, linguistics. A more recent linguistic technology might not, in the long run, have succeeded in changing anthropology into an exact science but it would at least have put anthropologists in touch with more advanced formalisms and would have helped them avoid phonologism. Likewise, although the semioticians' attempt to modernize linguistics and unify the methodology of the human sciences was not necessarily futile, they did not realize for a long time how effectively their objectives had already been attained by transformational grammar and the epistemology of science.

The structuralists' efforts at modernization put excessive pressure on the disciplines involved. Anthropologists aware of the limits of formalism criticized Lévi-Strauss' programme; linguists were puzzled by the frivolous use made of notions from their discipline; literary historians indignantly denounced what, in the early 1960s, was already called the structuralist ideology; finally, philosophers such as Derrida and Foucault used the concepts of Saussure, Hjelmslev and Zellig Harris to prove the impossibility of a genuinely scientific study of man.

But the 'backwardness' combatted by Lévi-Strauss was perhaps only imaginary, and the 'reputable' standards of epistemological investment that prevailed in physics and linguistics may not have been applicable to all the social sciences. The call for formal investment was rejected, and the revolutionary programme of scientific structuralism failed to lead to the genuine modernization of the social sciences. Instead, it promoted an ambiguous discourse which, disguised as structuralist ideology, made heavy use of traditional intuitive techniques. Lévi-Strauss himself often indulged in this kind of discourse which became the specialty of various brands of literary structuralisms: Lucien Goldmann's genetic structuralism is a good example of this mixture. In Lévi-Strauss's work, the intuitive techniques inherited from previous anthropologists severely lacked the old hermeneutic and philological controls. These were rejected by the structuralist revolution in the name of the new scientific ideals. But in the absence of rigorous regulative mechanisms, the scientific impulse degenerates into gnosis. This is quite a familiar pattern of action. It starts with a radical revolution based on inapplicable principles and unattainable objectives. It survives through the surreptitious use of pre-revolutionary methods as the only recourse against the ineffectiveness of the new principles. Utopian political regimes do not proceed any differently when, rather than admitting the impossibility of their programme, they blend a disorderly return to traditional practices with an unflinching affirmation of utopia. From this tension terror is born, for in order to survive, phantasms must either master reality or destroy it.

ON DISCRETIONARY INTELLECTUAL BEHAVIOUR

As for the specific physiognomy of French phenomenon in the 1960s, it derives less from the manifestation of the old utopia/terror scheme (for this kind of micro-degeneration abounds in intellectual history) as from the magnitude of the movement, the speed at which it spread, and the negligible resistance to it. The lack of opposition may be attributed to the weak position of linguistics and philosophy of language in France. The prompt diffusion of the movement can be explained both by French traditions and by changes in the cultural market. As for the magnitude and diversity of structuralism, from the rationalist utopia of scientific structuralism to the anti-rationalism of poststructuralism, the transition is an authentic reflection of the tensions prevailing in postindustrial countries: a system founded on economic modernization, freedom of expression and pluralist democracy engenders an adversarial culture which turns against the society that made it possible.

Marx analysed a similar configuration giving it the name 'German ideology'. The difference in our century is that the promoters of cultural revolutions and the Nietzschean denouncers of conventional values owe their existence not to the difficulties their countries are undergoing, as in Marx's example, but to the unprecedented opulence of modern democracies. In 1976, Daniel Bell feared that the rivalry between Protestant ethics and modernist counter-ethics would lead to the destruction of the moral texture on which modern pluralist societies are resting. The development of advanced societies belied such apprehensions. If, indeed, the foundation of the modernist counter-ethics lies, as Bell claims, in the dramatic increase of *discretionary social behaviour*, which in turn derives from an unprecendented increase in discretionary income, it must be expected that a decrease of the latter, or even just a credible threat of such a decrease, would weaken the influence of modernist counter-ethics. This is probably what we witnessed after the economic shocks of 1975 and 1980–1. Though these economic upsets may not have put the general prosperity of pluralist societies in doubt, they did at least make the chances of individuals effortlessly profitting from this prosperity more uncertain, thus indirectly reducing the seductive power of the modernist counter-ethics.

But during the 1960s, the great Western economies – both material and cultural – continued to progress without the slightest anxiety. Ambitious projects undertaken by the governments of that time bear witness to this atmosphere of confidence. The Johnson administration undertook simultaneously to build the Great Society and to wage the Vietnam war; de Gaulle's government developed social security, cultural centres, unemployment insurance and universal accessibility to higher education. The policies of expansion and redistribution adopted by the right and the left, suggest that the real debate of that era was about the *control of expenditure*. *Production*, indeed, seemed to be taken for granted, and the only issue at stake consisted in determining who would seize and distribute the extraordinary reserve of discretionary income and discretionary social behaviour made possible by advanced capitalism. Around the same time, the sudden proliferation of noisy and frivolous intellectual enterprises, the short-circuiting of the knowledge markets and the rebirth of gnosis showed a dramatic increase of *discretionary intellectual behaviour*.

It is not surprising that the tensions engendered by cultural frivolity led to the destabilization of the status quo, and that, in the field of scholarship just as in the economy, deliberate waste, programmatic hedonism and theoretical subversion became ubiquitous, symptoms of the anomie caused by excessive wealth. The ambiguities of structuralism acquire therefore a new meaning: the opposition between scientific and speculative structuralism reproduces that between the modernizing impulse and the triumph of discretionary behaviour. The metaphysicians of the 1960s used the modernization project of scientific structuralism as a background of their counter-modernizing programme. Their sudden turnabout says little about the abandoned branches of structuralism, since the accusation of positivism formulated against it is a decoy used by the radical wing to emphasize the charms of its own excesses. A reading of Derrida's *Of Grammatology* in the light of this hypothesis would certainly clarify its polemical strategies.

This configuration also helps us make sense of George Bataille's influence on speculative structuralism. Whereas the themes of Bataille's thought have little to do with the programme of moderate and scientistic structuralism, the author of *Accursed Share* has offered the metaphysicians of the movement a flawless justification of their theoretical practices. Dissipation and excess, these necessary gestures of anarchist and libertine thought, found a subtle and fervent theoretician in Bataille who, understanding their subversive potential very early on, made their consequences fully explicit. If the intellectual dissoluteness that ensued, which some qualified as nihilism, was received so well by speculative structuralism, it was less on account of theoretical kinship and more due to the fact that the poststructuralists, by virtue of their very position in the interplay of accumulation and expenditure, needed a canon for their licentiousness, a norm of the potlatch.

Scientific structuralism, then, owed its initial success to the decision to correct the alleged epistemological backwardness of the social sciences in France. The means employed to this end – the recourse to structural linguistics – proved inadequate and the group that should have provided a significant critique was not strong enough to do so. The attempted epistemological revolution rapidly degenerated into an ideological regime that stopped obeying the usual mechanisms that monitor knowledge. Lacking intellectual controls, structuralism polarized: one trend remained faithful to the scientific promise, while a radical trend opposing the scientific project used the structuralist conceptual framework to promote its own interests, in particular the opposition to humanist values. Favoured by the peculiar organization of the French intellectual market, the radical trend prospered thanks to the considerable stock of discretionary intellectual behaviour available in postindustrial societies.

This etiology is corroborated by developments in the United States and France between 1975 and 1985. A locally perceived backwardness explains the success of French poststructuralism in the United States better than the collapse of scientific standards. Owing to the decrease in student population, the corollary decline in postsecondary teaching jobs and the financial difficulties of universities during a period of economic uncertainty, peer evaluation in the American intellectual market at the end of the 1970s was as severe as ever. Yet these factors did not prevent the development of a strong American poststructuralist trend, quite similar to its French counterpart during those same years. True, the writings of the American poststructuralists remain confined to a small public. Moreover, American philosophy has been crucially involved in all major debates around language, logic and science from the beginning of the century, and so was never more than marginally affected by the rhetoric of speculative structuralism. The influence of poststructuralism did not extend beyond the departments of literature, film and theology, perhaps because, independently of French poststructuralists, American philosophers developed their own version of postanalytical thought. Some American philosophers (H. Putnam, J. Margolis) noted with interest the convergence of anti-intentional and anti-foundationalist themes in French and American philosophy; others (R. Rorty, I. Hacking) actively sought a synthesis between postanalytical philosophy and poststructuralism; some (H. Dreyfus) converted to one branch or another of French poststructuralism. Cultural critics (Hayden White, Jim Clifford, numerous feminist critics) experimentally used poststructuralist notions without necessarily subscribing to all theses of the trend. And yet, although neither philosophers nor the general public were seduced by it – perhaps because during the lean years 1975–82 excessive expenditure of intellectual resources seemed less appealing than a decade earlier – literary poststructuralism successfully gained control of a good number of literary departments during a period when peer judgement was at its most severe.

The explanation for poststructuralism's success in literary criticism lies elsewhere. From the 1950s, American literary studies suffered – or were believed to suffer – from stagnation, especially in contrast with the golden age of 1920–50, when the work of I. A. Richards, J. Crowe Ransom, Cleanth Brooks, Ivor Winters, Monroe Beardsley, W. Wimsatt, R. S. Crane and Kenneth Burke had defined an aesthetics of literature which, even after being rejected by younger critics, still continues to serve as the basis for most debates in contemporary American literary theory. With the founders gone, what were the chances of renewal? With Erich Auerbach, Joseph Frank, Meyer Abrams, Wayne Booth and Northrop Frye, American literary studies went through a period of balanced formalism, quite similar to that of French poetics of the 1960s. Thereafter, moderate and programmatic structuralism had little appeal for a milieu long dominated by textual formalism. In addition, literary scientism had and has no chance of success in a country in which the universities consider themselves to be the main depositories of high culture and humanist values. The political radicalism of the late 1960s and early 1970s did not generate enough movement within the humanities to be taken as a credible response to the anxiety of backwardness. On the contrary, through its violently anti-cultural choices, the radicalism of the 1960s added to the disarray in the humanities by emphasizing the social marginality of literature and, more generally, of the universities.

In the context of such anxieties, one can better situate the rise of deconstructionist criticism (Geoffrey Hartmann, Paul de Man, J. Hillis Miller and, in the following generation, Shoshana Felman and Barbara Johnson). The publications of these critics expresses doubts about their own place in the world of knowledge. With the help of Derridian dialectics, a doctrine based entirely on barely perceptible shades of meaning promotes marginality as a redeeming value; at the same time, the rejection of traditional criticism soothes the anxiety of backwardness. Similar to the strategy of the nineteenth-century transcendentalists, the Yale school, by opposing rationalist modernization, reiterates the crucial mission of literary studies in a world invaded by scientific utilitarianism. The criticism of logocentrism proclaims the humanist interpretations of literature obsolete, yet philology and hermeneutics exerted a strong influence on the members of this school as if, once the techniques of deconstruction had been adopted and the anxiety of backwardness appeased, the nostalgia of disciplinary traditions in turn received the right to express itself.

In France, at the other end of this scenario, the counter-modernizers opposed scientistic structuralism to promote speculative structuralism. In the absence of direct causal links, it is this aspect of the 1960s that best accounts for the family resemblances between poststructuralism and the explosion of May 1968: both were opposed to the ethics of accumulation and of postponement, both thrived under subversive and libertine expenditure. Made possible by prosperity, the spirit of this rebellion faded as soon as unexpected shortages started to threaten the well-being founded upon discretionary expenditure a few years later. And with the weakening of counter-ethics, the force of poststructuralism decreased as well. There were fewer novel ideas, fewer new disciples; the old labels started to be dropped, the name of the trend itself was rejected. The first wave of resistance took shape around 1977; several important participants recanted publicly. Some of the *maîtres à penser* disappeared. Towards the mid-1980s, the double failure of the forced modernization and of the ideological counter-modernization in the human sciences was apparent: in Paris, one could again talk about erudition, history and philology; about ethics and axiology too. Should one see in these fashionable topics the themes of a new turn? Is it possible that, having played at language games until dizziness set in, French thought, satiated with words, is now seeking the meaning of action, in accordance with Goethe's advice? Or, like other periods saturated with positivism, this one will privilege the study of culture?

These choices remain to be made. In the meantime, we should avoid the rhetoric of the end. As long as the causes that favoured the rise of various structuralisms continue to act – the 'relative deprivation' of the humanities and the social sciences, the tensions between the work ethic and the culture of dissipation, the prosperity in advanced countries that encourages discretionary behaviour – epistemological modernism, even after its novelty has worn off, will certainly maintain its influence. Promises, even ill-kept ones, retrospectively illuminate our life-paths: whether we applaud or deplore its disappearance, the linguistic mirage will leave behind an indelible memory of its radiance.

Post-Scriptum: The Heidegger Affair

Since the publication of the French edition of this book, another symptom of intellectual change has stirred the Parisian scene: the debate around Martin Heidegger, triggered by the realization that during the early 1930s the German philosopher had been a fervent supporter of National Socialism. At the same time, literature departments in American universities were briefly enlivened by the discovery that, as a young man, the late Paul de Man, one of the founders of deconstructive criticism, had regularly contributed to a pro-Nazi daily during the German occupation of Belgium.

The Heidegger debate reached considerable proportions. It started with a book by Victor Farias, *Heidegger et le nazisme (Heidegger and Nazism*, Paris, 1987) which provides a wide range of evidence about Heidegger's engagement with the National Socialist regime. Some of the facts had long been known, and, as Farias's critics were quick to point out, not all of the newer material was fully convincing. In addition, Farias's discussion avoids philosophical topics and often overinterprets Heidegger's most innocuous statements as anti-Semitic or pro-Nazi. Yet, despite these weaknesses, the book is a powerful demonstration (or reminder) that the philosopher who most influenced French thought in the twentieth century had openly supported the Nazis' rise to power and, after their defeat, never condemned them in unambiguous terms.

Paris is an ideal arena for spectacular intellectual polarization. Through 1987 and 1988, articles, books and special issues of journals devoted to Heidegger's political past flooded the market. Pierre Aubenque, Jean Baudrillard, Maurice Blanchot, Pierre Bourdieu, Michel Deguy, Jacques Derrida, François Fédier, Luc Ferry, Alain Finkielkraut, Elisabeth de Fontenay, Gérard Granel, Jeanne Hirsch, Philippe Lacoue-Labarthe, Emmanuel Levinas, Jean-François Lyotard, Alain Renaut, Tzvetan Todorov and many others took a public stand.

The defenders of Heidegger had no easy task. Some simply denied the facts or attempted to separate Heidegger's biography from his philosophy, arguing that any criticism of his work is an assault on Thought itself. Others accepted the evidence of Heidegger's intellectual involvement with Nazism but made the distinction between a romantic, utopian

National Socialism, free from anti-Semitism and the vulgar, Hitlerian variety. According to François Fédier (1988), for example, in the early 1930s visionary National Socialism would have represented little more than the desire shared by the entire German nation, including the left, to restore to Germany its dignity. Heidegger's adhesion to Nazism thus reflected a German national consensus. Disappointed by Hitler's betrayal of the true National Socialist ideals, Heidegger became a silent opponent of the regime. According to others, such as Jacques Derrida (1987), Heidegger never fully supported Nazism: a careful reading of his early public endorsements supposedly reveals a discreet opposition to racism in the name of spiritual values. Still others, such as Philippe Lacoue-Labarthe (1987) assert that Heidegger's philosophical opposition to humanism should not be seen as a proof of his Nazism; on the contrary, the National Socialist error was to take humanism seriously. The Nazi belief that a superior race can change the course of history was simply another form of the Enlightenment's confidence in humanity, albeit stripped of its universalistic pretensions. Only a Heideggerian deconstruction of humanism can provide the effective means of opposing Nazism.

All these approaches are marred with difficulties, but the last two particularly so. If Nazism is indeed a variety of humanism, the difference between its political programme and that of liberal societies needs to be explained. And if the difference is only one of the nuances, by what principle can one oppose Nazism? More practically speaking, how can one equate the self-confessed fallibility of democracies with the destructive self-confidence of totalitarian systems? Moreover, how can one claim that Heidegger's anti-humanism, which consists of the most vague and obscure statements, is the only genuine defence against Nazism? (Isn't it rather fortunate that half a century ago the adversaries of Nazi Germany had other weapons to rely upon?) The defence of anti-humanism and the legacy of Heidegger seem to be unconditionally linked. None of Heidegger's advocates who equate anti-humanism with anti-Nazism questioned the current relevance of Heidegger's philosophy. None has proposed an argument of the form: 'Among the concepts, methods and analyses Heidegger developed, A, B and C are illuminating and have been influential in fields D, E and F; his notions G, H and I, however, are insufficiently elaborated.' The very form of such an argument is precluded by the Heideggerian style of thought, which, as Pierre Bourdieu (1988) has keenly demonstrated, soars high above judgements in terms of results or influence. Yet, like science, literature and the arts, philosophy has always been evaluated in such terms. Philosophers applaud Leibniz's monadology and criticize his theodicy; why not, for instance, praise Heidegger's existential analytics and reject his notion of 'historiality', as Austrian, German and Anglo-American philosophers have? In France too, for a long time, Heidegger was the target of both admiration and criticism. Sartre's indebtedness to existential phenomenology did not prevent him from articulating his dissent from Heidegger's political opinions and anti-humanism. Unconditional Heideggerism is a relatively new phenomenon, whose occurrence needs explanation.

Why did Heideggerism attain such prominence in France during the 1960s and 1970s? And what does the Heidegger scandal reveal about contemporary French intellectual life? Luc Ferry and Alain Renaut (1988) do much to answer the first question. They submit that Heidegger's success as the French 'main left-wing philosopher' is largely a result of the postwar demoralization of Western Europe. The horror of two world wars, the rise of totalitarian regimes and the decay of the colonial empires discredited the intellectual ideals of Western European democracies. The principles of the Enlightenment, which had long governed liberal societies, were deemed responsible for the evils of the twentieth century: universalism had become Europeocentrism, rationalism had degenerated into technocracy, and democracy into state terrorism.

Since intellectuals play a critical role in liberal societies, and evils perceived as radical require radical opposition, Western European and especially French intellectuals turned to the radical critics of modern liberal society: Marx and Heidegger. Until the mid-1970s, Marxism satisfied the need for a radical anti-liberal doctrine and encouraged the hope that the programme of the Enlightenment might be achieved after all. Heidegger's conservative anti-modernism was outweighed by the Marxist confidence in a future, fully rational society. During the 1970s and 1980s, however, in the wake of the Soviet's invasion of Afghanistan and military repression in Poland, French intellectuals began to associate Marxism with imperialism and state terror. They were left with Heideggerism as the only radical critique of modern democracy.

To this situation can be added the factors I discussed earlier in chapter 6: the French tradition of strong but fleeting infatuations with literary geniuses alive or dead; the failure of the system of intellectual controls during the 1960s and 1970s; and the rise of discretionary intellectual behaviour with its conspicuous disregard for the moral premisses or the consequences of theories. In these circumstances, the fascination with Heidegger's thought became independent of anything he could have said or done, including his endorsement of the Nazis.

Why, then, should Heidegger's past support for National Socialism suddenly cause such a furor in 1988? True, earlier French translators of Heidegger had pruned some of the more compromising texts, and Farias's book provides new details about Heidegger's involvement with the Nazis. But Heidegger's political affiliation had been a matter of public knowledge since the end of the Second World War. The occurrence and the intensity of the Heidegger affair has more to do with changes in French politics and culture than with new facts about Heidegger.

First, the memories of Nazism and the war have begun to fade; the youngest witnesses of Hitler's rise and fall – those who in 1933 were, say, 15 years old – are now 70. Anyone aged 42 and under was born after the end of the Second World War. Moreover, while wars and massacres have occurred since then, for many the Nazi extermination camps, with their mixture of irrationality of purpose and technological execution, remain unique. Furthermore, by the early 1970s all the fascist regimes had disappeared in Europe and only a handful survived elsewhere. In the past few years, an intense effort has been made to find the last living witnesses of Nazism and record their testimony. The film *Shoah* is the most notable example of this effort. Ironically, the passage of time has not only made the recording of past horrors more pressing but also rendered it less effective. As the last survivors of Nazi concentration camps were recounting their past agony, a revisionist trend among German historians was emphasizing the resemblance between Hitler's and Stalin's repressive techniques, depicting the Nazis as simply one among several instances of modern political demonism. Furthermore, related to the decline of French Marxism, the resemblance between Hitlerism and Stalinism has become an accepted truth among French intellectuals in the 1980s.

Secondly, although asking whether the Nazi concentration camps were worse than those of Stalin is probably pointless, since there is a magnitude of evil which precludes quantification, the mere fact of asking such a question is significant. It indicates a new sensitivity to the human cost of radical projects and a willingness to apply humanist moral criteria to political operations. In France, after the decline of the *maîtres à penser*, the new humanist sensitivity was reinforced by the rise of what A. Finkielkraut calls *la pensée 80* (the thought system of the 1980s), that is, a rationalist-democratic consensus the most striking feature of which is the simultaneous growth of a liberal (i.e., neo-conservative) school of political thought and a rationalist left.

Perhaps no other element in French cultural life reveals this shift more dramatically than the new attitude towards the 1789 Revolution. François Furet's *Penser la Révolution française* (*Thinking the French Revolution*, 1978) successfully ended the traditional polemics between the right-wing rejection and the left-wing celebration of the Revolution. Several well-entrenched beliefs about the Revolution have since been severely scrutinized: that the Revolution was inevitable, that it arose out the class struggle between the Third Estate and the aristocracy, and that its human costs were negligible and excusable. Once the Hegel–Guizot–Marx explanatory model had lost its predominance, the Revolution started to look less like the inevitable result of historical progress and more like an adventurous series of political experiments. As such, it became subject to rational evaluation, especially in terms of human suffering. Hence the new interest in, and condemnation of, the period of the Terror of 1793. By implication a future Revolution is pointless, since democracy has been painfully achieved in the wake of the old one, and an involvement in grand historical projects waives neither moral responsibility nor punctilious respect of individual rights. For the new rationalist consensus, mass terror is the universal criterion for rejecting political systems, right or left, past or present.

Thirdly, by the early 1980s it had become clear that intellectual life in France and elsewhere could successfully survive the implementation of universal education. During the 1960s, with the quantitative explosion of higher education, the first generation of new students hoped to achieve the same intellectual level and social status as the graduates previously produced by the elitist system. But instead, under the pressure of sudden change, the general level of university education dropped, and along with it new graduates' chances of success. The tension between rising expectations and built-in disappointment undoubtedly contributed to the widespread student unrest in the late 1960s. It helps account for the rise of the *maîtres à penser*: those intellectual stars, shining high above the insignificance of the mass universities, offered the expanding intellectual public a compelling promise of salvation. But the students coming to university after the mid-1970s understood the realities of contemporary higher education better than their predecessors and adjusted their expectations accordingly. The universities also recovered after the initial shock and a brief period of disarray; although they could not uniformly attain the highest quality, they each reached some form of intellectual equilibrium.

The analogy with the development of mass democracy in our century is striking. Its sudden advent in Europe after the First World War led to disarray, political tensions and the success of mass dictators – Mussolini, Stalin and Hitler, as well as other lesser figures. But extended exercise of democracy in Western Europe (*pace* Ortega y Gasset) gradually divided the once homogeneous masses into various constituencies well aware of their own interests and adept at using democracy to achieve them peacefully. If, in the 1920s and 1930s, authoritarian leaders appeared desirable to many, in the 1980s even mild authoritarian rule was unthinkable in Western Europe.

Likewise, once the initial confusion of mass education had been overcome, the figure of the intellectual saviour lost its appeal. Mystifying and disappointing as it appeared during the 1960s, the new university gradually learned to split itself into innumerable groups, each defending its intellectual and political projects. Today, what some deplore as the fragmentation of the intellectual life represents the routine of academic pluralism.

Fourthly, and more locally, in contrast with the new democratic consensus during the mid-1980s, a temporary surge in the popular appeal of a right-wing xenophobic political party (Jean-Marie Le Pen's

National Front) alerted politicians and intellectuals to the recurrent danger of nationalism. Supporters of the National Front advocated a nationalist conservatism; although they carefully avoid biological racism, their blatant anti-immigration bias, as well as their populist rhetoric, recalled unpleasant memories.

Given these factors – the renewed interest in Nazism, the establishment of a rationalist consensus with an emphasis on human rights, the relative stability of higher education leading to the disappearance of the *maîtres à penser*, and the recurrent bursts of conservative nationalism – the revelations about Heidegger's political past, whether genuinely new or not, provided an exceptionally suitable ground for testing the strength of the new orthodoxy. The enemy of democracy and human rights who preaches dubious revolutions and refuses rational deliberation is the archetypal *bête noire* of the rationalist thinkers of the 1980s. The recent interest in the Nazis and the temporary success of the National Front require that he should have mingled with fascism. Finally, as a Master Thinker, he must have been or still be the object of an unconditional cult. No major figure satisfies these requirements as thoroughly as does Heidegger.

His writings display all the intellectual features of the above archetype. An idiosyncratic style, deliberately obscure, is put to the service of a strongly anti-modern message. Rationality, science, Enlightenment and democracy are more often contemptuously rejected than rationally criticized. After bringing his disciples to despair about the world, he mysteriously points to a radical alternative. Is this just utopian thinking on his part? Or a prophetic vision of *l'inouï* (the unheard-of), as his left-wing followers believe? Not at all, Farias reminds us: Heidegger's alternative to modern democracy is Hitler's National Socialism.

As a consequence, Heidegger's opponents present him as the incarnation of everything that must be expelled from French intellectual life if it is to prosper democratically: obscurantism, anti-humanism, revolutionary conservatism. He becomes the last, most powerful, yet easiest materialization of the Master Thinker to debunk. The last, because Heidegger, though considered by many as a contemporary philosopher, has at the time of the debate been dead for over ten years; the most powerful, because none of the Masters of the 1960s had or claimed to have Heidegger's stature and influence; the easiest to debunk, because as a German involved with the Nazis, he believed in a bygone nationalist ideology that few intellectuals would openly vindicate today. The attack on the distant past of a deceased foreigner unwittingly acquires a symbolic value: it implies that, though difficult and painful, all the issues involved in the debate belong to a remote intellectual and political horizon, be they Nazism, anti-humanism, or anti-democracy. For Heidegger's critics, his adhesion to Nazism deserves a three-fold condemnation: as past complicity with a right-wing murderous political system, as an obsolete model for contemporary left-wing anti-democratic thought, and as a representative of the extinct race of Master Thinkers. The intellectual level of the National Front being far below that of Heideggerism, the existence of a contemporary conservative nationalism barely affects Heidegger's offences.

If this assessment is correct, then those who attempted to defend Heidegger in the name of anti-humanism when Farias's book was published made a serious strategic mistake, since on political grounds Heidegger's accusers possess a decisive advantage. Those who revere Heidegger's thought should, at this point, attempt to move the debate to philosophical grounds, as Lacoue-Labarthe begins to do in some parts of his book. If this succeeds, the best way to safeguard Heidegger's memory would consist in ceasing to treat his thought as the unsurpassable model of philosophy. A re-evaluation of Heidegger's place in the context of twentieth-century German intellectual life is needed, as is a demonstration that Heidegger's philosophy is still relevant for contemporary moral and political concerns. Heidegger's admirers should realize that in relation to great philosophers, devotion should not inhibit criticism.

It is significant that the attack against Heidegger and, through him, the alliance between intellectual radicalism and anti-democratic politics focuses on the philosopher's life rather than his thought. Farias's book pays no attention to philosophy; many other participants in the debate have focused on minor texts, trying to derive from them biographical instead of philosophical lessons. This feature too is indicative of a change in the intellectual atmosphere. No one was more emphatically committed to humanism and left-wing politics than Sartre, yet 40 years ago, he examined Heidegger's political past and declared it irrelevant for an assessment of his philosophy. The intellectuals of the 1980s will not permit a distinction between a philosopher's ideas and his political choices. Having gone through war, tyranny and occupation, Sartre and his contemporaries – Dieter Bonhoeffer and Heidegger himself – were more sensitive than we are to the multiple layers human consciousness develops under political oppression; they acquired first-hand knowledge of the mechanisms through which totalitarian systems distort moral awareness. They understood that, though a philosopher or writer may have behaved despicably in such circumstances, his intellectual work might – just might – well remain unaffected by his personal failures. For those familiar with tyranny and war, the fact that Heidegger was an unrepentant supporter of some version of National Socialism did not necessarily entail that his philosophy was as Nazi as his politics. This does not mean, of course, that politics and philosophy have as little to do with each other as politics and mathematics. But the *affinities* between philosophy and politics (to use Bourdieu's term) are complex.

In contrast, for the French generation that has spent its entire adult existence in a peaceful, wealthy democracy, the most traumatic experience of political opposition (in a country in which both the radical left and the radical right are allowed to be active) was the playful rebellion of 1968. In the past decade, many members of this generation rejected the radical positions of the 1960s, articulating their newly found moderation in opposition to the Master Thinkers of the recent past. Yet their exposure to totalitarian regimes is limited to the Soviet system of the 1970s and early 1980s, which cannot sustain comparison with the great age of demonism. Consequently, it is difficult for a generation that identifies courageous opposition with articulate discourse to imagine situations in which silence is a form of courage.

It is even more difficult to grasp the complexity of the mediations between philosophical concepts and political consequences. In a relatively open dynamic society founded on the principles of the Enlightenment, every new political project in theory has a chance of being implemented; moreover, since in theory such a society makes decisions based on public deliberations, every political project must be openly defended in a coherent way. It is therefore in the interest of each political project to make its philosophy as explicit as possible. Consequently, citizens of liberal societies are quick to relate politics to philosophy and vice versa.

In contrast, in non-liberal societies – and this includes twentieth-century authoritarian regimes as well as older forms of absolutism – political projects are judged in secret by a small group of potentates according to the criterion of allegiance to the official ideology. In order to succeed, new political projects must hide as skillfully as possible their own underlying philosophy and demonstrate real or, more often, imaginary loyalty to the official philosophy. Thus, citizens of non-liberal states are particularly adept at minimizing the relationship between politics and philosophy.

This line of reasoning has already been used, though not very effectively, in defence of Heidegger's postwar silence about Nazism. Heidegger was no Boris Pasternak, courageous by restraint. Throughout his philosophical career, and particularly after Hitler's consolidation in power, Heidegger, like many other citizens of a non-liberal system, carefully aimed at dissociating philosophy from politics. This would not excuse his obstinate reticence to comment on National Socialism. But it may help explain his reluctance to include explicit political propositions in his philosophical work and to discuss texts of political philosophy.

Conversely, despite their sophisticated reading of Heidegger's texts, Ferry and Renaut, as good citizens of a liberal country, neglect the intricate mediations which lead from abstruse philosophical concepts to moral and political options. For example, Ferry and Renaut reveal an important contradiction in Heidegger's thinking. On the one hand, Heidegger defends a non-voluntarist view of the human condition, arguing that the essence of metaphysics and, by implication of Western civilization, consists in the inevitable forgetfulness of Being. On the other hand, he entertains voluntarist hopes in a historical action that would correct this forgetfulness. According to Ferry and Renaut, this contradiction explains Heidegger's involvement with the Nazis, whom he expected to redirect the history of Being. Now, this contradiction cannot be merely a philosophical mistake of Heidegger's *directly* leading to a mistaken political choice, for the good reason that the philosophical tension between non-voluntarism and voluntarism is present in every theological reflection on human freedom, beginning with St. Augustine's doctrine of the free and bound will. Similarly, in his writings on grace, Blaise Pascal carefully distances himself both from Pelagian voluntarism and from Calvinist abdication of responsibility. As his early readers correctly saw, Heidegger transposes this aporia, formerly developed by religious thinkers, into a lay language by constructing a model that translates the state of grace into proximity to Being and fall into forgetfulness, and by setting this story in a mythical time dimension called historiality.

If indeed reflection on existential freedom spontaneously engenders the tension between voluntarism and non-voluntarism, this means, first, that the links between Heidegger's philosophical contradiction and his political choice are *mediated* by the conflictual structure of freedom as a philosophical problem; and secondly, that modernity is just one of the possible contexts of this conflict. So we cannot, within a single philosophical argument, *both* denounce Heidegger's association with the Nazis *and* accuse him of taking the wrong side in the dialectics of the Enlightenment. The two offences are not necessarily related. To profess a contradictory philosophy of human freedom does not always lead to totalitarian political options. Conversely, the rejection of Nazism does not have to come from the positions of the Enlightenment. An analysis that would take as its conceptual basis not the Enlightenment but, say, the Augustinian doctrine of the fragility of human will would consider Nazism as a new terrifying image of human dereliction rather than as a result of either modernity or anti-modernism.

A second example involves Ferry and Renaut's moral evaluation of phenomenology, which, following Sartre, they portray as a philosophy of freedom. Now, as Husserl's phenomenology was primarily a foundationalist philosophy of knowledge, to derive an ethics from it is a problematic task. One familiar manoeuvre consists in asserting that, since the *transcendental ego* – that is, the ultimate source of epistemological legitimacy – is conceived by Husserl as devoid of any ontological determination, *humans* are beings without an essence and endowed with full freedom. But what warrants the identification between humans and the transcendental ego? Besides, how can one derive a full morality from a philosophy with such a severely constrained point of view as phenomenology? Sartre's dialectics of instant freedom and decisive commitment contains only the rudiments of a full-fledged ethics. Its description of human destiny as a chain of momentary decisions independent of the individual's past may appear enticing today in a period of considerable social mobility. But its conformity with our present behaviour remains illusory. The natural, rational and historical determinations of human freedom continue to exert a relentless pressure, even if one can pretend to overlook their existence. Moreover, phenomenology's inability to develop an ethics may not be the exception but the rule. Ethics, some argue, might well altogether be situated beyond the limits of speculative philosophy.

These considerations indicate that the philosophical problems raised by Heidegger's affiliation with National Socialism are more complicated than the participants in the debate seem to acknowledge. Justified as it is, the moral indignation over the political choices of a great thinker should not lead us to reduce Heidegger's philosophy to his political acts, nor to believe that contemporary self-righteousness has clarified once and for all the difficult relations between philosophy, morality and politics.

The same point applies to the more limited debate around Paul de Man. Both Heidegger and Paul de Man were influential academics who at some point in their careers professed National Socialist opinions. In their respective fields, both became central figures of anti-humanist radicalism. Both exemplify the affinity between right-wing and left-wing opposition to liberal societies. Moreover, they belong to the same intellectual tradition: Heidegger's philosophy influenced de Man directly, as well as through Derrida. But some dissimilar features are also worthy of notice. In 1933 Heidegger, as a world-renowned philosopher, lent the new Nazi regime some of his own prestige by becoming a party member and an enthusiastic university rector. In contrast, de Man's involvement with the Nazis, shocking though it is, was the work of a careerless young man in a defeated country. It engendered a series of unexceptional literary reviews which virtually no one, then or later, admired or even notice. Whether or not we accept Derrida's notion of a Paul de Man who radically broke with his past (1988), de Man's mature work, produced and published more than 20 years later, bears no *salient* relation to his wartime book reviews.

This being said, a responsible debate on de Man could be of considerable use. Such a debate should concentrate on his critical work. Even more than in Heidegger's case, those who wish to criticize or defend de Man's contribution to literary theory should refrain from commenting interminably on his wartime articles. Rather, they should focus on his intellectual profile, the background of deconstructionism and the sociological significance of its status in contemporary American academia. It is time to research the intellectual legacy and implications of deconstructionism; to speculate on its place in the Romantic and Nietzschean tradition which led to, but not exclusively to, National Socialism; perhaps to ponder under what historical and epistemological circumstances a specialized field such as literary criticism can aspire to be at the vanguard of philosophical opposition to the established values. Equally interesting would be a sociological examination of success in contemporary academia. In America, for reasons having to do with its long history of tolerance and pluralism, Master Thinkers have never attained the clout they have in France. In their stead a different breed developed: the Academic Masters, intellectual figures who attained both an outstanding distinction and influence in their specialty and a certain philosophical or political prestige beyond it: Margaret Mead, anthropologist; Leo Strauss, political philosopher; B. F. Skinner, psychologist; Noam Chomsky, linguist; and Paul de Man, literary critic. All generated controversial yet decisive changes in their respective disciplines; they commanded or still command unparalleled respect among their followers, who, unlike their counterparts in France, rarely come from outside the original field; and all exercised or still exercise a certain amount of influence on the mainstream culture. But, fortunately, since they have never become the objects of an unconditional cult, their work has periodically been subjected to severe criticism: Skinner's refutation at the hands of Chomsky, the innumerable polemics around Chomsky's own work, Derek Freemen's critique of Margaret Mead. We should hope that Paul de Man's work will be discussed in an equally rigorous manner, and that the discovery of his wartime articles will not serve as a pretext for dismissing an important figure of contemporary criticism. In a cultural landscape so immense, divided and mobile as exists in the United States, the changing fortunes of academic theories are hardly noticed outside the tiny worlds of specialists. Some deplore the placidity of American academia. But if, forgoing the high drama of the Heidegger affair, it hosted a comprehensive discussion of deconstructionism, moral responsibility and the political commitment of intellectuals, American intellectual life can reap lasting benefits.

Notes

Chapter 1 The Order of Language

There are numerous excellent discussions of the structuralist and post-structuralist trends in France. Richard Harland, *Superstructuralism: The Philosophy of Structuralism and Post-Structuralism* (London: Methuen, 1987) provides a balanced, informative approach. Jonathan Culler's *Structuralist Poetics* (Ithaca, NY: Cornell University Press, 1975) and *On Deconstruction: Theory and Criticism after Structuralism* (Ithaca, NY: Cornell University Press, 1982) cover literary criticism. Vincent Descombes, *Modern French Philosophy* (Cambridge University Press, 1980) acutely analyses the philosophical background of structuralism and poststructuralism in France since 1933. Jean-Marie Domenach, *Enquête sur les idées contemporaines* (Paris: Seuil, 1981) situates the structuralist and poststructuralist thinkers in the wider French intellectual context of the 1960s and 1970s, including history, sociology and the 'nouveaux philosophies'. John Fekete (ed.), *The Structural Allegory: Reconstructive Encounters with New French Thought* (Minneapolis: University of Minnesota Press, 1984) criticizes the period from a neo-Hegelian and neo-Marxist perspective.

Jean Piaget, *Structuralism* (New York: Basic Books, 1970); Phillip Petitt, *The Concept of Structuralism: A Critical Analysis* (Dublin: Gill and Macmillan, 1975); Terence Hawkes, *Structuralism and Semiotics* (London: Methuen, 1977) and Christopher Norris, *Deconstruction: Theory and Practice* (London: Methuen, 1982) successfully provide general introductions to these trends. Edith Kurtzweil, *The Age of Structuralism: Lévi-Strauss to Foucault* (New York: Columbia University Press, 1980) has a good bibliography which includes works on Henri Lefebvre and Alain Touraine. J. G. Merquior, *From Prague to Paris: A Critique of Structuralist and Post-Structuralist Thought* (London: Versus, 1986) is a strongly critical evaluation of Claude Lévi-Strauss's and Roland Barthes's intellectual careers set against the background of French intellectual history after 1945. For the historical background of structuralism, see also Jan M. Broekman, *Structuralism: Moscow, Prague, Paris*

(Dordrecht: Reidl, 1974). Peter Dews, *Logics of Disintegration: Post-Structuralist Theory and the Claims of Critical Theory* (London: Versus, 1987) criticizes poststructuralism from the point of view of the Frankfurt School. Allan Megill, *Prophets of Extremity: Nietzsche, Heidegger, Foucault, Derrida* (Berkeley: University of California Press, 1985) offers a history of French poststructuralist philosophy in the context of modern anti-Enlightenment philosophy. For an interesting attempt to relate French poststructuralism to developments in German and American philosophy see Quentin Skinner 'Introduction' in Skinner (ed.), *The Return of Grand Theory in the Human Sciences* (Cambridge: Cambridge University Press, 1985) and Kenneth Baynes, James Bohman, and Thomas McCarthy (eds), *After Philosophy: End or Transformation?* (Cambridge, Mass.: MIT Press, 1987).

For dependable anthologies, see Richard Macksey and Eugenio Donato, (eds), *The Structuralist Controversy: The Legacy of Criticism and the Sciences of Man* (Baltimore: Johns Hopkins University Press, 1970); Michael Lane (ed.) *Introduction to Structuralism* (New York: Basic Books, 1970); and Josué Harrari (ed.), *Textual Strategies: Perspectives in Post-Structural Criticism* (London: Methuen, 1980).

Chapter 2 Technology and Regression

Edmund Leach's *Claude Lévi-Strauss* (London: Fontana, 1974) is still the best short introduction to Lévi-Strauss's work. James Boon, *From Symbolism to Structuralism: Lévi-Strauss in a Literary Tradition* (Oxford: Blackwell, 1972) investigates the literary background of Lévi-Strauss's ideas. J. G. Merquior's *From Prague to Paris* formulates strong criticisms, as does Simon Clarke's *The Foundations of Structuralism: A Critique of Lévi-Strauss and the Structuralist Movement* (Brighton: Harvester Press, 1981). For more criticism on Lévi-Strauss, see James Boon and David Schneider, 'Kinship *vis-a-vis* Myth: Contrasts in Lévi-Strauss' Approaches to Cultural Comparison', in *American Anthropologist* 76, 1974, pp. 799–817; Dan Sperber's article in *Structuralism and Since: from Lévi-Strauss to Derrida*, ed. John Sturrock (London: Oxford University Press, 1979); Dan Sperber, *Rethinking Symbolism* (Cambridge: Cambridge University Press, 1975); Raymond Boudon, *The Uses of Structuralism* London: Heinemann, 1971); Mary Douglas 'The Meaning of Myth', in *Implicit Meanings* (London: Routledge, 1975); Michael Riffaterre, 'Describing Poetic Structures: Two Approaches to Baudelaire's *Les Chats*', in *Structuralism*, ed. J. Ehrmann (Garden City: Doubleday, 1970); Ernest Gellner, 'What is Structuralism' in *Relativism and the Social Sciences*, (Cambridge: Cambridge University Press, 1985). Lévi-Strauss criticized Vladimir Propp's analysis of folktales in an article reprinted in *Structural Anthropology* (New York: Basic Books, 1976), vol. 2, ch. 8. Vladimir Propp's little known, biting answer has been published in *Dispositio* 1, 1976, pp. 277–92. On Lévi-Strauss's use of linguistics, see Georges Mounin, 'Lévi-Strauss et la linguistique' in *Introduction à la sémiologie* (Paris: Minuit, 1970).

Hans Aarsleff, *From Locke to Saussure: Essays on the Study of Language and Intellectual History* (Minneapolis: University of Minnesota Press, 1982) provides a careful evaluation of Saussure's place in modern linguistics. On the cult of Saussure during the 1960s, see Marc Angenot's article in *The Structural Allegory*, ed. John Fekete. The first chapter of Geoffrey Sampson's *Schools of Linguistics* (Stanford: Stanford University Press, 1980) offers a concise analysis of nineteenth-century linguistics. See also R. H. Robins' classic *A Short History of Linguistics* (Bloomington: Indiana University Press, 1967). A stimulating collection of articles is Roland Posner (ed.), *History of Linguistic Thought and Contemporary Linguistics* (Berlin: de Gruyter, 1975), especially Lorenzo Renzi's 'Histoire et objectifs de la typologie linguistique'. Eugenio Coseriu 'Georg von Gabelenz et la linguistique synchronique' in *Word* 23, 1970, pp. 74–100 has clarified the relation between Saussure and his neogrammarian predecessors. See K. R. Janowsky, *The Neogrammarians* (The Hague: Mouton, 1972) and the still useful I. Iordan, *An Introduction to Romance Linguistics*, translated, revised, and augmented by J. Orr (London: Methuen, 1937). See also Rullon Wells, 'Linguistics as Science: The Case of the Comparative Method', in Henry M. Hoenigswald (ed.), *The European Background of American Linguistics* (Dordrecht: Foris, 1979).

On the Prague circle, see J. Vachek (ed.), *A Prague School Reader in Linguistics* (Bloomington: Indiana University Press, 1964); Paul Garvin, *A Prague School Reader of Aesthetics, Literary Structure, and Style* (Washington: Georgetown University Press, 1964); and Frantisek Galan, *Historic Structures: the Prague School Project* (Austin: University of Texas Press, 1985). Ladislav Matejka (ed.), *Sound, Sign and Meaning* (Ann Arbor: Michigan Slavic Contributions, 1976) provides a fascinating list of the lectures given in the Prague linguistic circle between 1926 and 1948 at pp. 607–22. The two articles in phonology that most influenced Lévi-Strauss's myth analysis are N. Troubetzkoy, 'La Phonologie actuelle', in *Psychologie du langage* (Paris: Alcan, 1933) and Roman Jakobson, 'Observations sur le classement phonologique des consonnes', in *Proceedings of the Third International Congress of Phonetic Sciences* (Ghent, 1938).

Chomsky's criticisms of classical phonology are formulated in 'Current Issues in Linguistic Theory' in *The Structure of Language*, J. A. Fodor and J. J. Katz (eds, Englewood Cliffs, N. J.: Prentice Hall, 1964). An interesting collection on the history of phonology is V. B. Makkai (ed.),

Phonological Theory Evolution and Current Practice (New York: Holt, 1972), which includes J. Vachek's article 'On Some Basic Principles of "Classical" Phonology'.

Chapter 3 The Transcendental Ties of Linguistics

On the structuralist debate, see the books by Harland, Culler, Merquior, Descombes, Domenach, Kurtzweil. On semiotics, see the anthologies edited by Thomas Sebeok, *The Tell-Tale Sign* (Lisse: Peter de Rider, 1975) and Robert E. Innis, *Semiotics: An Introductory Anthology* (Bloomington: Indiana University Press, 1985), as well as Terence Hawkes, *Structuralism and Semiotics*. François Furet's 'Les Intellectuels français et le structuralisme', in *Preuves* 192, February 1967, pp. 3–12, is still illuminating.

On Derrida and Saussure, see the calm, competent criticism of Bertil Malmberg 'Derrida et la sémiologie: Quelques notes marginales', in *Semiotica* 11, 1974, pp. 189–99. Culler's *On Deconstruction* examines in detail the relationship between structuralism and Derrida's thought. A pertinent criticism of Saussure's theory of meaning in the context of contemporary literary theory is put forward by John Holloway, 'Language, Realism, Subjectivity, Objectivity', in *Reconstructing Literature* ed. Laurence Lerner, (Oxford: Blackwell, 1983) and the recent study by Raymond Tallis, *Not Saussure* (London: MacMillan, 1988).

For a favourable evaluation of deconstruction written from the hermeneutic point of view, see David C. Hoy, 'Derrida', in *The Return of Grand Theory in Human Sciences*, ed. Quentin Skinner. The recent *Derrida* by Christopher Norris (Cambridge, Mass.: Harvard University Press, 1987) contains a good bibliography, mostly devoted to the philosophical and literary consequences of Derrida's influence. Derrida's criticism of Saussure is briefly presented in ch. 4. Rudolph Gasché, *The Tain of the Mirror: Derrida and the Philosophy of Reflection* (Cambridge, Mass.: Harvard University Press, 1986) discusses Derrida's epistemology against the background of German Idealism. On the relation between Derrida, Nietzsche and Heidegger, see Allan Megill's *Prophets of Extremity*. Peter Dews, *Logics of Disintegration*, makes a provocative comparison between Derrida's early work and Schelling's philosophy.

Brice Parain's only book available in English, probably not his best, is *A Metaphysics of Language* (Garden City: Doubleday, 1971). A few indications on the relations between structuralism in linguistics and logical positivism are given in the first chapter of F. J. Newmeyer, *Linguistics Theory in America* (New York: Academic Press, 1980). See also Laurence D. Smith, *Behaviorism and Logical Positivism: A Reassessment of the Alliance* (Stanford: Stanford University Press, 1986).

Chapter 4 Games of Dispersion and the Correspondence Fallacy

The beginning of this chapter is dependent on Alexandre Koyré, *From the Closed World to the Infinite Universe* (Baltimore: Johns Hopkins University Press, 1957) and Imre Lakatos, *The Methodology of Scientific Research Programmes* (Cambridge: Cambridge University Press, 1978). For a history of American structuralist linguistics, see F. Niemeyer's *Linguistic Theory in America*; Niemeyer's perspective, however, is marred by his unconditional Chomskianism, which makes him see earlier structuralism as a mere preparation for the Chomskian revolution. Martin Joos (ed.), *Readings in Linguistics* (Chicago: University of Chicago Press, 1957) brings together the most important papers of the American structuralists, but not Zellig Harris's 'Distributional Structure', in *Word* 10, 1954, pp. 146–62. *Readings in Linguistics*, vol. 2, ed. Eric Hamp, Fred Householder and Robert Austerlitz (Chicago: University of Chicago Press, 1966) adds several significant contributions of European structuralist linguists from 1929 to 1961.

On Foucault, there are numerous monographs ranging from the enthusiastic books of Hubert L. Dreyfus and Paul Rabinow, *Michel Foucault: Beyond Structuralism and Hermeneutics* (Chicago: University of Chicago Press, 1982) and Gilles Deleuze, *Foucault* (Paris: Minuit, 1986) to the more hostile *Oublier Foucault* by Jean Baudrillard (Paris, Galilée, 1977) and *Foucault* by J. G. Merquior (London: Fontana, 1985). Merquior's essay offers an extensive bibliography which includes most of Foucault's critics. Among those, see George Huppert 'Divinatio et Eruditio: Thoughts on Foucault', in *History and Theory* 13, 1974, pp. 191–207; Alan Megill's chapters on Foucault in *Prophets of Extremity*; Marcel Gauchet and G. Swain, *La Pratique de l'esprit humain. L'institution asilaire et la révolution démocratique* (Paris: Gallimard, 1980); Michel Perrot (ed.), *L'Impossible prison: recherches sur le système pénitentiaire au XIXe siècle. Débat avec Michel Foucault* (Paris: Seuil, 1980). See also the chapter on Foucault and the evaluation of the polemics between Foucault and Derrida in Luc Ferry and Alain Renaut, *La Pensée 68: essai sur l'anti-humanisme contemporain* (Paris: Gallimard, 1985), pp. 120–9. A more positive note is struck by the special double issue of *Critique* devoted to Foucault, nos. 471–2 (August–September 1986).

Chapter 5 On Conventionalism in Poetics

Recent translations of some of A. J. Greimas' work include: *Semiotics and Language: An Analytical Dictionary* (with J. Courtés) (Bloomington: Indiana University Press, 1982); *Structural Semantics* (Lincoln: University of Nebraska Press, 1983); *On Meaning* (Minneapolis: University of Minnesota Press, 1987), with an introduction by Paul Perro and a foreword by F. Jameson. Ronald Schleifer's *A. J. Greimas and the Nature of Meaning* (London: Croom Helm, 1987) is a favourable introduction to Greimas' ideas. Clément Legaré's *La Bête à sept têtes et autres contes de Mauricie* (Québec: Quinze, 1980) has been severely criticized by Claude Bremond, 'Sémiotique d'un conte mauricien. Sur deux études de Clément Legaré' in *Recherches sémiotiques/ Semiotic Inquiry* 2, 1980, pp. 405–23. Legaré answered in *Recherches sémiotiques/Semiotic Inquiry* 4, 1984, pp. 202–15. Claude Bremond's earlier critique of Greimas' narrative grammars is formulated in *Logique du récit* (Paris: Seuil, 1973).

The dispute between radical and moderate conventionalism in aesthetics rests on an implicit acceptance of a constructivist psychology of perception. The differences between theoreticians most often concern the nature and proportions of the materials that contribute to the perceptual constructs. But constructivism is neither the only available theory of perception nor necessarily the correct one; J. Gibson's *The Ecological Approach to Visual Perception* (Boston: Houghton Mifflin, 1979) suggests an entirely different approach. It is indeed likely that classical poetics, which assumed reference and representation to be unproblematic operations, spontaneously rested on theories of the ecological type. E. Winner, *Invented Worlds: the Psychology of the Arts* (Cambridge, Mass.: Harvard University Press, 1982) presents the various theories of perception and examines their aesthetic consequences. Menahem Brinker's important article 'Verisimilitude, Conventions, and Belief', *New Literary History* 14, 1983, pp. 253–67, criticizes conventionalist theories of realism. A realist account of narrative categories in Victor Turner, 'Social Dramas and Stories About Them', in *From Ritual to Theater* (New York: Performing Arts Journal Publication, 1982). On artistic conventions, see ch. 5 of my book *Fictional Worlds* (Cambridge, Mass.: Harvard University Press, 1986). I am also indebted to Arthur Danto, *The Transfiguration of the Common Place* (Cambridge, Mass.: Harvard University Press, 1981); F. Sibley, 'Aesthetic Concepts', *Philosophical Review* 68, 1959, pp. 421–50; J. Margolis, 'The Ontological Peculiarity of Works of Art', in *Journal of Aesthetics and Art Criticism* 36, 1977, pp. 45–50, and *Art and Philosophy* (Atlantic Highlands: Humanities, 1980); Kendall Walton, 'Categories of Art,' *Philosophical Review* 79, 1970, pp. 334–67. Hilary Putnam's articles on functionalism have been collected in his *Mind, Language, and Reality: Philosophical Papers*, vol. 2 (Cambridge: Cambridge University Press, 1975).

Chapter 6 On Discretionary Intellectual Behaviour

Most histories of twentieth-century French philosophy insist on the rise and fall of grand philosophies: Bergsonism, various brands of existentialism, Marxism, and structuralism. Vincent Descombes's *Modern French Philosophy* is the best recent account. Read in contrast with Jean Lacroix, *Panorama de la philosophie française* (Paris: Presses Universitaires de France, 1966) or with Colin Smith, *Contemporary French Philosophy: A Study in Norms and Values* (London: Methuen, 1964), it clearly indicates the change in the French intellectual climate from the early 1960s to the early 1970s. Alan Montefiore (ed.) *Philosophy in France Today* (Cambridge: Cambridge University Press, 1983) includes statements by several major French philosophers. The mutual ignorance of French and Anglo-American philosophy of science for the most part of this century is well reflected in F. Châtelet (ed.) *Histoire de la philosophie, XXe siècle* (Paris: Hachette, 1973), which contains no cross-reference between the chapters on French epistemology by Marcel Fichant and logical positivism by Jacques Bouveresse. At the end of the volume, a highly idiosyncratic list of twentieth-century philosophical landmarks provides a vivid image of the late 1960s' orthodoxy. On the history of analytical philosophy, see A. J. Ayer's *Philosophy in the Twentieth Century* (New York: Vintage, 1984) and Hao Wang's *Beyond Analytical Philosophy* (Cambridge, Mass.: MIT Press, 1988). On the migration of philosophers, see Herbert Feigl 'The Wiener Kreis in America', in *The Intellectual Migration: Europe and America, 1930–1960*, ed. Donald Fleming and Bernard Bailyn (Cambridge, Mass.: Harvard University Press, 1969). See also R. Rorty's classical anthology *The Linguistic Turn: Recent Essays in Philosophical Method* (Chicago: University of Chicago Press, 1967).

Sherry Turkle, *Psychoanalytical Politics: Freud's French Revolution* (New York: Basic Books, 1978) has been commented upon by Raymond Boudon, 'The Freudian-Marxian-Structuralist (FMS) Movement in France: Variations on a Theme by Sherry Turkle', in *The Tocqueville Review* 2, 1980, pp. 5–24. See also Boudon, 'L'Intellectual et ses publics: les singularités françaises', in *Français qui êtes–vous?*, ed. Jean-Daniel Reynaud and Yves Grefmeyer (Paris: La documentation française, 1981). On May 1968, see the excellent article by Philippe Benéton and Jean Touchard, 'Les Interprétations de la crise de mai–juin 1968', *Revue Française de Sciences Politiques*, June 1970, pp. 503–41, as well as the comprehensive presentation of the events in Bernard Brown, *Protest in*

Paris: Anatomy of a Revolt (Morristown, N.J.: General Learning Press, 1974).

A judicious presentation of theories of social change is Andrew C. Janos, *Politics and Paradigms: Changing Theories of Social Change* (Stanford: Stanford University Press, 1986).

References

Aarne, Antti, and Stith Thompson, 1961, *The Types of Folktale: A Classification and Bibliography*, Helsinki: Academia Scientiarum Fennica.

Aarsleff, Hans, 1982, *From Locke to Saussure: Essays on the Study of Language and Intellectual History*, Minneapolis: University of Minnesota Press.

Aron, Raymond, 1968, *La Révolution introuvable. Réflexions sur la révolution de mai*, Paris: Fayard.

Ayer, A. J., 1984, *Philosophy in the Twentieth Century*, New York: Vintage.

Barthes, Roland, 1963, *On Racine*, trans. R. Howard, New York: Hill and Wang, 1964.

——, 1966, *Critique et Vérité*, Paris: Seuil. *Criticism and Truth*, Athlone, 1987.

——, 1967, *Elements of Semiology*, trans. Anette Lavers and Colin Smith, London: Cape.

——, 1968a 'The Death of the Author', in *Image, Music, Text*, trans. S. Heath, New York: Hill and Wang, 1977.

——, 1968b, 'The Reality Effect', in *French Literary Theory Today*, Tzvetan Todorov (ed.), Cambridge: Cambridge University Press, 1982.

Bataille, Georges, 1988, *The Accursed Share*, trans. R. Hurley, New York: Zone Books.

Baudrillard, Jean, 1977, *Oublier Foucault*, Paris, Galilée.

Baynes, Kenneth, James Bohman, and Thomas McCarthy (eds), 1987, *After Philosophy: End or Transformation*? Cambridge, Mass.: MIT Press.

Bazell, C. E., 1952, 'The Correspondence Fallacy in Structural Linguistics' in *Readings in Linguistics, II*, Eric Hamp, Fred W. Householder, and Robert Austerlitz (eds), Chicago: University of Chicago Press, 1966.

Bell, Daniel, 1976, *The Cultural Contradictions of Capitalism*, New

York: Basic Books.

Benéton, Philippe and Jean Touchard, 1970, 'Les Interprétations de la crise de mai-juin 1968', in *Revue Française de Sciences Politiques*, June 1970, pp. 503–41.

Bloch, Bernard, 1946, 'Studies in Colloquial Japanese. II: Syntax', *Language*, 22, pp. 200–48.

Bloomfield, Leonard, 1933, *Language*, New York: Holt.

Boon, James, 1972, *From Symbolism to Structuralism: Lévi-Strauss in a Literary Tradition*, Oxford: Blackwell.

—— and David Schneider, 1974, 'Kinship *vis-à-vis* Myth: Contrasts in Lévi-Strauss Approaches to Cultural Comparison', in *American Anthropologist* 76, pp. 799–817.

Boudon, Raymond, 1971a, 'L'Intellectuel et ses publics: les singularités françaises', in *Français qui êtes-vous?*, Jean-Daniel Reynaud and Yves Grefmeyer (eds), Paris: La documentation française.

——, 1971b, *The Uses of Structuralism*, London: Heinemann.

——, 1980, 'The Freudian-Marxian-Structuralist (FMS) Movement in France: Variations on a Theme by Sherry Turkle', in *The Tocqueville Review*, 2, pp. 5–24.

Bourdieu, Pierre, 1988, *L'Ontologie politique de Martin Heidegger*, Paris: Minuit.

Bouveresse, Jacques, 1984a, *La Philosophie chez les autophages*, Paris: Minuit.

——, 1984b. *Rationalité et cynisme*, Paris: Minuit.

Bremond, Claude, 1973, *Logique du récit*, Paris: Seuil.

——, 1982, 'Sémiotique d'un conte mauricien. Sur deux études de Clement Legaré' in *Recherches sémiotiques/Semiotic Inquiry*, 2, pp. 405–23.

—— and Jean Verrier, 1982, 'Afanasiev and Propp', trans. T. Pavel and M. Randall, in *Style*, 18, 1984, pp. 177–95.

Brinker, Menahem, 1983, 'Verisimilitude, Conventions, and Belief', *New Literary History*, 14, pp. 253–67.

Broekman, Jan M., 1974, *Structuralism: Moscow, Prague, Paris*, Dordrecht: Reidl.

Brooke-Rose, Christine, 1980, 'The Evil Ring: Realism and the Marvelous', in *Poetics Today*, pp. 67–90.

Brown, Bernard, 1974, *Protest in Paris: Anatomy of a Revolt*, Morristown, N.J.: General Learning Press.

Carnap, Rudolf, 1936–7, 'Testability and Meaning', in *Philosophy of Science*, 3, pp. 419–71; 4, pp. 1–40.

Châtelet, F. (ed.), 1973, *Histoire de la philosophie, XXe siècle*, Paris: Hachette.

Chomsky, Noam, 1955, *The Logical Structure of Linguistic Theory*, New York: Plenum Press.

——, 1964, 'Current Issues in Linguistic Theory', in J. A. Fodor and J. J. Katz (eds), *The Structure of Language*, Englewood Cliffs, N.J.:

Prentice Hall.
Clarke, Simon, 1981, *The Foundations of Structuralism: A Critique of Lévi-Strauss and the Structuralist Movement*, Brighton: Harvester Press.
Compagnon, Antoine, 1983, *La Troisième République des Lettres*, Paris: Seuil.
——, 1984, 'Le débat du *Débat*', in *Le Débat*, 32, pp. 176–7.
Constant, Benjamin, 1816, *Adolphe*, trans. Carl Wildman, London: Hamilton, 1948.
Coseriu, Eugenio, 1970, 'Georg von Gabelenz et la linguistique synchronique', in *Word*, 23, pp. 74–100.
Culler, Jonathan, 1975, *Structuralist Poetics*, Ithaca, NY.: Cornell University Press.
——, 1982, *On Deconstruction: Theory and Criticism after Structuralism*, Ithaca, NY: Cornell University Press.
Danto, Arthur, 1981, *The Transfiguration of the Common Place*, Cambridge, Mass.: Harvard University Press.
——, 1985, *Narrative and Knowledge*, New York: Columbia University Press.
Deleuze, Gilles, 1986, *Foucault*, Paris: Minuit.
Derrida, Jacques, 1963, *Edmund Husserl's 'Origin of Geometry': An Introduction*, trans. John. P. Leavy, Jr, Stony Brook, N.Y.: Nicholas Hays, 1978.
——, 1967a, *Speech and Phenomena and Other Essays on Husserl's Theory of Signs*, trans. David B. Allison, Evanston: Northwestern University Press, 1973.
——, 1967b, *Of Grammatology*, trans. G. Spivak, Baltimore: Johns Hopkins University Press, 1976.
——, 1987, *De l'esprit*, Paris: Galilée.
——, 1988, 'Paul de Man's War', in *Critical Inquiry*, 14, pp. 590–652.
Descombes, Vincent, 1980, *Modern French Philosophy*, Cambridge: Cambridge University Press.
——, 1983, *Objects of All Sorts: A Philosophical Grammar*, trans. L. Scott-Fox and J. Harding, Oxford: Blackwell, 1986.
Dews, Peter, 1987, *Logics of Disintegration: Post-Structuralist Theory and the Claims of Critical Theory*, London: Versus.
Domenach, Jean-Marie, 1981, *Enquête sur les idées contemporaines*, Paris: Seuil.
Douglas, Mary, 1975, 'The Meaning of Myth', in *Implicit Meanings* London: Routledge.
Dreyfus, Hubert L. and Paul Rabinow, 1982, *Michel Foucault: Beyond Structuralism and Hermeneutics*, Chicago: University of Chicago Press.
Duchet, Claude, 1969, 'Roman et objects: l'exemple de *Madame Bovary*', in *Travail de Flaubert*, Paris: Seuil, 1983.
Ducrot, Oswald, et al., 1968, *Qu'est-ce que le structuralisme?*, Paris: Seuil.

Eco, Umberto, 1976, *A Theory of Semiotics*, Bloomington: Indiana University Press.

Fédier, François, 1988, *Heidegger: anatomie d'un scandale*, Paris: Laffont.

Feigl, Herbert, 1969, 'The Wiener Kreis in America', in *The Intellectual Migration: Europe and America, 1930–1960*, Donald Fleming and Bernard Bailyn (eds), Cambridge, Mass.: Harvard University Press.

Fekete, John (ed.), 1984, *The Structural Allegory: Reconstructive Encounters with New French Thought*, Minneapolis: University of Minnesota Press.

Ferry, Luc and Alain Renaut, 1985, *La Pensée 68: essai sur l'anti-humanisme contemporain*, Paris: Gallimard.

——, 1988, *Heidegger et les modernes*, Paris: Grasset.

Flaubert, Gustave, 1857, *Madame Bovary*, trans. F. Steegmuller, New York: Random, 1957.

——, 1951, *Oeuvres*, vol. 1, A. Thibaudet and R. Dumesnil (eds), Bibliothèque de la Pléiade, Paris: Gallimard.

Foucault, Michel, 1966, *The Order of Things: An Archeology of the Human Sciences*, trans. Alan Sheridan-Smith, New York: Random House, 1970.

——, 1969, *The Archeology of Knowledge*, trans. Alan Sheridan-Smith, London: Tavistock, 1972.

Fumaroli, Marc and Gérard Genette, 1984, 'Comment parler de la littérature?', in *Le Débat*, 29, pp. 139–57.

Furet, François, 1967, 'Les Intellectuels français et le structuralisme', in *Preuves* 192, pp. 3–12.

——, 1978, *Penser la Révolution française*, Paris: Gallimard.

Galan, Frantisek, 1985, *Historic Structures: the Prague School Project* Austin: University of Texas Press.

Garvin, Paul, 1964, *A Prague School Reader in Aesthetics, Literary Structure, and Style*, Washington: Georgetown University Press.

Gasché, Rudolph, 1986, *The Tain of the Mirror: Derrida and the Philosophy of Reflection*, Cambridge, Mass.: Harvard University Press.

Gauchet, Marcel and G. Swain, 1980, *La Pratique de l'esprit humain. L'institution asilaire et la révolution démocratique*, Paris: Gallimard.

Gellner, Ernest, 1985, 'What is structuralism', in *Relativism and the Social Sciences*, Cambridge: Cambridge University Press.

Genette, Gérard, 1966, *Figures of Literary Discourse*, trans. Alan Sheridan, New York: Columbia University Press, 1982.

Gibson, J., 1979, *The Ecological Approach to Visual Perception*, Boston: Houghton Mifflin.

Gombrich, E. H., 1960, *Art and Illusion*, Princeton: Princeton University Press.

——, 1965, 'Visual Discovery Through Arts', in *Psychology and the Visual Arts*, James Hogg (ed.), Harmondsworth: Penguin.

Goodman, Nelson, 1968, *Languages of Art*, Indianapolis: Bobbs-Merrill.
Greimas, A. J., 1966, *Structural Semantics*, Lincoln: University of Nebraska Press, 1983.
——, 1970, *On Meaning*, Minneapolis: University of Minnesota Press, with an introduction by Paul Perron and a foreword by F. Jameson, 1987.
——, 1976, *Maupassant: la semiotique du texte*, Paris: Seuil.
——, 1982, *Semiotics and Language: An Analytical Dictionary* (with J. Courtés), Bloomington: Indiana University Press.
Habermas, Jürgen, 1987, *The Philosophical Discourse of Modernity*, trans. F. Lawrence, Cambridge, Mass.: MIT Press.
Hamon, Philippe, 1973, 'Un Discours contraint', in R. Barthes et al. *Littérature et réalité*, Paris: Seuil, 1982.
Hamp, Eric, Fred Householder, and Robert Austerlitz (eds), 1966, *Readings in Linguistics II*, Chicago: University of Chicago Press.
Harland, Richard, 1987, *Superstructuralism: The Philosophy of Structuralism and Post-Structuralism*, London and New York: Methuen.
Harrari, Josué (ed.), 1980, *Textual Strategies: Perspectives in Post-Structural Criticism*, London: Methuen.
Harris, Zellig, 1946, 'From Morpheme to Utterance', in *Language*, 22, pp. 161–83.
——, 1954, 'Distributional Structure', in *Word*, 10, pp. 146–62.
Hawkes, Terence, 1977, *Structuralism and Semiotics*, London: Methuen.
Hjelmslev, Louis, 1943, *Prolegomena to a Linguistic Theory*, trans. F. J. Whitfield, Madison: University of Wisconsin Press, 1961.
——, 1954, 'La Stratification du langage', in *Word* 10, pp. 163–88.
Holloway, John, 1983, 'Language, Realism, Subjectivity, Objectivity', in Laurence Lerner (ed.), *Reconstructing Literature*, Oxford: Blackwell.
Hoy, David C., 1985, 'Derrida', in Quentin Skinner (ed.), *The Return of Grand Theory in Human Sciences*, Cambridge: Cambridge University Press.
Huppert, George, 1974, 'Divinatio et Eruditio: Thoughts on Foucault', in *History and Theory* 13, pp. 191–207.
Husserl, Edmund, 1913, *Logical Investigations*, vol. 1, trans. J. N. Findlay, New York: Humanities, 1970.
Innis, Robert E., 1985, *Semiotics: An Introductory Anthology*, Bloomington: Indiana University Press.
Iordan, Iorgu, 1937, *An Introduction to Romance Linguistics*, trans, rev. and augmented by J. Orr, London: Methuen.
Jakobson, Roman, 1938, 'Observations sur le classement phonologique des consonnes', in *Proceedings of the Third International Congress of Phonetic Sciences*, Ghent.
——, Gunnar Fant, and Morris Halle, 1952, *Preliminaries to Linguistic Analysis*, Cambridge, Mass.: MIT Press, 1963.

Janos, Andrew C., 1986, *Politics and Paradigms: Changing Theories of Social Change*, Stanford, Stanford University Press.

Janowsky, K. R., 1972, *The Neogrammarians*, The Hague: Mouton.

Joos, Martin (ed.), 1957, *Readings in Linguistics*, Chicago: University of Chicago Press.

Jørgensen, Jørgen, 1931, *A Treatise of Formal Logic*, Copenhagen: Levin and Munsgaard; London: Oxford University Press.

Kaisergruber, Danielle, David Kaisergruber, and Jacques Lempert, 1972, *Phédre de Racine. Pour une sémiotique de la représentation classique*, Paris: Larousse.

Koyré, Alexandre, 1957, *From the Closed World to the Infinite Universe*, Baltimore: Johns Hopkins University Press.

Kuhn, Thomas, 1962, *The Structure of Scientific Revolutions*, Chicago: University of Chicago Press.

Kurtzweil, Edith, 1980, *The Age of Structuralism: Lévi-Strauss to Foucault*, New York: Columbia University Press.

Lacoue-Labarthe, Philippe, 1987, *La Fiction du politique*, Paris: Bourgois.

Lacroix, Jean, 1966, *Panorama de la philosophie française*, Paris: Presses Universitaires de France.

Lakatos, Imre, 1978, *The Methodology of Scientific Research Programmes*, Cambridge: Cambridge University Press.

Lane, Michael (ed.), 1970, *Introduction to Structuralism*, New York: Basic Books.

Leach, Edmund, 1974, *Claude Lévi-Strauss*, London: Fontana.

Legaré, Clément, 1980, *La Bête à sept têtes et autres contes de Mauricie*, Québec: Quinze.

——, 1984, 'Poucet et le géant', in *Recherches sémiotiques/Semiotic Inquiry*, 4, pp. 202–15.

Lévi-Strauss, Claude, 1958, *Structural Anthropology*, New York: Basic Books, 1963.

——, 1971, *The Naked Man*, trans. John and Doreen Weightman, New York: Harper, 1981.

Lewis, David, 1969, *Convention*, Cambridge, Mass.: Harvard University Press.

Lyotard, Jean-François, 1979, *The Postmodern Condition: A Report on Knowledge*, trans. by G. Bennington and B. Massumi, Minneapolis: University of Minnesota Press, 1984.

Macksey, Richard and Eugenio Donato (eds), 1970, *The Structuralist Controversy: The Legacy of Criticism and the Sciences of Man*, Baltimore: Johns Hopkins University Press.

Malmberg, Bertil, 1974, 'Derrida et la sémiologie: Quelques notes marginales', in *Semiotica* 11, pp. 189–99.

Margolis, J., 1977, 'The Ontological Peculiarity of Works of Art', in *Journal of Aesthetics and Art Criticism*, 36, pp. 45–50.

——, 1980, *Art and Philosophy*, Atlantic Highlands: Humanities.
Matejka, Ladislav (ed.), 1976, *Sound, Sign and Meaning*, Ann Arbor: Michigan Slavic Contributions.
Megill, Allan, 1985, *Prophets of Extremity: Nietzsche, Heidegger, Foucault, Derrida*, Berkeley: University of California Press.
Merquior, J. G., 1985, *Foucault*, London: Fontana.
——, 1986, *From Prague to Paris: A Critique of Structuralist and Post-Structuralist Thought*, London: Versus.
Montefiore, Alan (ed.), 1983, *Philosophy in France Today*, Cambridge: Cambridge University Press.
Morin, Edgar, Claude Lefort, and J. M. Coudray, 1968, *Mai 1968: la brèche*, Paris: Fayard.
Mounin, Georges, 1970, *Introduction à la sémiologie*, Paris: Minuit.
Nora, Pierre, 1980, 'Que peuvent les intellectuels?' in *Le Débat*, 1, pp. 3–19.
—— and Marcel Gauchet, 1988, 'Mots-Moments', in *Le Débat*, 50, pp. 171–89.
Norris, Christopher, 1982, *Deconstruction: Theory and Practice*, London: Methuen.
——, 1987, *Derrida*, Cambridge, Mass.: Harvard University Press.
Parain, Brice, 1942, *Recherches sur la nature et les fonctions du langage*, Paris: Gallimard.
——, 1947, *L'embarras du choix*, Paris: Gallimard.
——, 1971, *A Metaphysics of Language*, Garden City: Doubleday.
Pavel, Thomas, 1985, *The Poetics of Plot: The Case of English Renaissance Drama*, Minneapolis: University of Minnesota Press.
——, 1986, *Fictional Worlds*, Cambridge, Mass.: Harvard University Press.
Perrot, Michel (ed.), 1980, *L'Impossible prison: recherches sur le système pénitentiaire au XIXe siècle. Débat avec Michel Foucault*, Paris: Seuil.
Petitt, Phillip, 1975, *The Concept of Structuralism: A Critical Analysis*, Dublin: Gill and Macmillan.
Piaget, Jean, 1970, *Structuralism*, New York: Basic Books.
Picard, Raymond, 1965, *Nouvelle critique ou nouvelle imposture?*, Paris: Pauvert.
Propp, Vladimir, 1928, *Morphology of the Folktale*, trans. L. Scott, rev. Louis A. Wagner, Austin: University of Texas Press, 1968.
——, 1946, *Les Racines historiques du conte merveilleux*, trans. L. Greul-Appert, Paris: Gallimard, 1983. English trans. of two chapters in V. Propp, *Theory and History of Folklore*, trans. A. Y. Martin and R. P. Martin, Minneapolis: University of Minnesota Press, 1984.
——, 1976, 'Study of the Folktale: Structure and History', in *Dispositio*, 1, pp. 277–92.
Putnam, Hilary, 1961, 'Some Issues in the Theory of Grammar',

in *Noam Chomsky: Critical Essays*, G. Harman (ed.), New York: Doubleday, 1974.

——, 1975, *Mind, Language, and Reality: Philosophical Papers*, vol. 2, Cambridge: Cambridge University Press.

Renzi, Lorenzo, 1975, 'Histoire et objectifs de la typologie linguistique', in Roland Posner (ed.), *History of Linguistic Thought and Contemporary Linguistics*, Berlin: de Gruyter.

Revel, Jean-François, 1976, *Pourquoi des philosophes, suivi de La Cabale des dévots*, Paris: Laffont.

Ricoeur, Paul, 1963, 'Structuralisme et herméneutique', in *Esprit*, (11), pp. 596–627.

——, 1967, 'La structure, le mot, l'événement', in *Esprit*, 35(5), pp. 801–20.

——, 1984, *Temps et Récit II: La Configuration dans le récit de fiction*, Paris: Seuil.

Riffaterre, Michael, 1970, 'Describing Poetics Structures: Two Approaches to Baudelaire's *Les Chats*', in J. Ehrmann (ed.), *Structuralism*, Garden City: Doubleday.

——, 1978, 'L'Illusion référentielle', in R. Barthes et alii, *Littérature et réalité*, Paris: Seuil, 1980.

Robins, R. H., 1967, *A Short History of Linguistics*, Bloomington: Indiana University Press.

Rorty, Richard (ed.), 1967, *The Linguistic Turn: Recent Essays in Philosophical Method*, Chicago: University of Chicago Press.

Roustang, François, 1986, *Lacan, de l'équivoque à l'impasse*, Paris: Minuit.

Sampson, Geoffrey, 1980, *Schools of Linguistics*, Stanford: Stanford University Press.

Sartre, Jean-Paul, 1976, *Critique of Dialectical Reason*, trans. A. Sheridan-Smith, London: New Left Books.

Saussure de, Ferdinand, 1878, *Mémoire sur le système primitif des voyelles dans les langues indo-européennes*, Leipzig: Teubner.

——, 1916, *Course in General Linguistics*, trans. Wade Baskin, New York: McGraw-Hill, 1959.

Schleifer, Ronald, 1987, *A. J. Greimas and the Nature of Meaning*, London: Croom Helm.

Sebeok, Thomas, 1975, *The Tell-Tale Sign*, Lisse: Peter de Ridder.

Sibley, F., 1959, 'Aesthetic Concepts', *Philosophical Review*, 68, pp. 421–50.

Skinner, Quentin, 1985, 'Introduction', in Skinner (ed.), *The Return of Grand Theory in the Human Sciences*, Cambridge: Cambridge University Press.

Smith, Colin, 1964, *Contemporary French Philosophy: A Study in Norms and Values*, London: Methuen.

Smith, Laurence D., 1986, *Behaviourism and Logical Positivism: A Reassessment of the Alliance*, Stanford: Stanford University Press.
Spacks, Patricia Meyer, 1986, *Gossip*, Chicago: University of Chicago Press.
Sperber, Dan, 1975, *Rethinking Symbolism*, Cambridge: Cambridge University Press.
Sturrock, John (ed.), 1979, *Structuralism and Since: from Lévi-Strauss to Derrida*, Oxford University Press.
Tallis, Raymond, 1988, *Not Saussure*, London: MacMillan.
The Quest of the Holy Grail, trans. P. Matarasso, Harmondsworth: Penguin, 1977.
Thuillier, Pierre, 1982, *Socrate fonctionnaire. Essai sur (et contre) l'enseignement de la philosophie à l'Université*, Bruxelles: Complexe.
Tocqueville, Alexis de, 1840, *Democracy in America*, vol. 2, trans. H. Reeves, New York: Vintage, 1945.
Todorov, Tzvetan, 1970, *The Fantastic: a Structural Approach to a Literary Genre*, trans. Richard Howard, Cleveland: Press of Caser Western University, 1973.
——, 1984, *Literature and its Theorists: A Personal View of Twentieth Century Criticism*, trans. Catherine Porter, Ithaca, N.Y.: Cornell University Press, 1987.
Troubetzkoy, N., 1933, 'La Phonologie actuelle', in *Psychologie du langage*, Paris: Alcan.
Turkle, Sherry, 1978, *Psychoanalytical Politics: Freud's French Revolution*, New York: Basic Books.
Turner, Victor, 1982, 'Social Dramas and Stories About Them', in *From Ritual to Theater*, New York: Performing Arts Journal Publication.
Vachek, J. (ed.), 1964, *A Prague School Reader in Linguistics*, Bloomington: Indiana University Press.
——, 1972, 'On Some Basic Principles of "Classical" Phonology', in V. B. Makkai (ed.), *Phonological Theory Evolution and Current Practice*, New York: Holt.
Walton, Kendall, 1970, 'Categories of Art', *Philosophical Review*, 79, pp. 334–67.
Wang, Hao, 1980, *Beyond Analytical Philosophy*, Cambridge, Mass.: MIT Press.
Wells, Rullon, 1979, 'Linguistics as Science: The Case of the Comparative Method', in Henry M. Hoenigswald (ed.), *The European Background of American Linguistics*, Dordrecht: Foris.
Winner, Ellen, 1982, *Invented Worlds: the Psychology of the Arts*, Cambridge, Mass.: Harvard University Press.
Wölfflin, Heinrich, 1915, *Principles of Art History: The Problem of the Development of Style in Later Art*, trans. M. D. Hottinger, New York: Dover, 1950.

Index

Aarslef, Hans, 19
Adorno, Theodor, 87
algebra, *see* language, difference
Althusser, Louis, 4, 6
anarchism, epistemological, 86–8
anthropology, British functionalism, 22, 23; and linguistics 10–11, 22–5
Aristotle, 43, 47
Aron, Raymond, 135
attention, in art and literature, 116–17
Augustine, 154

Bacon, Francis, 85
Balzac, Honoré de, 123, 124
Barthes, Roland, 3, 4, 5, 6, 39, 41, 96–9, 110, 112
Bataille, Georges, 142
Bazell, C. E., 77, 78
Bell, Daniel, 141
Benda, Julien, 133
Bergson, Henri, 128, 134
biuniqueness, 31, 34
Bloomfield, Leonard, 51, 80, 88
Boas, Franz, 22
Bonhoeffer, Dietrich, 152
Boudon, Raymond, 134–5
Bourdieu, Pierre, 152
Bourricaud, François, 134
Bouveresse, Jacques, 2
Bréal, Michel, 19
Bremond, Claude, 4, 106
Bresnan, Joan, 81
Brinker, Menahem, 111
Brooke-Rose, Christine, 111, 120–2
Bruno, Giordano, 75, 76
Burke, Edmund, 87
Burkhardt, Jacob, 9

Carnap, Rudolf, 56, 57
Chekhov, Anton, 92, 103, 120
Chomsky, Noam, 26, 30, 39, 57–8, 78, 81, 83
classes of equivalence, 53
Cleland, John, 122
Compagnon, Antoine, 2, 96, 127
conscience, and language, 40–3, 44
Constant, Benjamin, 113, 115–18, 120
context, distributional, 53, 83–4; linguistic and extralinguistic, 41
conventionalism, in aesthetics, 112–13; 118–24
Copernicus, Nicolaus, 92
correspondence fallacy, 77–9, 91
Couturat, Louis, 128
Culler, Jonathan, 102, 132–3
Cusanus, Nicolaus, 75

Danto, Arthur, 9
Deleuze, Gilles, 133

demonstrative effects, 177
Derrida, Jacques, 3, 4, 5, 6, 14–17, 44–73, 75, 76, 77, 88, 94, 126, 139, 142, 155
Descartes, René, 85
Descombes, Vincent, 2, 129
description, in literature, 113, 115–18, 122; classical shortcut, 116; realist detour, 117
difference, and algebra of language, 69–70; and deferral, 50–1, 66; between Being and beings, 67, 69; in Bloomfield, 80; and linguistic signs; 71–2; according to Saussure, 69–70, 72–3; and writing, 67–70
Dilthey, Wilhelm, 20
disciplines, proliferation of, 18
discourse, in Foucault, 88–92, discursive formations, 88–9, 92
discretionary behaviour, social, 141; and intellectual, 141–2
distributionalism, 79–85
Dreyfus affair, 96, 127, 129
Duchet, Claude, 111
Duhem, Pierre, 93, 128

Eco, Umberto, 38
emergence, 122–4
emic *vs* etic units, 32–4
empirico-transcendental sidestepping, 7, 92–3
end, of history, 9; rhetoric of the end, 8–15; as deconstruction, 13–15; as division, 11–13; as salvation, 10–11
Enlightenment, 86–7

Fant, Gunnar, 77
Farias, Victor, 146, 151, 152
Fédier, François, 147
Ferry, Luc, 2, 148, 153–4
Fillmore, Charles, 81
Finkielkraut, Alain, 149
Flaubert, Gustave, 113, 117–20, 123
formalism, in human sciences, 102–3; in linguistics, 58–61; in narrative semiotics, 106–9; in philosophy of language, 68
Foucault, Michel, 3, 5, 6, 11–14, 19, 85–95, 139
foundationalism, critique of, 63–5
Freud, Sigmund, 126
Fumaroli. Marc, 2
functionalism, 92, 122–3
Furet, François, 149

Gadamer, Hans Georg, 102
Galileo, 92
Gasché, Rodolphe, 93
Gauchet, Marcel, 93
Genette, Gérard, 2, 4, 39, 119
glossematics, 56–61
gnosis, 36–7, 109
Godzich, Wlad, 102
Goldmann, Lucien, 140
Gombrich, Ernst, 111–14, 115
Goodman, Nelson, 112–14, 116, 118
Greimas, Algirdas J., 4, 100–9, 126
Guattari, Felix, 133

Habermas, Jürgen, 2
Halle, Morris, 77
Hamon, Philippe, 111, 120–2
Harris, Zellig S., 26, 78, 79–82, 90, 139
Hegel, G. W. F., 7, 40, 54, 89, 126, 129; opposition in England and Austria, 127
Heidegger, Martin, 61, 64, 66, 69, 87, 126, 130, 146–55
Hempel, Carl, 63
hermeneutics, 38–9
Hilbert, David, 128
Hjelmslev, Louis, 6, 45, 48, 51, 54–61, 67, 71, 76, 78, 126, 139
Hockett, Charles, 80

human sciences, 23
humanism, synchretic, 3; and structuralism, 5
Humboldt, Wilhelm von, 10, 89
Huppert, Georges, 93
Husserl, Edmund, 20, 44–7, 52, 54, 62–5, 126, 129, 154

ideal objects, 61–3, 65
illusion, in art, 111–12; referential, 110
indetermination, conceptual, 74–6, 82, 92–3
indexical expressions, 52–4
intentionalism, in aesthetics, 99–100
invariance, 31, 33–4
isomorphism, in linguistics, 78

Jakobson, Roman, 11, 77–8, 126, 131
Jameson, Fred, 103
Jespersen, Otto, 102
Jones, Daniel, 56
Joos, Martin, 88
Jørgensen, Jørgen, 55

Kafka, Franz, 122
Kant, Immanuel, 61–6, 129
Kepler, Johannes, 76–7, 83, 92
Kleene, Stephen, 61
Kuhn, Thomas, 93

Lacan, Jacques, 3, 5, 133
Lacoue-Labarthe, Philippe 147, 152
Lakatos, Imre, 93
language, natural, 47–9, 65; as algebra, 60, 69–70; and conscience, 40–3, 44; as ideal object 65–6; *langage vs. langue*, 49, 50, 54, 68, 69–70; as proto-logic, 59–60
Lanson, Gustave, 96–7
Légaré, Claude, 101
Lévi-Strauss, Claude, 3, 4, 5, 6, 9–11, 23–37, 39, 76, 77, 84, 88, 104, 105–6, 126, 133, 138–40
Lewis, David, 119
linearity, 31, 33
linguistic turn, 2; in France, 16–17
linguistics, and comparative philology, 19, 21; creation of modern, 20–1; in France, 130–2; historical and synchronic, 23–4; history of, 18–21; according to Hjelmslev, 56–61; and metaphysics, 70–1; and phenomenology, 68–73; as science, 54, 70
literary criticism, American, 142–4; *nouvelle critique*, 96
local determinacy, 31, 34
logical positivism, 56–9
logocentrism, critique of, 15
Lyotard, Jean-François, 2, 8

Mach, Ernst, 20, 56
Madvig, J. N., 19
Maistre, Joseph de, 87
Malmberg, Bertil, 135
Man de, Paul, 146, 155–6
Margolis, Joseph, 122–3
Marlowe, Christopher, 122
Marx, Karl, 87, 126, 130, 137, 140, 148
Masaccio, 117
Mauron, Charles, 98
Mead, Margaret, 22
meaning, as difference, 80; as distribution, 78, 80; *see also* sign
Merquior, J. G., 93
methodology, 18, 20, 71; according to Foucault, 88–92; in anthropology, 22–5; in linguistics, 19–20, 79; and thematics in science, 71
modernization, intellectual, 18–19, 125–6, 134–40; of

anthropology, 22–5; delays, 136–8
Molière, Jean-Baptiste, 133
Mounin, Georges, 135
myth, Lévi-Strauss on, 26–37

narrative poetics, 109–11, 113–24
narrative, and philosophy, 8
Neurath, Otto, 56
Nida, Eugene, 80
Nietzsche, Friedrich, 66, 87, 126, 130
Nora, Pierre, 1
Nozick, Robert, 134

Oedipus myth, 27–8
Olbers, Heinrich, 74–5, 77
orality, 47

Parain, Brice, 40–3, 45, 131
Pascal, Blaise, 154
Paul, Hermann, 19
phenomenology, 40, 44–53, 54, 61–73; Derrida's critique of, 64–5; and linguistics, 68–73; and philosophy of mathematics, 62–3, 65
philosophy in France, and the Dreyfus affair, 127; German influence, 126–7; influence of analytical philosophy, 128–31; of language, 126–30
phonetic specifiability, in phonology 30, 31–2
phonetics, acoustic and articulatory, 77–8
phonology, 23; classical, 30–1; as instrument of modernization, 139; and myth-analysis, 28–7
Picard, Raymond, 39, 96
Pike, Kenneth L., 80
Plato, 64
poetics, in France, 138–9; *see also* narrative
Poincaré, Henri, 128
Popper, Karl, 57, 63, 93, 102
Post, E., 61
Propp, Vladimir, 104, 105–7
Putnam, Hilary, 92, 103, 123

quasi-transcendentals, 93–4
Quine, W. v. O., 58, 67, 88, 92

Racine, Jean, 98
Rawls, John, 64, 134
realism, in literature, 111, 114, 115–24; classicist realism, 115; psychological schematism, 115–16; realist detail, 111
reference, *see* meaning, sign
Renaut, Alain, 2, 148, 153–4
representation in art, as denotation, 112; as illusion, 111; in literature *vs*, painting, 117; pictographic, 114; and structural features, 119–24
Rickert, Heinrich, 20
Ricoeur, Paul, 39–40, 103
Riffaterre, Michael, 110
Rimmon-Kenan, Shlomith, 102
Rousseau, Jean-Jacques, 6
Rousset, Jean, 4
Roustang, François, 2
Russell, Bertrand, 128–9, 138

Sapir, Edmund, 10
Sartre, Jean-Paul, 3, 152, 154
Saussure, Ferdinand de, 3, 6, 10, 20–1, 24, 39, 43, 56, 61, 67, 68, 71, 72, 76, 94, 104–5, 126, 133, 139
Schlegel, Friedrich, 19
Schleicher, August, 19, 20
semantics, and distribution, 78, *see* meaning
semiosis, 46
semiotics and semiology, 38–9, 42, 45–8; 68; semio-linguistics 100–9; semiotic generativism, 107–9; semiotic square, 100–1,

104–7
Sibley, Frank, 122
sign, linguistic, 10, 45–7; arbitrariness, 10, 22–5, 54, 71; indicative and expressive, 44–50; and meaning, 104–5; phenomenology of, 44–50, 70; and reference, 104; and trace, 72–3
sociology of knowledge, 87
Spacks, Patricia Meyers, 116
Spinoza, Baruch, 36
structuralism, causes of success in France, 133–40; contradictions, 132–3; features of, 3–7; and hermeneutics, 38–9; and linguistics, 5; and literature, 97–100; and May 1968, 135–6; moderate, 4, 139; scientistic, 4, 139–40, 142–3; speculative, 4, 142; style of, 8; as utopia, 140
subject, death of, 53, 63, 67; return of, 8, 63–4
Swain, G., 93
synonyms, 48

Tel quel, 15
Tocqueville, Alexis de, 8, 117, 133
Todorov, Tzvetan, 2, 4
Tolkien, J. R. R., 120
Toulmin, Stephen, 102
trace, and arche-trace in Derrida, 72–3, 75
Turkle, Sherry, 133–4

verification, empirical, 57–8
Verrier, Jean, 106
Vienna School, 20, 68, 127, 128

Wells, Rullon, 80
White, Hayden, 103
Whitney, W. D., 19
Whorf, B. L., 10
Wittgenstein, Ludwig, 63, 68, 138
Wölfflin, Heinrich, 122
writing, transcendental or arche-writing, 51, 55, 66, 67–9, 75

Zumthor, Paul, 4